THE home zone

THE **home**
zone MAKING THE
MOST OF YOUR
LIVING SPACE

RYLAND
PETERS
& SMALL

London New York

SENIOR DESIGNER **Paul Tilby**
SENIOR EDITOR **Clare Double**
LOCATION AND PICTURE
RESEARCH MANAGER **Kate Brunt**
PICTURE RESEARCHER **Emily Westlake**
PRODUCTION **Patricia Harrington**

ART DIRECTOR **Gabriella Le Grazie**
PUBLISHING DIRECTOR **Alison Starling**

First published in the United Kingdom
in 2002 by Ryland Peters & Small
Kirkman House
12–14 Whitfield Street
London W1T 2RP
www.rylandpeters.com

10 9 8 7 6 5 4 3 2

Text by Ros Byam Shaw, Caroline Clifton-Mogg, Leslie
Geddes-Brown, Vinny Lee, Fay Sweet and Judith Wilson.

Text, design and photographs copyright
© Ryland Peters & Small 2002

A CIP record for this book is available from the
British Library.

ISBN 1-84172-268-5

contents

INTRODUCTION

It is a natural instinct to want to live in a home that is comfortable, well appointed, and finished with decorative pieces and colours which add beauty and please us. But, instinctive as this desire may be, getting our home to be more dream and less disaster does not necessarily come easily. It can seem a daunting task.

As with most things in life the best place to start is at the beginning, but one person's beginning can quite easily be another's finishing line. That is why a book like *The Home Zone* is so useful, combining as it does both the aspirational and the functional side of decorating and designing life. It is a rare individual, other than a professional designer, who understands the practical and the aesthetic in equal measure. For most of us, one element is easier than the other: lighting plans – easy; which lights to have – difficult, and so on. In *The Home Zone*, the first section illustrates some inspirational styles – ideas to give you ideas; the second part takes you through each room in a more concentrated manner; and the third section gets right down to the domestic nitty-gritty, with information on everything from lighting and flooring to window treatments and soft furnishings. You can tackle large and small projects with equal confidence.

The Home Zone will give you a clarity of purpose that will help to define your design aspirations. I am a great list maker, particularly where anything to do with the house is concerned, and before reading this book it might be useful to note down absolutely all the projects you would like to undertake in your home – large or small, practical or decorative, urgent or still a daydream. You may not do them all, but you are bound to do some of them and anyway, everything appears less daunting when written down. The further beauty of making a list – or even lists – is that, when ideas are set out on paper, relationships between seemingly unrelated tasks become apparent: repainting the walls in one room, for example, could coincide with rewiring and introducing a new lighting system there; installing a new shower in a previously unused small bedroom might be combined with a new or revamped storage system for linens, clothes and related objects.

It is important to think laterally about how you want your home to work. Many of us live in spaces which were designed in another time for people who lived very differently to the way we live now, both in terms of how they passed their days, and what sort of decoration they favoured. Priorities are different today: try and think of the space in which you live in a broad, total sense, rather than compartmentalized into separate rooms with specific uses; think about how you really want to use the space in terms of how you spend your time when there.

When faced with an empty, unprepossessing room, bear in mind that every room has a personality – it is up to you to find it. And every room, no matter how uninspiring initially, will have something in it that pleases you – even if it is something very small indeed. Think positive – the room may be narrow, but perhaps it is flooded with morning light; conversely, it may be very dark, but beautifully proportioned.

Another way to make the right decisions is to try and think about a project, and the space available, in the way that an interior decorator would: take nothing for granted, and be flexible about both the layout of the rooms and the furniture within them; decide what you really want and how you want it to work. Most of what you own is movable. Just because it has stood for a length of time in one room or against one wall doesn't mean that it always has to. It might look better in another place in the room; it might even – revolutionary thought here – look better in another room altogether, or with a completely different function; a cupboard that has always been used to hold china and glass, for example, might make a pretty and unusual linen cupboard. Furniture – particularly, of course, old furniture – does not merely have one life or even one use. Your eyes may have got used to it fulfilling a certain role, but that doesn't mean to say that there is not a different life or role waiting for it, and you could be pleasantly surprised with the change. On a more familiar scale, thinking of alternative functions for familiar pieces of furniture is perhaps like rooting round in your wardrobe and producing a new, successful outfit from familiar, sometimes forgotten, pieces of clothing, used in a different way or in different combinations.

Although it is certainly not necessary that every room in a house be decorated in the same style – indeed it is usually preferable that they should not be – there should always be a visual link between rooms and between any connecting areas. It may be of colour or texture, but aim for flow throughout the space rather than staccato movements.

If you are buying new things for a room, large or small, do not automatically reject something on the grounds of its high cost. Very often, the expensive purchase – the beautiful cushion, the handmade cupboard handles – will be the thing that lifts the whole room and gives it a signature. Better by far, in my view, to save money on the utilitarian than forfeit the unique and rare, for they are the things you will always remember – and if you do not buy them, you may always remember them with regret.

If you are by now raring to get down to work, I must inject a word of warning. Working on a house can become addictive. Like those cosmetic surgery junkies one reads about, you will often find that when you have tackled one home project successfully, however small it might have been, there wells within you an unstoppable urge to go on to the next. It might be something as small as getting round to clearing out the junk-filled cupboards in the living room, or finally organizing some bedroom curtains that are the right length and keep out the morning light. But beware – if it works, it will be catching. Flushed with success, you will find yourself looking around you with an eager eye for new challenges, and before you know where you are the whole place will be being revamped, recoloured and rearranged.

I have done a few houses myself in my time – sometimes in their roofless entirety, sometimes just a bit of decorative tweaking. Actually there is no such thing as just a bit of decorative tweaking – once you start, you find more and more things that you are itching to change. Something that I would never do now would be to buy a home that is described as 'needing no work': taste is so individual that anyone with even the mildest of opinions on decoration is bound to want to change the status quo. When I first worked on a house it was done out of necessity, but I realize that it has now developed into a habit – a mild addiction; I say that I could stop at any time, but I wonder. It is a bit like having a baby – wonderful idea before it happens, not much fun while it's going on, but a thrilling and completely satisfying end result – at least, until one starts to see where improvements could be made (in childhood terms this part is rather like those sweet cuddly babies becoming teenagers). This means that over a period of time – several years usually – I begin to think 'Well, perhaps what we really need is this', or 'Next time wouldn't it be nice to have one of those', and before I know where I am – and certainly before the other people living in the house know where they are – we are off again, either in the same house or, more often than not, starting again somewhere new. And each time that I do it, I think it will be the never-to-be-repeated best – the perfect home, a machine for living and so on. The house that we have now, for instance, is all I could want – it is pretty, suits us very well, everything works and it is a pleasure to come home to; and yet, and yet, perhaps the sitting room could be a bit wider, and the kitchen has always been a little dark... As I say, when you're hooked, you're hooked. But it could be worse – you could be hooked on stripping down vintage motorbikes, or making models of cathedrals from matchsticks.

With a book like *The Home Zone* – indeed, with any source of advice or suggestions on how to renovate and decorate a house or flat – it is important not to feel daunted by the quantity of advice and suggestions offered. Rather than feeling that all ideas are essential and that in some way your schemes are inadequate if not every part of them has been carried through, think of the ideas more as one of the large banquet menus of the nineteenth century – but service *à la française* rather than service *à la russe*, the former being the occasions on which many different dishes were laid out on the table at the same time and guests helped themselves only to those dishes which tempted them, rather than being offered each dish in succession, as in the service *à la russe*. And, as it is inspiration that is offered here, not commandments, remember that when you study the different inspirational styles shown, although each one is perfect in its entirety, style is in the end a completely personal thing. Many a good room is created using a little of this and a little of that, mixing periods, styles and colour. The important thing is to ensure that each room is harmonious, and that everything within it is in proportion with everything else, and, of course, that you are completely happy with it. Homeliness is often a rather derided virtue these days, but what it conveys – a home in which you and your family are happy to live and in which you feel comfortable and relaxed – must surely be the most important consideration of all when planning any changes or improvements in your home. So read on and enjoy the experience!

Caroline Clifton-Mogg

inspirational
interiors

SIMPLE & NATURAL

A neutral palette, spanning ice to taupe, and natural textures, from crunchy linen to rough wood, makes this relaxed look easy to achieve. Work with clear-cut furniture silhouettes, choose plains over patterns and leave ample room for the play of space and light.

The relaxed mood so characteristic of simple, natural rooms has catapulted the look into our design consciousness in recent years. Soothing to the spirit, tranquil to the eye, it's hard to resist the charm of a white-toned interior, unlined curtains diffusing sunlight, pale garden roses in a jar. Yet, while those components are crucial – the crisp white fabrics, textured wood and stone surfaces – there's scope to personalize. This is a look to dress up or down, according to whim, season or colour preference.

Don't disregard pure simplicity because you have a home jammed with children and pets. It can be immensely practical. White-painted walls are easy to touch up, cotton loose covers may be washed, and natural surfaces are simple to clean and maintain. This is also a cost-effective look. Precisely because colours are neutral, they won't go out of fashion, so your initial financial outlay will last longer. 'Utility' fabrics like drill or calico are inexpensive, as is basic white paint, and the 'distressed' junk-shop or auction furniture essential to the style may be bought cheaply, then repainted or loose covered.

Opposite below:
Concentrate on pared-down architectural features that contribute to a tranquil mood. This unadorned grate allows the eye to go straight to the beauty of the fire, and the pleasing mix of natural textures, from brickwork to wood.

Main picture:
White walls, cotton loose covers and painted boards are essential basics. Enhance the whites' purity by adding minute colour splashes. Fresh flowers provide an instant fix; so, too, does one item in a dark contrasting neutral.

Above left: **In a sparse white room, the play of sunlight and shadow has valuable decorative potential. Leave windows unadorned, or choose unlined window treatments, to allow sun to cast graphic patterns on walls and floors.**

Below left: **The natural look is easy to transfer to a modern interior. Stick to the characteristic whites and natural surfaces – slate, wicker and wood – but choose furniture in boxy shapes.**

When a room is sparingly furnished and decorative details pared down to a minimum, visual emphasis inevitably falls on its bare bones. Take time to evaluate what you have to work with. Of course elegant sash windows and panelled shutters will give a head start. But it's not a disaster if the room lacks architectural distinction. Adding simple Swedish-style MDF panelling to one wall or laying a reclaimed wood floor can make a huge difference. Replacing a faux period fireplace with a boxy style also sets the right tone.

While a white-on-white colour scheme is the basis for the look, consider the natural light in your room before finalizing decisions. Pure brilliant whites may be uncomfortably dazzling in a sunny area, or look too blue in the cooler light of a north-facing aspect. It's also worth remembering that bright white is not the antidote to a naturally dark room: soft-toned greys are a better choice. Whites can range from blue-white to lavender-white,

through to greys, putty, and creams. Not all whites will look good together. For this reason, combine all potential paints, fabrics and flooring samples in the room to be decorated, to see how they look in varying lights. This will also ensure that brighter whites won't make varying tones look dirty.

Walls should be plain, yet that needn't mean matt paint. Vinyl silk paints give off an attractive light-reflecting sheen, then there are subtle white-on-white self-patterned wallpapers. If you want to add texture to a basic white wall, consider painting over tongue-and-groove panelling or bare brickwork; or paint different walls in varying off-whites to highlight natural shadows. For extra contrast, white walls may be combined with one wall in pale pink polished plaster, or concrete. And remember that an all-white room may actually lose its architectural definition. By using several grey-whites for details such as cornicing, you will enhance the details.

Flooring needs to be natural-textured and pale-toned. If you have good floorboards, use them; even if they're in a slight state of disrepair, it is still worth taking time to sand and repair them. Boards may be waxed, stained, limed or treated with Swedish white oil and soap to give a pretty bleached effect. Alternatively, paint them in white or grey-blue. If you want a wood floor and the existing boards are past redemption, replace them with reclaimed boards, which are naturally worn in, rather than laying a shiny laminate wood floor, which will look uncharacteristically new. Go for paler woods, such as oak and maple.

In a kitchen, hall or bathroom, the neutral tones and hard-wearing surfaces of stone floors are practical, from the creamy notes of limestone to grey slate. Consider under-floor heating to take away the chill of stone underfoot. Try to use a mix of hard and soft floors if running the natural look throughout your home, but keep to the same tones. Instead of carpet, try knobbly seagrass, coir or sisal, or, for a bedroom, a softer wool–sisal mix. These days there's a huge choice of colours, from pale honey to grey-green, as well as weaves, from herringbone to giant crunchy knots. Look out for unusual natural options, such as bamboo, which is ideal for a bathroom.

Fabrics should be predominantly plain, in appropriate shades across the white spectrum, from whites and off-whites to natural linen tones or pigeon grey. Look for those with loose weaves and matt finishes, and try to mix a number of different textures, an essential tip for giving interest and lift to lots of plains. Look at cottons, linen, denim, and 'utility' materials like calico or canvas, from drill to cotton duck. Fabrics for window treatments should be fluid enough to hang in a relaxed way; textiles for loose covers should look crisp. Although the basis of the simple and natural look is white-on-white, choose a few fabrics which will introduce accent colours. Consider darker greys, biscuit, or soft flesh pinks and Swedish grey-blue.

Soft furnishings must be well made, and the simpler the style, the more important this is. For windows, if you are not overlooked and have the right architectural features, go for white-painted panelled shutters and eschew curtains. Most of us have more need for privacy, however. Plain blinds, from a white blackout roller blind to linen or cotton Roman blinds or thin cotton roll-up Swedish styles are all options. Always line Roman blinds – in bright light, everything (from rods to

Opposite left: **If there isn't a suitable pale wood table and chairs for the natural look, a dining room is easily transformed with snowy white linen, white china and glass. The less fussy the tableware shapes, the better.**

Main picture: **Kitchens should be simply designed, with flat panel doors and minimal handles, so that the emphasis is on the surfaces. Choose natural stone worktops and floors, and wood or painted wood. Too much white and the kitchen looks clinical. Look out for unusual veneers, such as burr walnut, which looks good with stainless steel.**

Right: **Pale wood units are a versatile option for the natural look. Teamed with stainless-steel surfaces they look contemporary, or paved with creamy stone worktops they appear more rustic.**

Below right: **If a dining room sits between an open-plan kitchen and sitting room, choose sophisticated furniture, but in pale, bleached woods. This choice will sit as well with a white sofa as in a white and steel kitchen.**

rings) will show. Curtains need to hang simply: go for tie, tab, gathered or ring headings, on an unpretentious iron, thin wood or brass pole. Unlined drapes look great, but for warmth and privacy do add white roller blinds.

Other soft furnishings need to be equally informal, and loose covers, not tight upholstery, are a key element to the look. Have loose covers cut on the baggy side; the finish is more relaxed, and allows room for shrinkage after cleaning. And give due thought to cleaning, because white covers must be washable or at least dry-cleanable. Utility fabrics, while cheap and robust, do shrink substantially, and should be pre-shrunk before making up. Keep loose cover detailing understated, with minimal piping, easy ruffles, and

Opposite above left: **For a truly plain and simple look, dress up the bed in crisp, almost monastic fashion. Regular pillows, and a flat white sheet or bedspread are the only true essentials. Keep clutter to a minimum.**

Opposite above right: **A serene mood is paramount in the bedroom. Go as bare and plain as you dare, using natural light to provide decoration. Here, perspex shutters filter light; translucent blinds or unlined curtains will also do the trick.**

Opposite below: **A fast-track way to the simple look is to concentrate on symmetry. Positively Zen-like in its pairing of identical pillows, rugs and bedside tables, this white and taupe bedroom exudes calm.**

This page, clockwise from top left: **The pure and simple bathroom relies on natural surfaces, from limestone and marble to wood and glass, designed along chunky yet sleek lines. Allow for good storage to minimize clutter: pick giant wicker baskets or leather or wood boxes to introduce more natural textures. Contrast surfaces with contemporary plain white sanitary ware and modern chrome fittings. The ultimate in simplicity is a wet room, with walls and floor in identical stone. It's easy to get carried away with the monastic mood and forget about comfort. But bedrooms and bathrooms need fluffy towels, plump cushions and tactile fabrics.**

buttons or simple ties for fastenings. A set of identical white linen or cotton loose covers is a great way to unify a mismatched set of furniture, or a set of dining chairs. For headboards or the odd armchair, contrast the loose covers with tight upholstery in hessian, jute or natural linen.

Furniture should be in natural materials, especially wood and stone. Go for distressed or raw-looking surfaces rather than anything over-polished. Metals, too, make a wonderful contrast to an all-white background: aged finishes like rusty wrought iron, or the faded gilding of a mirror. Yet not everything has to be antique. Contrast the curvier shapes of period pieces with boxy, modern silhouettes and smooth, utility surfaces: a rectangular slate-topped coffee table, perhaps, or the dull sheen of a zinc kitchen table.

When arranging a simple and natural room, the aim is to maintain an air of space and light, without furnishing it so sparsely that the look becomes unwelcoming. So take time to play around with the furniture, until the balance is right. Employ as many tricks as you can to encourage natural light into the room to enhance the white-on-white theme. A big mirror propped against one wall, white-painted floors and curtains which push right away from the window all help. Precisely because of its simplicity, this is the perfect style to consider in a small room.

If you're worried that the room looks too sparse, concentrate on the subtle details which help it to look 'lived in'. A real log fire, the play of sunlight on a bare white wall, casually placed garden flowers on a table will all bring it to life, as will sensual comforts such as plump feather-filled cushions and a warming mohair throw. And, while decorative accessories should be kept to a minimum, they should work hard to earn their places in the room. Choose personal items that people will want to examine and pick up, anything from a few well-chosen black-and-white family photos, simply framed, to knobbly beach pebbles or giant creamy church candles. Scale them up, choosing one large bowl over several small ones, but leave plenty of space for the room to breathe – don't stuff every surface. The essence of the simple and natural look is peace and tranquillity. It's also the perfect example of less is more.

Top: **Loft apartments are ideal backgrounds for a sleek and modern look, but their inevitably big, industrial windows and high ceilings need a practised eye to furnish. Work on a large scale, and use the typically long, lean outline of contemporary sofas and tables to balance the space. A curved lampshade or squashy beanbag will soften the straight lines.**

Above and right: **You can create a softer or more masculine take on the modern look using different fabrics and colours on the same basic furniture and surfaces. Above, brown matt wool upholstery and black leather seats are perfect for a bachelor pad; right, a similar sofa, upholstered in white, and teamed with tub chairs, takes on a more feminine note.**

Opposite main picture:
Vast expanses of plain wall, teamed with equally plain upholstery, risk looking sterile. This is where contrast of texture helps. Here reflective glass mixes with soft fabric, and polished concrete floors with matt white walls. The play of light can replace pattern, but flashes of bright accent colour, either as vases or painted directly onto the wall, will also lift a neutral interior.

Left: **Take care with a grey-on-grey scheme, so it doesn't look either too harsh or too clinical. Experiment with shades from gull white to charcoal, then lift the tones using metallics, warm woods and glass. If you don't want to add colour, black-and-white photography can look stunning with graphites.**

SLEEK & MODERN

Cutting-edge rooms demand boxy furniture, streamlined surfaces and moody tones from graphite to gunmetal, biscuit to beige. Texture is key. Capture the gleam of glass and smooth stone, touchy-feely leathers and the confident gloss of lacquer and stainless steel.

Spawned by the cool, empty interiors of late Nineties minimalism, the sleek and modern look isn't one to be undertaken lightly. It's also a consciously urban fashion. Taken to extremes, it offers no midway path; there's no mixing of furniture types, no compromise on styles. This makes it perfect for decorating addicts wanting an excuse to sell their last decade's furniture and start afresh. Yet, if you prefer a more comfortable take on the modern look, there are still plenty of style elements to adopt. And who knows – the mantra of functionalism and order might just rub off a little, and make your home a serene place.

In practical terms, what first appears to be a high-maintenance and expensive look has plenty of benefits for today's time-pressed home owners. With the style's emphasis on hard surfaces, from limestone floors to stainless-steel walls, cleaning is relatively easy, provided you're armed with the correct products and a penchant for buffing. Equally, the top-quality wools, leather and faux skins for upholstery are robust and less likely to stain. Of course you can spend a small fortune on solid wood floors and polished plaster walls. But you don't have to. There are plenty of good-looking equivalents like concrete,

This page and opposite above left: **With their flat-fronted cupboards, cubed or rectangular outlines, and pared-down style, modern kitchens need subtle detailing to stop them looking clinical. Vary cupboard fronts with frosted glass or coloured laminate, or by mixing pale wood with white. Under-cabinet lighting can give interest to a plain steel or glass splashback.**

Opposite: **If dining tables and chairs are part of an open-plan living area, they must look good with a sleek kitchen or stylish sofas. Choose modern tabletops which won't need a cloth: laminate, stone, cement, wood or glass all look smart and are robust as well. Try no-nonsense seating in modern materials like polypropylene – so you can introduce flashes of colour – or aluminium.**

or wood veneers laid over MDF, which look similar and cost half the price. And while you may need to invest in some new pieces of furniture to get the right silhouette, the sleek look, taken literally, needs only a few key pieces.

As the look is visually dramatic, consider the style of your home before starting off. It's great for lofts, new-build houses, and open-plan urban apartments; less easy to carry off in suburban houses with a warren of small rooms. It's also perfect if all the architectural detailing has been removed from your home because the simpler the background, the better. If you are about to embark on building work, certain details enhance the look. A cavity fireplace, with stainless-steel surround and contemporary fittings, shadow gaps instead of skirtings, and a run of flush, built-in cupboards are great basics. If you do have ornate mouldings or a marble fireplace, it's a crime to rip them out. The clash of ultra-modern with period details can be stunning.

Get the surfaces right, and the other details will fall into place. As soft furnishings play such a small part, you can afford to concentrate on unusual surfaces. Eschew matt surfaces for a sheen or gloss. Essential materials to consider are stone, from marble and limestone to granite; metals, from stainless to waxed mild steel; glass, from toughened clear to sandblasted; and solid wood or wood veneers. Rather than dividing your surfaces into separate floor, worktop and wall categories, think radical. Toughened glass looks as good for a bathroom worktop as, more conventionally, for a shower screen; and stainless steel is as dramatic on the kitchen floor as for the splashbacks. The key is that the surfaces look expensive, even if they aren't.

For walls, you might choose that classic minimalist staple of brilliant-white paint, but there are plenty of other options. For example, glossy lacquer paints are newly available in dark moody colours, or experiment

Right: **Stainless steel doesn't have to look masculine or utilitarian in a bathroom. Here, wrapped around the softer lines of an oval bath, it provides a sleek and pretty take on contemporary surfaces. Also look out for oval all-stainless-steel baths.**

Centre right:
Modern bathrooms are designed to be super-efficient rooms for washing, rather than places in which to linger. Keep things functional by wall-mounting your sanitary ware – even the toilet – a particularly useful space-saver for a small bathroom. Pick surfaces that can be used on floors and as splashbacks, to give a visually cohesive look, also a useful trick for small rooms.

Above far right:
The ultimate minimalist bathroom combines glass, stainless steel and very contemporary fittings. There should be no clutter, so plan bathroom cupboards behind glass doors.

Right: **If an en suite bathroom is visible from the bedroom, take care to marry the two looks. Take tips from modern hotel design, and sink the basin into a stone worktop, with glass shelves for cosmetics.**

with a metallic wall finish. As a contrast to shiny furniture, walls may be textured, from stretched Seventies-style hessian to dark wood veneers, or in a bathroom add a panel of stainless steel or sandblasted glass. Other stone wall finishes might include polished plaster, or trendy concrete block work.

Floors and worktops will probably constitute your greatest investment, particularly in a kitchen or bathroom. In recent years, the choice of stone has increased hugely. Limestone comes in every colour from soft grey to beige and almost white. Then there's granite, in shiny or honed forms, slate and marble. For a budget stone look, consider concrete (for floors and worktops), or for a matt, city-slicker look there are rubber floors, from plains to patterns, or lino. Wood is also ideal, but go for rich, dark tones, from wenge to iroko, and the wider and glossier the floorboards, the better.

With the emphasis on natural stone and metal surfaces, it's inevitable that the classic sleek and modern colour schemes are variations on the monochrome. You can pick from cool white-on-white, mixed with natural tones or with silvery metallics. Or there is the quite masculine palette of grey-on-grey, from graphite and gunmetal to pale blue-greys and off-whites. Soften the monochrome tones by adding in sharp accent colours, from lilac and scarlet, through to burnt orange, aubergine or citrus yellow, either in a piece of contemporary furniture or used on walls or in scatter cushions.

Many a rigorously designed modern interior has been ruined by a sloppy choice of furniture. You simply can't put a leather chesterfield into a modern stone and glass room. Far better to store inappropriate pieces, and budget for an inexpensive sofa that looks right. The high street is full of good copies of designer pieces. The essential silhouette to choose is boxy and slim; a sofa may be long and low to the ground, or Seventies-style L-shaped, armchairs square, bedheads slick and rectangular. To team with your upholstered pieces, choose glass- or stone-topped coffee tables, the amazingly useful and lean sideboard, and contemporary dining chairs, from perspex to steel. Furniture surfaces may be dark wood, brilliant gloss paint, lacquer or glass, all with stainless-steel detailing.

Fabrics need to be matt and slick, appropriate for the tight, figure-hugging silhouettes of sofas and chairs. Sleek isn't uncomfortable, however. Think about wool, from flannel to bouclé, and alcantara, leathers and Seventies-inspired vinyls. Plains are most effective, but the odd graphic, geometric print can look good. The pared-down silhouette extends to windows, too. Choose treatments that are streamlined and allow for light-play: Venetian blinds with metallic or wood slats, perforated cotton roller blinds and sliding Japanese panels. Increasingly, contemporary blinds companies are offering exciting trim options, from crystal beads to leather detailing. Curtains should be sculptural in firm folds of white linen or contemporary metallic or synthetic fibres.

Stick to the basic principles of form and functionalism to accessorize this most urban of looks. If you have cherished accessories, store them in built-in cupboards and choose instead one or two large-scale pieces: a giant cylindrical glass vase, or a burnished Vietnamese platter. You don't have to spend a fortune on abstract art. Ask an art supplier to make up a giant canvas, and paint it in muted shades to match your scheme.

Top left: **Look for pared-down furniture in the bedroom. Experiment with low platform beds on steel legs, futon wood styles or contemporary steel frames. A plain, upholstered divan, pushed up against the wall without a headboard, gives a similarly sleek look. Dress the bed in minimal vein, with tightly tucked-in sheets.**

Top right: **The more clinical the bedroom, the better, so clothes and accessories need to be well hidden in a row of flush, flat-fronted cupboards.**

Paint them to match the walls, or experiment with sandblasted glass, stainless-steel or laminate fronts.

Above: **This dividing wall acts as a headboard, an important design feature. Choose either a panel of wood laminate, used on top of MDF, solid wood or a plain, upholstered rectangular headboard in a matt fabric. Overscale it to extend high above the bed, and a good 30cm (1ft) to either side. For the really functional bedroom, build in wall lights as well.**

Opposite top left: **Let the period appeal of a rustic architectural feature shine, by dressing the rest of the room in plain, simple colours and fabrics. Comfortable details such as a thick padded mattress, cushions or deep-pile wool rug are crucial too.**

Opposite centre, left and right: **Pick unfussy antique furniture that has a lovely shape, and set interesting pieces against a plain wall to show off a pretty outline. Classic chair and table styles will endure for ever, so are an investment.**

Opposite below: **Mix and match patterns freely. Classic stripes may include ticking, antique or new, deckchair canvas, wovens or printed designs. For florals, consider embroidered textiles, prints, upholstery weaves and traditional chintz.**

Left, above and below: **The most successful country interiors combine warmth, comfort and a relaxed mood. Fresh flowers, books and candles all add to the ambience.**

COUNTRY & RUSTIC

Relaxed in spirit, naturally tactile, the country look combines warm and faded colours, homespun textiles and the patina of antique woods. For the classic mix of antique chintz and tapestry, or the cleaner lines of modern rustic, keep things simple and informal.

The traditional country look has cleaned up of late. Gone are the frills and groaning pine dressers, the shiny chintz and the china ornaments. In their places have arrived rustic textiles, hard-working surfaces, and a faded colour palette, making the perfect backdrop for the new stars of the country look: pretty antique pieces, from furniture to textiles. No matter if they are distressed or worn; what counts is that they are unique, decorative and functional. The new look has its roots half in the Shaker ethos, with its clean lines and pale colours, and half in 'modern country', the latest preoccupation with sparse furniture and raw, honest textures. The key is that nothing should look too new: instead, the rooms in your home should seem to be naturally evolved and well loved. An informal mood counts most of all. At the heart of any successful country interior is the clarion call to find a sofa, pick up a book and settle down.

As a decorative style, the country look is guaranteed to be low maintenance and family friendly. If you live in the country, you will already know that an outdoor lifestyle dictates the need for washable floors, upholstery that withstands pet hairs and kids, and warm, cosy window dressings to keep out the chills of inclement weather. If you live in the city, you can still capitalize on that practicality. Country style is also inexpensive to carry off, and its classic looks will endure. Because it relies on a mixture of furniture styles, it's the ideal way to deal with hand-me-down family furniture, junk-shop buys, and possessions collected over the years. You won't need to buy new furniture, just sort through what you already have. And rigorous sorting is crucial. For country style, don't read jumble or clutter.

While the classic country cottage has low ceilings, small rooms and even smaller windows, making the perfect background for antique rustic pieces, you can still adapt the look for a different property. It will work successfully, in plainer vein, against the taller ceilings and sash windows of a standard Victorian terrace. Certain elements can even work successfully in an urban loft apartment: an overstuffed, ticking upholstered wing chair or cherrywood farmhouse table provides a marvellous conflict of styles. If you don't have rustic architectural features, it's better to work with a plain room than to attempt to add obvious fake beams or leaded windows. And, if your country property does boast outstanding details, such as a stone fireplace, use them as the visual inspiration for your scheme.

When choosing everything from wall surfaces to furniture, remember that things must look slightly battered or distressed; there's no place for spanking new upholstery or garish gilding. So conserve rather than restore. Look at what you have to play with. There's a definite charm to a nineteenth-century sofa with its stuffing peeking out, to mirrors whose glass is gently foxed, and broad floorboards worn to a slope from generations of passing feet. And if you don't have the real thing, you can always fake it. Many a new pine chest of drawers or door can be given the country look with watered-down vinyl matt paint, some wire wool and finishing wax.

On walls, you can achieve the worn-out look by using dead matt emulsion paint, broken stencilled patterns (large abstracts only, no flowers or leaves) in faded shades, or by stripping off all wallpaper and leaving the pretty patterns of the plaster underneath. If plaster is bumpy, so be it: the contours are part of the country charm. Consider, too, the appeal of painted or unpainted brickwork. Wallpaper certainly fits in with the rustic look, but go

for faded shades and avoid small patterns. There's potential here to use florals, but go for rambling large-scale blooms and use sparingly in a bedroom or bathroom, as the only pattern in the room. Woodwork should always be painted in eggshell, as it has minimal sheen, or dead flat oil paints, now available from specialist period paint suppliers.

In terms of colour, it's not so much the exact shade you pick that matters, but the tone. Fresh pastels or any colours with too much white should be avoided in favour of washed-out or muddy tones. Adding a little black pigment to ready-mixed paints is one way to take the edge off their brightness. Instead of fresh white paintwork, experiment with woodwork in the same tone as the wall colour, or choose one of the 'old' whites available from specialist paint ranges. Historical paint ranges are also brilliant sources of muddied colours, ranging from pale stone and lichen shades to salmon pink, moss and terracotta. And if you're stuck for inspiration, you can't lose if you look out of the window. Nature's tones, whatever the season, are guaranteed to provide a suitably earthy palette.

Flooring should be robust, easy to clean and naturally textured. But it should also be cosy underfoot. The ideal combination of function and comfort is to expose good wood boards or flagstones if you have them, then (for warmth) add faded kilims, sisal mats or traditional wool herringbone runners on top. Wool carpet is perfectly acceptable in a country home, but save it for the upper floors, where muddy boots are well out of the way. If you pick a neutral grey or beige, then more interesting antique rugs can be

Opposite above: **For the ultimate rustic kitchen, ignore purpose-made cupboards entirely, and store everything from pans to food on an eclectic mix of mismatched, distressed furniture. Look for open shelves, long serving tables to be used as a sideboard, and a mix of chairs. To match the look, the cooker should be a free-standing range, and the sink a butler's style on a stand.**

Opposite below: **The Aga is an essential country kitchen ingredient, so** build a relaxed, unfitted kitchen around it. Wall cupboards may have wood or painted-wood doors in plain, panelled or glazed styles. Base cupboards for pans and pots can be combined with a dresser for china and glass. No country kitchen is complete without a central table, either in plain scrubbed pine, or with an oilcloth or cotton cloth on top. Stick to muted colours: soft blues, greens, pinks and cream, and matt, easily maintained surfaces like tiles, paint and wood.

This page: **Adopt the more casual habit of eating in the kitchen, and table and chair choices can become more informal. If you have chosen a particular rustic look for the kitchen – Shaker, perhaps – then pick simple furniture that fits the theme. Ladder backs, antique church pews, old school stools, and French country chairs are all excellent choices. If chairs are** mix-and-match second-hand, then paint them in different colours for fun. Tables will most likely be wood, from pine to cherry, or more unusual fruitwoods through to mahogany. With simple, classic styles, the dining room can easily be accessorized with basic chunky plates and glasses for everyday use, or dressed up with a linen cloth and antique ceramics and crystal for dinner parties.

Left and below:
To create a pared-down rustic look, keep to very simple bed and window treatments. Some pattern is nice; stripes give a fresh, crisp finish, or use strips of fabric in a contrast shade to trim a Roman blind, tablecloth or the leading edge of plain linen curtains.

Below left: **In the country bedroom you can layer textiles and use fabrics to dress up the bed. Think about quilts, cushions, bolsters, eiderdowns and valances. Layer them onto an iron or simple wood bed frame, rather than a padded headboard.**

placed on top. In a kitchen or bathroom, natural lino is an appropriate choice, or terracotta, slate or limestone. Under-floor heating is definitely worth the investment if you go for stone.

A tantalizing mix of textiles is a crucial part of country style. This is the one place where you can afford to experiment with pattern, and there is a huge choice. At the really traditional end, there are overblown faded chintzes, needlepoints, tapestries and paisleys, in classic patterns and textures. For a simpler look, choose ginghams, madras cottons and stripes, from ticking to deckchair canvas. Think about contrasting different textures, from the deep pile of velvet to tight-woven cottons. And mix your patterns with plenty of plain fabrics, which is the key to keeping the country look simple. While floral chintzes look overpowering *en masse*, a single cushion on a calico-covered armchair has enormous charm. This is a great opportunity to experiment with antique textiles, and don't worry if they have a few holes. Good places to hunt out remnants, from mattress tickings to linen sheets, are antiques fairs and car boot sales.

When planning soft furnishings, comfort counts as much as style. Thick, heavy curtains are a must, whether cosily interlined, or assembled from a tapestry or blanket flipped at the top to create a pelmet. Hang drapes from heavy wood or brass poles and rings. Keep to plain and simple cotton or linen Roman blinds, or traditional cream holland blinds to team with curtains. Use wooden shutters if you have them, and if the look seems too

Left: **You can create a very pretty country bedroom without masses of florals. A decorative metal bed, sophisticated painted furniture, and muslin curtains are the essentials.**

Above: **The panelling and fresh blue and white of American country style are perennially popular. Patchwork quilts, Oxford pillowcases, and crisp white linens are basics.**

Right: **A practical bathroom floor could be lino, vinyl, sisal or carpet. Walls may be painted or tongue-and-groove-lined. A roll-top bath is a must, but sanitary ware doesn't have to match. Restored period pieces (and taps) have more character.**

sparse, hang muslin or Swiss voile panels in front for softness. Steer a course between a mix of tight upholstery – upholstery nails can look very decorative teamed with simple fabrics like cotton duck or ticking – and baggy loose covers. If a sofa has seen better days, gently drape a quilt or needlepoint panel over the back of it. Battered leather chairs are increasingly popular as part of the modern country look, and look especially fetching with faded floral cushions.

When arranging furniture, aim for an unusual mix of different periods of furniture, and styles, from Louis XV gilt to Victorian button-back chairs. Combine country fruitwoods with painted, distressed pine, cast iron with upholstered pieces, or marble tops with scrubbed pine. Don't overstuff rooms; instead, allow enough space to enjoy the contours and textures of each piece. Once you're confident creating that casual mix, extend it to the kitchen and bathroom. For the rustic look it's much more fun to abandon the idea of an off-the-peg design, and treat these functional rooms as any other: a free-standing bath, kitchen range or cupboard is infinitely more appropriate and welcoming than a built-in, fitted design.

Employ restraint when it comes to filling rooms with possessions. Of course the country look is all about bookshelves stuffed with books, kitchen shelves piled with plates and family photographs in the toilet. But try to pick out just the prettiest things, and keep the rest for a rainy day. Remember that 'country' has widened its brief, so that in among the flower-sprigged china and botanical prints there should be some surprises: chunky creamy ceramics, distressed terracotta pots, and twigs from the garden, plopped into the milk jug.

Right: **Choosing the right furniture silhouette is vital. Look for sofas with curved backs and deep, sweeping seats, boxy little Thirties-style armchairs, round and oval stools, and elongated, slim tables. For cushions, slim rectangles and round and bolster shapes are all appropriate.**

Below left: **Gilded, metal furniture featuring knot or looped details, curlicues or squiggles suggests salon chic. Such details might be found on lamp bases, mirror frames, glass-topped tables or dressing tables. Stick to burnished effects rather than vulgar bright gilding.**

Below right: **The truly elegant drawing room has more than its fair share of symmetry. Twin sofas, a pair of chairs either side of a fireplace, or artwork arranged symmetrically are all possibilities.**

Left: **Daybeds are vital pieces in the contemporary elegant sitting room. Reminiscent of Thirties boudoirs and salon style, they may be boxy and modern, or sinuous and curvy; what matters most is that cushions and bolsters are plump. Use one as the focus of a smart drawing room.**

Above: **Shapes and colours needn't all be curvy and pale to make the mood elegant. As long as natural light is soothing and well controlled, and fabrics tactile, boxier outlines will work. Expensive-looking leathers, suedes and lacquer do the trick here.**

For this combination of salon chic and fresh modernity, team luxurious textiles with curvaceous furniture, decked out in pale tones from shell to pistachio and ice blue. Think elegance, symmetry and subtle glamour.

CONTEMPORARY ELEGANCE

Hovering between the sophisticated textiles and tailored shapes of the twenty-first century, and the signature glamour of the Thirties, this style is elegant yet accessible. Not to be confused with its younger sister, boudoir style, this may be a look consciously adopted by anyone 'growing into' a second or third home, and perfect for pied-à-terre city life or singletons minus pets or kids. Even in a family home, grown-ups could adopt the look for the adults' bedroom. While it's not exactly style on a budget, and is distinctly high maintenance, it has its compensations. Whether you view it as couture home style, or the interiors version of immaculate grooming, it's set to keep us on our toes, Hoover and duster firmly in hand.

With its signature pastel colours and silky fabrics, this look gives the impression of being expensive, yet there are cost-effective ways to recreate a similar luxury feel. Quite apart from the ruinous cost of real silks and animal skins, it's worth investigating sophisticated, synthetic equivalents because they look just as good and are dry-cleanable to boot. These days, you can even find washable suedes. If you don't want to bypass at least a dash of real silk – on cushions, perhaps, or to upholster an occasional chair – then invest in stain-guarding. You can also conjure up an extremely elegant look by adding one or two key luxury pieces to an essentially bare, restrained room.

We all know the film-star charm of a high-ceilinged first-floor drawing room, sweeping staircase or pairs of tall French doors and, if you have them, they may inspire you to try contemporary elegance. Some studio flats, for example, boast such features because they are part of a larger house conversion. If your rooms are more modest, you might take a marble fireplace, parquet floor or simpler French doors as a

Above: **In among proper sofas and armchairs, add smaller salon-style chairs, from Louis XV armchairs to velvet-covered pouffes and lyre-backed gilded chairs with satin seats. Chosen not so much for comfort as for the way they set a mood, they can be decoratively covered in anything from a remnant of hand-painted silk to plain linen with an embroidered monogram.**

Left, right and below right: **Kitchens can also match the style. Sleek, expensive-looking surfaces include glossy granite, marble and slate worktops, unusual wood veneers from maple to walnut, and plenty of sophisticated black. Keep appliances and taps functional yet smart in stainless steel.**

Below: **Dining chairs can also feature sophisticated, curvy outlines. For a smarter look, choose upholstered, waisted chairs in moleskin, suede or linen (but think first about how they will be cleaned). Everyday, yet supremely elegant kitchen-dining chairs include the classic Arne Jacobsen 3107 chair (below), whether in bleached wood or its many pastel varieties.**

starting point. And even if you are beginning with four basic white walls, remember that salon chic is determined as much by textiles and furniture shape as by architectural distinction.

The quality factor is crucial. Finishes must be immaculate, and plumbing first rate. Doors should snap shut with a satisfying thud, and carpets should feel soft underfoot. If you're on a tight budget, you might invest in a few quality fittings – a giant antique mirror, for example – and keep everything else simple. As a tranquil mood is essential to the look, invest in great lighting so that ambience is easy to control. Plan for a selection of uplighters, downlighters and table lamps, controlled from a single switch and with a dimmer. Pretty lamps with cone or waisted silk shades, ornate metal wall lights or angled downlighters, to highlight art, are all options.

Surfaces should be either very matt or reflective, and the best look has a good mix. For the reflective style, consider fondant-coloured walls overpainted with opalescent washes, a ceiling stuck with silver handmade paper, or metallic wallpapers. For matt, choose wallpaper with sophisticated stripes, pale damask patterns or abtract designs such as bamboo. Fabric, from padded and battened linen to silk, may be used on walls. Then there are wood veneers in exotic woods like burr oak or walnut, or mirrored panelling.

For floors, pale wood boards or traditional oak parquet are highly appropriate. Although this is a style with its roots in plains, a wood floor can be successfully dressed up with a pure wool rug in a graphic design. Or buck current trends and lay a pale neutral carpet. Sisal–wool mixes are another option, as are the more expensive but very chic linen and Brussels weaves. For sophisticated bathrooms, pale limestone, marble or ceramic tiles in a traditional black-and-white chequerboard are good choices.

The strongest theme for colour is neutrals, especially shades of ivory, bone and pearl combined with darker chocolate and mocha. But look too at 'neutral colours', which are paler than true sorbet shades, and range from pinkish beige and shell, through to eau-de-Nil, lilac and celadon green. Good accent colours might be plum, graphite or metallics. When picking fabrics, don't restrict colour to cushions: there's something unashamedly luxurious about a prettily coloured sofa or occasional chair in palest silk.

Top left and right: **To create the right mood in a bathroom, at least a sliver of marble, polished granite or limestone will help, if only for a bath or basin surround. It may seem a large investment, but you can buy inexpensive plain white sanitary ware to go with it. Consider elegant options for taps. Either choose state-of-the-art chrome fittings or period-style taps and shower mixers – and avoid gold-effect taps.**

Centre left: **Read luxury for contemporary elegance, and create a bathroom that looks and is indulgent. Details such as choosing a bigger than normal bath, placing it in the centre of the room, or adding two basins, will make all the difference. Great lighting in a bathroom feels luxurious too. Instead of glaring overhead downlighters, install uplighters or lights either side of the mirror for the most flattering make-up illumination.**

Centre right and right: **A bathroom-cum-dressing room is a popular trend. Consider sinking bowl-style basins into a continuous worktop, either marble, glass, limestone or solid wood. Drawers and cupboards beneath the worktop can hold everything from towels to bathroom essentials. If a worktop isn't an option, pretty and glamorous basin styles include bowl-effect basins, from glass to stone, on simple stands.**

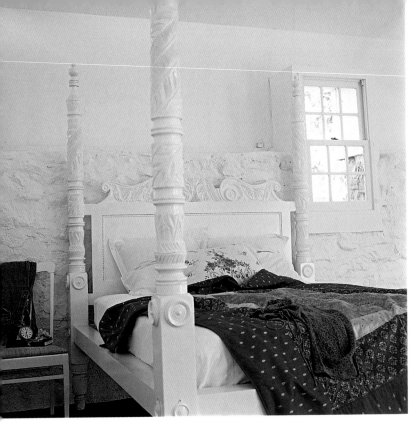

Opposite, clockwise from top right: **Inevitably, the bed is centre stage in the elegant bedroom. It needs to look very luxurious, crisp and of good proportion. First consider the headboard. Leave rounded, padded types for clear-cut rectangular styles; the taller, the better. Upholstery can be anything from neutral linen to moleskin or suede; choose these in** preference to harder-edged wood styles. A tailored valance is also essential on a divan, with neat knife pleats at each corner. Either match the valance to the bedhead, or choose a contrast fabric. Create a truly indulgent bed with plenty of pillows, including square continental ones, and ensure linen is pin-neat in crisp cotton, linen, or with hemstitch details. Eschew fat, bumpy quilts in favour of a flat bedspread, and add a tactile throw, perhaps in mohair or cashmere, neatly folded. Keep bedroom colours to a cool, neutral palette, with touches of pale pink, lilac or chocolate for extra sophistication. A long, low bedroom stool at the end of the bed, upholstered in animal skin, creates a final glamorous touch.

Fabric texture is key. As well as silks and satins, consider linen, velvet and moleskin; suede, leather and faux animal skins are also excellent. Experiment with a good mix of textures – cashmere curtains teamed with organza inner curtains, perhaps, or a zebra faux-fur throw lined with pink satin. Let yourself be indulgent when choosing soft furnishings. Curtains may go in two directions: either tailored, sculptural folds, perhaps with pin-tucking or contrast edging at the hem, or hanging full and loose. If you're using silk, check if it will fade (many of the cheaper silks do). Hang drapes from narrow metallic poles, perhaps with curlicue finials, or from fabric-covered pelmets, Thirties style. Blinds should be sheer; blind-makers now have a good selection of sophisticated synthetic fabrics, or find a specialist company that makes blinds from delicate fabrics without needing lining.

The whole point about contemporary elegance is that furniture should have beautiful sweeping silhouettes and plenty of curves, so plan soft furnishings to give a mix of figure-hugging tight upholstery, and tailored loose covers featuring corner pleated skirts, and minimal detailing. Think

Above: **A four-poster bed is the last word in elegance, but you need to choose the right style. Steer well clear of very ornate designs or overpowering fabric hangings, and choose instead painted wood, decorative metal frames or a contemporary, Shaker-style four-poster in pretty, warm woods such as cherry. This white bed is tranquil.**

Centre: **The right mix of lighting is particularly important in bedrooms. Try a number of wall lights and bedside lights, operated from a central switch with a dimmer, rather than overhead lighting. Reading lights should be at the correct height to give a powerful beam. Choose metal, fabric or parchment shades in simple cone or waisted shapes.**

Right: **Clutter is out in the contemporary elegant bedroom, so ensure you have enough storage for clothes and personal items. If necessary, think about banishing wardrobes to a spare bedroom, to keep the master bedroom clear. As well as the bed, another essential is a comfortably plump, well-upholstered daybed, armchair or small sofa.**

about cushions: long, bolster styles and pilule shapes are particularly appropriate. Try to get a contrast of furniture shapes, from the more contemporary long, lean silhouette to the elegant curves of antique pieces. No sitting room or bedroom, for example, is complete without a contemporary daybed, a couple of Louis XV salon-style chairs, and fat, upholstered stools. A glass-fronted drinks cabinet is also fun. Other furniture needs glossy finishes – lacquer or highly polished wood – or curly metal detailing, whether on a decorative standard lamp or mirror frame. Glass and mirrors, with their glamorous reflections, are also essential, from an overmantle mirror with gilded frame to glass chandeliers or a mirrored dressing table in Thirties vein.

Accessorize contemporary elegance with a confident hand, but keep it simple. A large sculpture or collection of period glass will look more arresting than many smaller objects. Give thought to what hangs on the walls. Contemporary art or symmetrically arranged paintings, in soft colours, will mix well with the elegant furniture. Don't restrict yourself to the sitting room; great art looks good in a sophisticated bathroom too. Try to lose the clutter. If at all possible, place technology, from TV to CD, in a cupboard and books behind closed doors. And pick flowers carefully – go for tall stems and luscious scents, from glamorous lilies to roses.

Left: **You can achieve striking decorative effects simply by juxtaposing the clean, simple lines of one piece of furniture, perhaps a sofa, with the more romantic curves of an older, eclectic find.**

Below: **Mixing old and new doesn't have to mean blowing your budget on precious antiques or expensive designer buys. With the increasing interest in twentieth-century classics, just as enjoyable a mix may be achieved by gathering together an Eames classic, perspex Sixties chair and assorted other styles.**

OLD & NEW

There's fun to be had in the mixing of old and new, creating idiosyncratic looks that can't be bought off the peg. Highlight the clash of antique and modern with quirky decorative touches, or throw it into sharp relief by contrasting with a simple, pure interior.

We all recognize the appeal of a home in which the owner has mixed old and new with a confident eye and daring spirit. Because the result is unique, we are by turns intrigued and inspired by it: each room offers a visual surprise. This form of decorating also allows for a highly personal interpretation of style. The freedom to mix across historical periods and decorative categories, without feeling bound to follow any rules, is guaranteed to provoke exciting new looks. Even better, you can mix and match as little or as much as you like. Combining old and new can be done modestly, by juxtaposing one or two quirky antique accessories in a room, or on a grand scale, taking over a whole house. Aim for a fun, experimental mood, but to avoid the Miss Havisham cliché keep a tight rein on clutter. Mixing old and new is all about constant change, so when you bring the next great discovery home put something else away.

Provided you have a well-developed sense of what you like, or the enthusiasm to experiment, mixing old and new is one of the easiest and most relaxed looks to achieve. As it is all about trial and error, you won't make mistakes, just discoveries. Many a well-respected decorator and antique dealer will admit to constantly rearranging furniture in a room to achieve the right mood, or to delivering a mad piece of furniture to a home, just to 'look and see'. This is also one of the most user-friendly styles to fit in with a busy or family lifestyle, as nothing is too precious. What matters is its decorative appeal. 'Old' doesn't have to mean antique – instead, it can be defined as junk or second-hand – and 'new' doesn't necessarily mean expensive designer acquisitions, it can just as easily mean a high-street furniture-sale bargain, or an interesting hardware purchase from the shop around the corner.

When planning decorations to go with eclectic furniture and accessories, first decide if you want to create a blank canvas for the blend of your possessions. Of course the most gallery-like choice will be white walls, wood or sisal flooring and natural upholstery. But you can ring the changes here. Walls might be painted a vivid colour; flooring could be textured stone or rubber in a strong shade, because a funky backdrop will still throw possessions into sharp relief, and make them fun to live with. What counts is that the decorations don't tie the interior to particular pieces; you're aiming

Above: **Mixing old and new decorative styles and periods can look truly original. It often helps to keep a theme in mind. Here the room takes an ethnic motif – for furniture, decorative accessories and rugs.**

Right: **An all-white background, and neutral flooring and upholstery, throw the emphasis onto an elegant mix of antique and modern pieces. This is a very natural, relaxed look.**

Above: **Highly functional kitchens so often lack character. Just by choosing a theme – here, old weighing and measuring equipment – the most frequented room in the house is transformed into the most interesting. This combination of catering-style stainless steel and antique wood promotes a relaxed and fun mood.**

Left: **Sometimes, the architecture of your home will provide decorative cues or links. Here, the giant industrial-style light fittings cross the divide between minimal white kitchen and spacious loft apartment.**

to create a classic backdrop for an ever-changing selection of things. And pieces don't need to 'match' the architectural vocabulary of the house, either. There might be an exciting contrast in an elaborately carved eighteenth-century door panel, propped in a contemporary interior, or a giant beanbag placed against Georgian wood panelling.

In direct contrast to the gallery effect, you might choose an exotic mix of furnishings, and use the decorations themselves to create a clash between old and new. Consider twenty-first-century finishes – a metallic wallpaper or polished plasterwork – contrasted with a Gustavian-style armchair or a marble-topped washstand. Or reverse the process using traditional patterns and fabrics. You might choose a *toile de Jouy* wallpaper, combined with Sixties perspex dining chairs, or a lounge-lizard modern sofa, complete with in-built computer terminal, set next to antique chintz curtains. If you don't want such a direct juxtaposition, then choose unusual, textural wall and floor treatments that will add just a touch of exoticism to each room.

Below right and left:
Choosing classic white bathroom fittings, and neutral surfaces, from white tiles to wood boards, frees you to add old or new touches. Great with classic white are gilded, distressed mirrors, calico-covered armchairs or mirrored retro side tables; or try a bright polypropylene or metal bathroom cabinet or a funky set of scales.

Above: **The ultimate unfitted kitchen follows no style guidelines, yet it helps to pick a theme. In this kitchen, disparate fittings, from the American-style retro fridge, to the work table and butler's sink, work because of a strong utility theme and the continuity of the pure white colour scheme.**

Left: **A classic, very simple kitchen can be accessorized with contemporary fittings or antique accessories according to fashion. This mix of white-painted units, tiled floor and marble top will endure for a decade.**

A leather-tiled or colourful Moroccan-tiled floor, burnished metal wall or *trompe l'oeils* on cupboard doors would all do the trick.

If you prefer to restrict matters to mixing old and new furniture, then you can do so in many different ways. Choose all pieces in one colour and finish; for example, all white or all cast iron. With upholstered chairs, unify many styles from contemporary to antique using a single fabric: Schiaparelli pink cotton will look as exciting on a Victorian slipper chair as on a modern seating cube. You can also categorize by shape – square pieces, curvy ones – or by a theme. In this way, for example, a kitchen might be personalized with a huge collection of kitchenalia through the ages. And don't forget to rethink your definitions of 'old'. Instead of going for real antiques, you might want to stick within the twentieth century, searching out modern classics to set against this decade's trends.

Sometimes the inclusion of just one or two items from a very different decorative period can be enough to turn an ordinary interior into something spectacular. This can work either way. An ultra-modern white and stainless-steel kitchen might benefit from the addition of a scrubbed wooden farmhouse table, teamed with contemporary chairs, to take the sterility off the design. More conventionally, interior designers frequently add the clean lines of a modern perspex table to a room full of traditional antiques. Similar results may be achieved with accessories. The surprise of a hi-tech lamp silhouetted against an oil painting, or a stone bust as the only decoration in a sleek and functional limestone bathroom, can have extraordinary appeal.

However consciously you mix old and new together, the resulting look will, by definition, be the most personal and comfortable style to live with. It's the natural progression of every home, however carefully tended and revamped, to gather pieces from different periods. In turn, such a style allows you to be constantly on the search for new finds, and – because the look is so eclectic – you won't need to abandon one style and start afresh with another. For the interiors fan, that's surely the best excuse ever to shop.

Above: **Although a bold mix of styles is always arresting, it takes time and effort to get right. Picking one or two large objects to draw together disparate pieces is a good starting point. This might be a great piece of art, or an unusual furniture piece. In this bedroom, the artwork is the central focus for an eclectic mix of glass table, wooden bed and retro leather chair. It's a great style if you like to gather favourite things in your bedroom.**

Above left: **Sometimes, it's not so much the mix of old and new styles that creates an impact, as the surprise of placing a beautiful antique piece into a simple white interior. Here, the dark wood and pretty outline of the bed look fresh and distinctly contemporary.**

Above right: **The decorative frame of an antique bed can be 'dressed' to create different moods. Hung with antique textiles and decked with lace-edged pillows, this bed might look over the top. But accessorized with classic, fresh white linen and crisper textiles, it takes on a fresh, modern look.**

Left: **Don't be afraid to experiment with an antique bed in a contemporary interior. Using an old design is often the way to engineer a truly romantic mood. The process works in reverse, too. A steel-framed four-poster, set against Georgian panelling, will have a similarly stunning effect.**

room
by
room

kitchens
& eating
areas

The kitchen is the engine room of a home. It is where the practical business of storing and preparing food takes place, but in recent years it has also diversified to become a dining and family room as well. This important space should be carefully planned so that it is an efficient yet enjoyable and welcoming place to be.

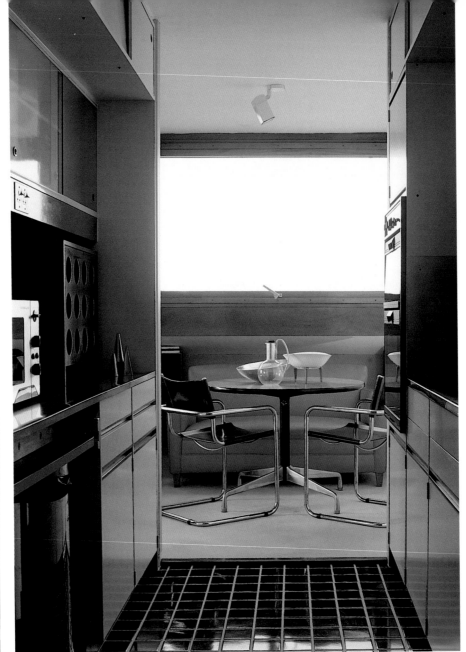

Far left: **Most standard units come in a limited range of sizes. Mix these regular units with specially made ones, free-standing furniture or features such as shelves or wine racks to achieve a neat fit in your space. If your kitchen is open-plan or doubles as a dining area, a display of decorative items will play down its practical side.**

Left: **A galley-style kitchen, with units on either side, focuses attention on the dining area beyond, but also allows the kitchen to gain natural light from the window. Glazed ceramic floor tiles also help to reflect daylight.**

Opposite main picture: **Practical work surfaces need not be dull: this industrial corrugated steel is attractive but also hard-wearing.**

Planning your kitchen

Before planning a kitchen it is important to identify what sort of space you really need: family-friendly, for example, or designed for cordon bleu cookery? Analyse the area available and your lifestyle. Start by thinking about what type of kitchen will suit your home and your needs. How many people will use the space? How will they use it? Are you a working, single person who mainly eats out, or does the kitchen need to double as a playroom and dining area? How many people would you like to be able to seat? Then, take a piece of paper and a pencil and map the outline of the room, marking in the solid features such as windows and doors, and also the utility outlets. Next sketch in the machines and equipment that you need to install, keeping in mind whether or not they need to be near water pipes and power points.

The basic guideline to planning a kitchen is to achieve a 'work triangle'. The points of this imaginary triangle are where the sink, hob, cooker, and fridge are positioned. These features should be separate but within easy reach of each other. The triangle gives you easy access between the main work areas in the kitchen, enabling you to cook in comfort. In most cases the triangle will need to give a little, depending on the length and configuration of your walls. The triangle may also have to bend to work around the main thoroughfare or traffic route in the kitchen. Ideally the main route of access and exit to and from the kitchen should not intercept the work triangle because this will interrupt the flow of activity – and may lead to accidents if people are crossing the pathway of a cook with a hot pan in their hand.

Opposite, top to bottom: **Good storage planning will pay off, and in small kitchens every nook and cranny will be needed. Pivoting shelves reach the back of a corner unit; useful but attractive lengths of link chain provide storage for frequently used tools without blocking the window; niche storage for dry goods and books.**

Opposite: **Colour is a practical, effective way of taking the hard edge off a steel or industrial-style kitchen, and is useful for giving a dual-purpose room a more relaxed feel. Here hot orange warms the cool blue of the metal facades and accessories.**

If the room is large, a central island or work station will help to break down the distances between each point. In a family room you may find that a sturdy dining table can double as additional worktop. Another alternative is to have tall stools around an elevated work surface so that it can also be used as a breakfast bar or casual dining area.

At the planning stage, aim to position appliances with similar functions together: for example, dishwasher, sink and washing machine are best kept near each other so that all the plumbing and wet work can be conveniently grouped. It's useful to have the fridge and freezer together, too. Not only are their functions compatible, but it will also make unpacking shopping easier.

Where possible, these chilling and freezing machines should be positioned away from hot machines such as cookers and tumble dryers, which might affect their cooling functions. If a fridge does have to be placed next to a wall-mounted oven or a stove, then place an insulating panel between the two. Most modern machines should be adequately insulated within their casing, but an extra panel is a worthwhile precaution.

When looking at machines and appliances, take into consideration not only the space that you have available in the kitchen but also the way you cook. Do you honestly need a six-ring hob, cooker and grill, or do most of your meals go into a microwave? Are a double sink and drainers necessary if you have a dishwasher? Try to achieve a sensible balance of space, machine size and capacity.

Storage is also important, but again consider how much you really need. You'll need more shelf space if you are a once-a-month supermarket shopper, less (but more fridge space) if you buy fresh food two or three times a week.

Safety and hygiene are priorities in a kitchen, with its hot pots and pans and sharp blades, and mix of raw and cooked foodstuffs. Ensure that the area is uncluttered and easy to move around in and that there are plenty of suitable surfaces for resting hot pots and preparing food with sharp knives, as well as a non-slip floor surface and work surfaces that are easy to clean thoroughly.

Top: Solid unit doors make small kitchens look smaller. Clear or opaque glass, mesh or reflective surfaces such as polished steel or punched panels can have the opposite effect. If you choose glass, make sure it is laminated safety glass for kitchen use.

Pale wood surrounds and white walls also add to the feeling of space and light.

Above: In this long, narrow kitchen a trolley is useful for transporting ingredients and taking cutlery and china from the sink or dishwasher to its home or the table. Simple cupboard and drawer handles provide a good, easy grip and suit a streamlined galley style like this one. Avoid ornate styles: they can be difficult to grab with greasy hands, and will also be troublesome to clean.

Above: **In this kitchen there are two dining options – a snack or breakfast facility at the edge of the island unit, well away from the heat of the hob, and a more traditional table and chairs in the centre of the room.**

Right: **There are two distinct eating areas here: the long table and bench for family dining, and a small pull-out table for a single diner. The pull-out table can also be used as an additional serving station or a place to prepare vegetables. It is designed to roll neatly back into a niche in the unit, and the front is edged with a matching drawer facade so it is camouflaged when not in use. The bench and table will push back against the wall to save space, too.**

Kitchen-diners

Kitchens that double as dining spaces have to be versatile and therefore well planned. They need to accommodate the practical kitchen functions as well as the more relaxing and sociable process of dining, and be adaptable so that they function for both family meals and, if there is no separate dining room, for more formal entertaining.

The main rule is to make sure that the dining table you choose is a suitable size for the space. Diners need to be able to push their chairs back and move comfortably around the table without knocking against surrounding cupboards and machines. Remember to site the table sufficiently far away from heat sources such as hobs and ovens, so that diners do not become overheated (or even burnt). And, ideally, guests should face away from the pile of pots waiting to be washed.

If your kitchen is a modest size, use a small table or a foldaway style with flaps that can be fixed in place when

required, so that it won't dominate the kitchen when it is not being used. If possible, extend a worktop to make a breakfast bar, with stools tucked underneath. For more generously sized rooms larger tables, with removable leaves or insets, can also be useful as they will provide plenty of working space for the room's kitchen role but can be reduced in size for smaller or intimate meals.

If the surface of your table is wood, or other material vulnerable to scratches or marks, cover it with plasticized cloth or a similar protective, easy-to-clean surface for cooking, preparing food or feeding young children. Otherwise, choose a practical melamine or laminated tabletop. This can always be covered with a linen or cotton tablecloth to give a less utilitarian feel when you entertain.

Lighting plays a very important role in changing the mood of a room like this. For example, task lights directed over work areas can be dimmed or turned off for

Main picture: **The stylish mid-twentieth-century chairs, with their curving backs, become a decorative feature in these simple surroundings. A free-standing cabinet, displaying glassware, gives a more homely aspect to the room.**

Above: **Here, pale wood chairs and table complement this white kitchen. White is the perfect shade to make a kitchen feel crisp, fresh and clean, while crockery and utensils displayed on open shelves stop the room looking too clinical.**

dining and a softer ambient light with a decorative lighting feature, such as candles, centred on the table. For family mealtimes or busy breakfasts, lighting needs to be stronger and more targeted, so an adjustable pendant light (with a dimmer switch) can be a useful option positioned directly over the table.

Decoration also plays a vital role in accommodating the two activities. Above all the decor should be practical, and surfaces durable and easy to wipe clean. Storage should be plentiful so that the bulk of kitchen gadgets and utensils can be stowed away out of sight when dining is the primary function of the room.

Simple decorating schemes generally work best in a kitchen-diner. Aim to plan decoration to make a functional and hygienic base for the kitchen, then add extra flourishes when you lay the table for dining. A bright cloth, glittering glasses, and china and cutlery can all be used to build up decorative interest on the table. In smaller spaces, aim for a sympathetic decorative scheme that will link the dining and kitchen functions rather than exaggerate their different uses. For example, if you have a hi-tech steel-clad kitchen, then the dining furniture should be contemporary and in a similar style or finish. In a traditional scheme – for example, a painted and wood kitchen – the furniture should be complementary in style, with perhaps country-style wood chairs with rattan seats and a classic sealed wood table as the focus of the room.

Good ventilation and an extractor fan are necessary to make a kitchen comfortable for eating (and, of course, cooking) in. The build-up of steam from boiling water and pots, the heat from grills, stoves and hobs and the various aromas of cooking food can make a room overheated and stuffy. If the room is not adequately ventilated, the heat and smells will linger. A good hood and extractor fan over a hob area are a great asset, and louvred windows or window vents will also help to reduce the steam and heat.

Above and above right: **In a small kitchen without space for a free-standing table, this folding, pull-out surface, which has a matching drawer facade, is an ideal snack bar. The surface is made in two sections, which double back neatly, and slides back on** steel runners. **The variety of tones in the natural slate flooring, laid in a diamond pattern, brings together the colours used in this scheme – the cool silver of the cooker and storage jars, the soft blue of the units above and the pale brown tone of the wood.**

Left: **This island unit doubles as a breakfast bar and the stools provide a comfy perch. The island has been picked out in a pale yellow-cream that contrasts with and separates it from the green units behind. It also forms a barrier between the working kitchen and the rest of the room, so the kitchen is visually self-contained in this open-plan space. To prevent the strong colour becoming overpowering, there are areas of plain white wall and ceiling, and the floor is covered with a light, speckled polished granite.**

In many homes the kitchen's role has expanded to incorporate a number of other functions. It is no longer just for food preparation and dining, but also accommodates children's play, TV watching and general relaxation. In new homes the kitchen is generally built larger than it was thirty years ago, and in many older homes owners have extended their kitchen, often with a light-filled conservatory-style room, or knocked down an internal wall to create a larger all-purpose living space. In loft developments – perfect for open-plan living – people make the most of the openness, using temporary dividers, such as folding or movable walls, to define or enclose areas.

As with kitchen-diners, good ventilation is vital in these larger rooms. Although steam and water vapour will generally disperse, smells and moisture may linger, and if you have upholstered furniture, curtains or other soft furnishings near your cooking area, they may absorb the moisture and smells, as well as grease, which can cause damage and staining.

Storage in multi-purpose spaces should be generous. It can also double as display, so that groups of glasses or matching plates become part of the overall appearance of the room. Try to allocate storage so that it is specific to the function of that part of the room. This reduces muddle and will also cut down on journeys from one area to another. Kitchen storage should cope with foodstuffs and washing equipment; the dining area needs cupboards to hold crockery, glass, table linen and cutlery; and the living area requires a section for books, magazines and home entertainment items.

In an open-plan kitchen different functions will need different lighting: task lights for food preparation and cooking, perhaps under wall-hung cabinets and over the hob, and softer background lighting for the table. Areas can also be defined by rugs, mats or flooring finishes. For example, the cooking area could have a utilitarian tiled or slate floor,

Open-plan kitchens

Opposite far left: **A wall of open shelving, painted bright yellow, contrasts with the neutral tones in the rest of the room. The shelves have been constructed around narrow windows to provide a view and also to allow natural light in at worktop level.**

Opposite centre: **Colour has been used here to play down the industrial look of this steel kitchen and make it compatible with the multi-purpose room.**

Left: **Here an island unit doubles as a breakfast bar and casual dining table, to be used with adjustable wooden stools. It also forms a useful barrier between the working part of the room, with the sink and oven, and the entertaining area.**

with the dining and living sections based on a softer, warmer wood floor. Rugs can also bring a softer feel to a dining or sitting area. (If laid over a polished wood or similarly shiny surface, they should be placed on non-slip backing.)

Open-plan and multi-purpose kitchens are popular with families because an adult can prepare a meal while still being able to see and talk to other family members or guests, while small children can be kept out of danger – but still easily visible by an adult – in a play area separated from the kitchen by a child gate or screen.

Above: **In this converted factory an industrial-style steel-clad kitchen is softened by a leather daybed and simple, classic furniture in the living and dining area. Although there are three distinct functions housed here, each has its own defined space.**

Left: **In this L-shaped room the main dining and living section occupies the longer leg, while the kitchen and casual eating areas are in the more compact end. This configuration contains the kitchen neatly, although it is still part of the same room. Colour has been used to link areas and define their uses: the red leather seats of the Fifties chrome stools link with the more formal skirted covers on the dining chairs.**

Island kitchens

A kitchen 'island' is a free-standing, usually central, block of worktop. Island kitchens revolve around this station and are usually spacious rooms where the island acts as a central point between the three points of the work triangle.

The shape of the island varies – it can be square, oblong or even curved. It may be decorated so that it stands out as a feature from the rest of the units and scheme, or it may be finished to match the overall scheme. Well-finished edges are important; they should be smooth and rounded so that they do not catch on clothing or hurt passers-by.

The island itself is a very flexible piece of furniture. The simplest model may be a food preparation and storage

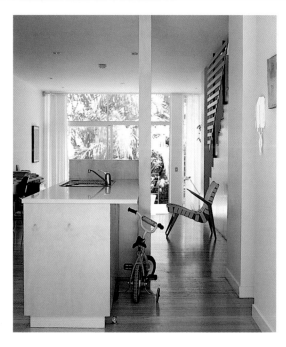

Opposite above:
The rounded end of an island unit is extended beyond its base to create a simple breakfast bar deep enough for informal meals. This kitchen's built-in storage with sliding, roll-top panels keeps the majority of the kitchen machines and gadgets out of sight but still easily accessible.

Opposite below: **In this large kitchen, the island unit contains a sink and forms part of the work triangle between the large fridge-freezer and the stove. It is also a good way of reducing the distances between one side of this spacious room and the other; it provides a central point and work surface, cutting down on walking around while cooking. The gleaming copper pans give the room a decorative focus.**

block on wheels. A static, plumbed and wired version offers other options. The area beneath the worktop can be left empty, fitted for storage such as drawers and cupboards, or house machines, perhaps a dishwasher or even a second fridge. The top can be inset with a hob or griddle. With power points the island can be a work station for anything from food processing to coffee making.

Another advantage is that an island can be raised to provide an area that is comfortable for you to work at standing; taller and smaller people are therefore not restricted by standard-height kitchen units. Alternatively, some standard units can be raised on adjustable legs, and to add extra height a butcher's block or thick chopping board can be fixed into a recess or surround (to stop it slipping) on the surface.

The true working area of an island unit, especially a large or square design, is around its edges. The central part may not be readily accessible, but it is an ideal point over which to hang pots and pans – the area will not be in direct contact with or at head height of a person working at the unit, but it and any hanging utensils are still accessible by an outstretched arm. But remember that pots and pans left on display in a central area like this will be a feature – so they should be good quality and perfectly clean.

Top: **This unit has a flush facade with recessed handles so that a person can work close to it in comfort. The work surface overhangs on the other side; a stool could be stored underneath here, to pull out when needed. The below-surface storage contains** herbs and spices used for cooking on the hob above. Storing them in the unit makes seasoning easy. Pans hang overhead within reach.

Above: **This island creates a corridor on one side while providing a work area for the kitchen on the other.**

Unfitted & country-style kitchens

When installing a kitchen, one of the first questions you have to ask yourself is whether you want it to be fully fitted, free-standing or a combination of both. Fitted kitchens are often the best option in small rooms because they can be tailored to fit into every available centimetre, so maximizing your worktop and storage area.

Unfitted kitchens give you the flexibility to add and subtract pieces of furniture as you go along or as your budget permits. In addition, you can take the furniture with you when you move, whereas fitted units stay in place. You may opt for a bit of both, fitted units containing appliances such as the sink, which has to be plumbed in, and wall-mounted cookers, which need to be wired and vented, with free-standing furniture in between.

The mix-and-match option is also a cheaper way of redoing an existing kitchen. Instead of ripping everything out and starting from scratch, you can leave a number of the existing units, such as those containing fixed appliances, in place. You can then choose to replace other units, or fill in any spaces, with unfitted furniture. The latter two configurations create very personal kitchens because they are individually devised. Fitted kitchens are

Below: **A Scandinavian-inspired setting has a modern double oven and hob, but both are vented through a traditional-style chimney.**

Top right: **Dressers can be created by hanging a row of shelves on a wall over cupboards. You could use standard fitted units below and** custom-made shelves above. The unit doors may be painted *trompe l'oeil*-style to give the impression of panelling, or gain a decorative MDF border, fixed to the door and painted.

Above: **A light curtain makes a softer option than solid unit doors.**

Above right: **Cream is a good background colour for displaying china against. It is also warmer and less stark than pure white.**

Opposite above left: **Chequerboard patterned floors are classic and work well with many styles. The old enamel stove adds a rustic touch to this setting. All vintage equipment should be reconditioned and checked before use.**

Opposite above right: **This modern kitchen is designed to look old. The paintwork has been rubbed to give a worn look and the units echo traditional country style.**

Opposite below: **This unfitted kitchen has been constructed from a variety of furniture, most of which is finished with matching handles.**

generally bought from a manufacturer's stock selection and are configured in a uniform way, although you can customize standard units with decorative details or by adding different door handles.

Unfitted kitchens are generally associated with the country look because the rustic kitchens of times gone by were essentially unfitted, made up of a couple of cupboards, sometimes a dresser and a good, solid wood table. Function was the order of the day, although dresser shelves were sometimes arranged with a display of best china or other decorative tableware.

As a rule the country look remains loyal to natural materials. Wood plays a key role, as do stone and terracotta flooring and plain, glazed ceramic tiles. But this particular

decorative style is wide-ranging because it comes from many countries. If you want to play up Mediterranean influences, introduce stronger hues and a primary colour – red, blue or yellow – mixed with liberal amounts of white. For Scandinavian overtones, try a palette that has a grey tint, elegant lavender blues and soft mossy green.

American country style is most widely associated with the beautifully simple Shaker look: well-made, practical panelled cupboards with round wooden knobs, peg rails and walls painted white or off-white. Cupboards are usually painted cheerful colours such as cranberry red, mid-blue and yellow-green.

Neutral country style means cream, or warmer tones with more yellow, and natural wood. This background is warm but not overpowering, so you can add decorative accessories, pretty fabric or china. The kitchen will be a perfect, uncomplicated backdrop for these items.

Country furniture is usually wood – painted, stained or waxed. The pristine fresh look of painted furniture is ideal for some styles but others need a little more character and age. Painted surfaces can be rubbed down with sandpaper or wire wool, giving the corners a worn appearance as the wood peeks through the upper layer of paint. Bear in mind that wood needs waxing or sealing to protect it from wear, and always use a chopping board on your wood table. This is protective and easy to remove for washing.

Another aspect of the unfitted and country-style kitchen is that you can find great pieces of furniture if you employ a little lateral thinking. A ceramic Belfast sink can be countersunk into a small wood table, which will also double as a sink surround. An old chest of drawers, perhaps with a couple of damaged drawers, can be adapted to form the base of an island work station, and a section of a broken marble tabletop or a dairy or butcher's shop worktop can be adapted to form a perfect meat-chopping or pastry-rolling surface in a domestic kitchen.

Opposite above left: **The flue of this stove has been plumbed out through an existing chimney breast, but the opening has been sculpted in an unusual shape.**

Opposite above right: **A selection of furniture has been assembled to form this kitchen. The sink, resting on top of a set of shelves, is plumbed in beneath wall-mounted taps. Blue paint makes the scheme coherent.**

Opposite below left: **Vintage patterned tiles mix with plain contemporary ones to form a splashback.**

Opposite below right: **Existing features such as an old painted cupboard and stone floor provide a source of inspiration for this decidedly rural look.**

Top right: **A reclaimed stone sink resting on brick pillars is easily incorporated into an arrangement of free-standing units.**

Centre right: **An old wood table is positioned to form an island unit. The style and colouring of the table complements the existing antique fireplace.**

Right: **Ceramic tiles can be beautiful as well as useful. Their easy-to-clean surface has made them a long-standing kitchen favourite. Here they soften a kitchen in modern traditional country style.**

Left: **This central beam shelf is a useful and decorative storage feature.**

A room to relax, read or party in, the living room must be all things to all people – flexibility and beauty are just the start. The smaller it is, the harder it has to work, so plan it minutely and it will pay you dividends. Add soothing colours and all your favourite things.

living rooms

Planning your living room

For the lucky few, the living room is a dedicated sitting room, a tranquil space for winding down in, even a cool style statement in terms of the objects and furniture on display. But for the greater majority, it is the nerve centre of the home, where family life, TV-watching, computer-shopping and socializing coexist, day in, day out. The living room is a harder working room than most of us realize. So give it due attention. Plan it as carefully as the kitchen or bathroom, and the whole family will reap the rewards.

Before you do anything else, take a mental trawl through your lifestyle and ask some salient questions. How much time will be spent in the room, and what activities will go on there? What favourite possessions do you want to show off? What needs to be stored? Where is technology to go, from TV to CD? If you entertain frequently, can space be rearranged

easily? Finally, pay attention to mood. If this is the one room where you can relax, be sure there is excellent control over natural and artificial light, sound and comfort levels.

Correct furniture arrangement is paramount. Good planning means you can watch TV in comfort (because there's a coffee table nearby), and chat easily with friends (because the chairs are close enough). Careful space management may even squeeze in enough room for a separate seating area for quiet reading or card games. See whether there is a natural focal point in the room, be it a fireplace or a great view, because incorporating that into a scheme can be a useful decorative starting point. It sounds a cliché, but drawing a scale plan of the room and cutting out to-scale shapes of existing furniture really will help. In terms of human traffic flow, remember that space between furniture always seems less once translated into three dimensions, so err on the generous side.

Plan where to house the technology at the outset, and the room will look slick. It's not an issue whether or not the TV is on show, but do try to conceal trailing wires. On-show options include purpose-built trolleys (often on contemporary castors), perspex cubes (so the TV seems to 'float'), and a wall-mounted folding 'arm' (useful in tiny spaces). Alternatively, conceal 'the box' within a built-in cupboard, low sideboard or in a purpose-built alcove, so only the screen is on show. The video player doesn't have to sit directly below the TV and is more practically stored in a cupboard next to the stereo, near the videos and CDs. If you

Opposite: **A real or real-effect fire is a natural focal point, and is always worth the investment. Match mantelpiece styles to the rest of the room. Don't be sentimental about keeping a period fire surround if your look is contemporary; replace it with a modern hole-in-the-wall style.**

Below: **When different living areas coexist, simply facing seating away from the dining table can be just as effective as a physical division.**

Left: **When planning furniture layout, think through every possible living-room activity. Is there a light and low table by a reading chair and an armchair by the phone? For entertaining, is there room for extra seats, and places to put drinks?**

Below left: **For the ultimate contemplative sitting room, devoted to music, books and conversation, pare everything to the minimum. Let the visual focus fall on a great view and stylish furniture.**

must have a computer in the living room, screen it carefully from the main sitting area. And save rewiring the house with built-in speakers for the next move. Instead, paint existing speakers to match the walls, or disguise them in a wicker basket on top of a shelf unit.

Good lighting can make or break a living room. If possible, replace central pendant lighting – it casts ugly shadows – but don't do away with overhead lighting altogether. Every living room needs the option of bright light sometimes. Strategically placed downlighters not only provide ambient illumination (add a dimmer, so you can control the level), but may be angled to cast specific beams over paintings. Plan for more side lights than you think you'll need, and put all lights on a central switch with a dimmer. Don't forget good task lighting, for reading, and a smattering of styles to add decorative interest.

Controlling natural light is equally important. Everyone longs for a sunny living room, but if sunlight is too dazzling consider screening it with translucent roller blinds, Venetian blinds or American-style shutters, alone or in addition to curtains. If the room is naturally shady, place at least one chair and table next to a window to capitalize on daylight.

Choosing a style and refurbishing is the exciting part, but give great thought to your budget. A living room demands investment pieces of furniture, from sofas to bookshelves, not to mention metres of fabric and the almost ruinous cost of making up soft furnishings. It can be an expensive business. So try to compose a classic scheme which will endure over at least a decade – thus helping to spread the cost – which may be updated with trendier accessories.

First look at what you have. A sofa may be reupholstered in a new fabric, or a battered side table given a new, distressed paint finish. If buying a new sofa, try to pick an enduring style – antique ones are often the best – which can be given contemporary upholstery. And if you need new curtains, consider ready-mades. There are some great, inexpensive styles in high-street stores. Remember, it's always better to invest in a good curtain or loose cover maker and use a budget fabric, than the other way round.

Go classic, too, when choosing the colours and surfaces of the room. A neutral colour scheme, wood or sisal flooring and hard-wearing fabrics, from linens to wool, are the order of the day. A neutral background provides the best backdrop for pretty possessions and art, and is easily updated with fresh splashes of colour. Don't be afraid to make the living room the most sophisticated room in the house, particularly if you like to entertain. A gilded mirror or precious painting will set the right 'public' tone and be enjoyed by everyone.

Main picture: **Plan good storage for a hard-working living room, so that books, magazines and videos can be tidied away quickly. Anything dual-purpose, from a coffee table with drawers to floor-level cupboards which support the TV and a dining-cum-work table, will help the room work harder still.**

Opposite above: **Zone a small living space correctly, and it becomes dual-functional. Create two separate living-work areas with back-to-back storage units or a desk butted up to a sofa. Squeeze bookshelves into every corner.**

Opposite below and below: **There are various devices for separating areas without compromising the spirit of open-plan living. A change of floor levels, simple wall divisions or a subtle shift in furniture style or colour – plastics versus leather, primaries contrasted with neutrals – also rings the changes.**

Zoning your living space

Above: **A neutral colour scheme helps to unify, rather than demarcate, zones within an open-plan apartment. This means the space looks bigger, and it's a flexible arrangement as furniture moved from one zone to another will suit either setting.**

In a small home, where rooms must be dual-functional, or in a loft or open-plan apartment, in which a seating or dining area will be just one of several activity zones, it's essential to define 'living space' boundaries. Everyone needs to know there's a specific area for relaxing. The demarcation may be anchored physically, using partitions or by the placement of furniture, or visually, using colour to define areas.

Either way, think first about the flow of human traffic. In a small home, locate the living area in a quiet spot, away from busy access routes from front door to kitchen, or the playroom to the staircase. In an open-plan space, locate sofas well away from central kitchen and play areas, and nearest to the bedrooms, for guaranteed peace. When kids are around, this also cuts down on straying sticky fingers.

If building work is an option, then there are myriad ways to divide zones. Mezzanine floors and raised platforms are particularly suited to lofts or radical house conversions. If knocking down walls to create an open-plan space, leave some sections, to create natural divisions between spaces. Or replace walls with a fixed glass brick or sandblasted glass wall. More flexible options include traditional double doors, pivoting or fold-back panels, or sliding canvas 'walls'.

A carefully placed U- or L-shaped seating configuration is the simplest way to define a living space; alternatively, try two identical sofas, facing each other, with a central coffee table. These arrangements mean you are sitting looking inwards, so they feel instantly cosy. Contemporary sofas lend themselves particularly well to specific groupings, as many are available as modular units to rearrange.

Do remember that while furniture can, and will, define a space, silhouettes shouldn't be so bulky as to destroy the view through an open-plan area, or fill up too much space in a small room. Choosing low sofas, substituting a daybed for a sofa, or swapping a boxy armchair for a slimmer one can all help. One of the most common problems in a city terraced house is how to unify two halves of a knocked-through living room. By putting sofas back to back in the centre of the room, you will create two well-defined seating areas.

Colour is a powerful tool. In a white-painted loft with wood floorboards throughout, the living zone might be highlighted by painting the wall nearest to it in a bright or pastel shade. Alternatively, matching colourful upholstery for chairs and sofa will set the zone apart, perhaps in direct contrast to monochrome natural materials and furniture used elsewhere. Bold accessories can also be a defining

influence. Think about cheerful abstract rugs in blocks of colour, a painted wall canvas, or bright metallic bookcases.

If you prefer not to have striking contrasts, then keep all furniture, from sofas to dining chairs, firmly within a monochrome palette, so that the eye travels easily across an open-plan space. This also allows more freedom for moving furniture as the mood takes you. In a small house, a strict, muted colour scheme also avoids jarring contrasts.

Tailored lighting also helps to 'zone' a space. In an open-plan apartment, try to have downlighters on a different circuit to, say, the kitchen area, otherwise the sitting area will look too brightly lit. At the very least, fit a dimmer switch. You can have fun choosing lighting for specific areas. Centrally arranged downlighters will pool light onto a specific seating spot. Inset floor lights can lead the way to a sitting or dining area, or a string of fairy lights can encircle it. Within the zone, play around with options of glowing side lamps, wall lights, standard lamps or bright task lighting.

Opposite: **If space permits, provide two separate seating areas: one for conversation or television, the other a quiet space for reading or listening to music. Unify both using an identical colour scheme. In a large room, several clusters of seating help the room seem intimate.**

Below left and right: **If sitting and dining areas are squeezed into a smaller area, arrange furniture so it doesn't impede the view across a room. Low-lying furniture, glass or perspex tables, and woven or wire chairs all create the impression of space and light.**

Below: **Conversions of industrial buildings into domestic homes call for the creation of ingenious multi-purpose living spaces. Experiment with mezzanine levels, platform rooms, and internal 'pod' rooms within a large space. When dealing with a totally open-plan environment, always try to sandwich the dining area between kitchen and sitting area; no one, however tidy, wants to relax right next to dirty pots and pans. Here, a cohesive colour scheme, boxy silhouettes repeated throughout kitchen, dining room and sitting room, and cleverly concealed TV area all create a simple, streamlined living space.**

Compact living

Most of us have less living space than we would like, and some, from terraced-house owners to studio dwellers, are especially space-challenged. Yet squeezing a relaxing living area into a one-space home often provokes creative solutions. Accept that your living space needs to be flexible, practical and utterly neat, and you've won half the battle. Also remember that in a small space everything, from the kitchen to the front door, is on display. So either decide that's acceptable or work out ways to hide certain features.

In open-plan homes, choose a unifying decorative theme in terms of colour and surfaces. In a small space, there's little point in zoning; the emphasis should be on cohesion. This not only simplifies the look, but also helps blur boundaries between different activity areas. Adaptable surfaces, which are as appropriate in a kitchen as in a living area, include wood, glass, stainless steel and leather. With these, pick a neutral scheme: classic all-white or – if going for colour – no more than three specific shades, to avoid visual confusion.

Think about choosing dual-purpose and flexible furniture. A daybed can double as a sofabed, a coffee table with drawers becomes a storage unit, a fashionable seating cube acts a side table. Stacking dining chairs are also a boon. Rather than one huge sofa, consider two mini sofas – a design much beloved by contemporary furniture designers – or a number of armchairs teamed with a daybed. Stick to similar furniture styles throughout. You need to be able to mix and match different pieces across the whole area, so aim to choose chair styles, for example, which look as good tucked under the dining table as positioned next to the sofa.

If you're not comfortable having everything out on show, investigate ways to separate living and work areas. Kitchens are notoriously difficult to disguise, but – provided you stick to a minimal galley – may be hidden behind purpose-built folding glass or MDF doors, sliding painted or wallpapered panels, or pivoting metal or glass doors. Avoiding structural changes, free-standing bookshelves and mobile screens can create a suitable barrier. Face living-room furniture away from the kitchen, preferably towards a pretty window or fireplace, and each area will take on a well-defined mood.

Above left and opposite:
It is often better to put up with an open-plan kitchen as part of one large room than ruin its proportions with a solid dividing wall. Galley kitchens are easily disguised behind sliding screens or folding doors. If adopting the minimalist look, match cupboards' fascias to cupboards in the living area – blurring the boundaries between work and relaxation zones.

Above top and bottom:
Not all divisions need to be solid. In this relaxed interior with eclectic furnishings, plain white cotton and muslin drapes are an enticing alternative, and can be tied back or let down to create impromptu screens between bathroom and sitting area.

Opposite: **Allow for the possibility of chopping and changing displays according to season or mood. Paintings propped on shelves or on a mantelpiece have more flexibility than wall-hung versions; set aside a few simple frames which may take fresh images or photos from time to time.**

Left: **Plain walls create the best background for displays of contemporary art. Work out the best picture arrangement on the floor first, and measure appropriate gaps; then hang them on the walls.**

Below: **Open shelves running the breadth of fireplace alcoves and chimney breast provide a fresh take on the conventional cupboard and shelf option. If storing papers or photos on open shelves, give a cohesive look by choosing attractive files or storage baskets: cardboard and wicker are both good choices.**

Bottom: **Create 'invisible' storage by building a fake wall 50cm (20in) or so from the original wall. Then use the space to build a series of different-sized cupboards with flush doors, or inset storage alcoves.**

Storage & display

However busy it becomes in reality, the living room should have the potential to look and be tranquil and tidy. That's why great storage is crucial. Long before deciding on storage styles, think long and hard about what really needs to be stored in the living room. Depending on the size of your home, it may be possible to relocate certain items – old photos, perhaps, or out-of-favour CDs – to the attic or basement. If space is tight, have regular clearouts. Things you keep in the living room should be items for enjoyment only – music and books, treasures and mementoes.

Built-in storage has the advantage of being tailor-made to suit your possessions, from book heights to TV size, and can match your chosen decorative style. Try to think beyond the conventional option of a bookshelf and cupboard in each fireplace alcove, which makes a room smaller. Closed storage options include a whole wall of panelling, with individual doors that pop open to reveal cupboards, small alcoves inset into the wall – which hold everything from the TV to a vase – or shallow cupboards, wall-mounted or built into an alcove, with frosted glass, MDF or perspex doors.

The advantage of free-standing storage is that it comes with you when you move. Don't just think of bookshelves: other options include mix-and-match units offering shelves and cupboards, traditional commodes or storage ottomans, or, less conventionally, a sideboard or plan chest. Inside each item, provide easy access to items like CDs and videos by placing them in cheap plastic racks, and keep bulky things such as photo albums low down so they are easy to lift out.

Above and left: **You can build bookshelves into many alcoves – under the stairs, around a door, in a redundant fireplace or, conventionally, flanking a chimney breast. They needn't be painted white:** **match the colour to the walls for a more integrated look.**

Opposite: **For a contemporary look, arrange books vertically and horizontally on simple open-ended shelves.**

Opinions differ as to whether books should, or shouldn't, be included in a living room. In a very elegant room, many colourful spines may spoil a decorative scheme. In general, however, books add a lived-in, comfortable air. Don't just fit bookshelves into an alcove. Shelves can be fitted around a door, open shelves fixed just below the ceiling, or spanning a bare wall. Spend time arranging shelves neatly, otherwise books quickly look messy. And they don't have to be book-filled. Several contemporary shelves, with a broad front edge, look fabulous propped with framed family portraits.

The best living rooms bear the personality of their owner. So collect favourite things in here, from serious art to stones gathered on the beach. Less is more in terms of display. A mantelpiece may need only a cluster of ceramic vases to look good. (Don't rely on flowers to enliven a room, as they are not always available in winter.) Pay attention to picture display, too. Instead of dotting paintings around the room, hang a cluster on a single wall – infinitely more arresting.

Creating the comfort zone

A peaceful and cosy ambience is the prime objective in any living room. In pursuit of this, choose comfortable furniture that helps everyone relax. Look for deep seats, high arms that will support the head if lounging, and well-stuffed seat cushions. A daybed is great for listening to music, a wing chair ideal for reading. If choosing new upholstered pieces, never be embarrassed to stretch out in the shop: everyone has their own comfort priorities. Look for a mix of scatter cushions. Fat, feather-filled ones are great, but a sturdy bolster or neck-roll shape is helpful for reading support.

Colour, more than any other single object, will affect the room's mood. Try to think beyond fashionable shades, and pick a scheme that is soothing, relaxing and will endure. A neutral base is safest, but go for the warmest neutrals you can, favouring pink or yellow tones of taupe rather than grey, creams and flax shades rather than pure white. If having colour is a priority, then it is cheaper to put it on walls rather than on upholstery; walls are easier to repaint or repaper. Go for tranquil soft pastels, from putty pink to Swedish grey-blue, or really deep tones of terracotta, ochre or olive.

And give due attention to flooring. Despite the lack of softness underfoot, many people still prefer the smarter look of floorboards, rather than picking carpet. Think about your lifestyle. If you're the type to sprawl on the floor, or you have young children, then laying a wool rug over the boards in the central sitting, TV-watching area is ideal. There's a

Left: **The style and shape of cushions and upholstery can make or break the comfort factor. As well as square cushions, experiment with rectangular shapes – from very narrow to substantial pillow versions – and go for squashy feather-filled cushions. The same rules apply to upholstered furniture. Avoid over-zealous upholstery that's straining at the seams.**

huge choice of rug designs, from traditional to contemporary, or a bound sisal rug will fit well with a neutral colour scheme. An animal hide, from ponyskin to cow, is another option.

Treat yourself to tactile finishes. As well as upholstery fabrics and curtains – and there is every fabric option, from velvet to wool, and moleskin to satin – add cushions, a warming throw, a deep-pile rug or a velvety footstool. While a daybed with fabric hangings, or a curvy deep sofa with lots of cushions, provide obviously romantic-looking living-room options, even hard-edged contemporary furniture will seem cosseting when teamed with the right textiles.

In pursuit of that all-important ambience, gather together as many tools as you can to create a tranquil mood. Low lighting, the flicker of firelight, deliciously scented fresh flowers and plenty of candles are just some essentials.

Opposite above and below: Warm, rich wall colours impart an instantly cosy atmosphere to a living room. Experiment with shades from terracotta to scarlet and warm ochre to chocolate brown. Balance the vivid walls with neutral upholstery, flooring and window treatments.

Above: Combine a variety of light sources to create ambience. Firelight, candlelight and mood lighting from table lamps provide the basic mix.

Above right: **The living room should contain your favourite things, and the more exotic and personal the mix, the better. Experiment by mixing original art, hand-painted textiles or lampshades, and antique textiles.**

Right: **All the best sitting rooms have a quiet corner for contemplation, be it a luxurious daybed or an armchair close to the fire. Include a table for books and a coffee cup, decent task lighting, and plenty of cushions for comfort.**

From childhood we dream of a room of our own – a private place, an escape from the noise and demands of other people. As adults we may choose to share this intimate space with the one we love, but our bedroom remains a personal retreat and a place to feel safe.

bedrooms

Opposite: **In this studio, a single spacious room is bedroom and living room, united with a subdued palette and clever choice of spare, multi-functional furnishings. The bedroom area, partially hidden by a flexible wooden screen, is lined with discreet floor-to-ceiling cupboards. The bed can be folded up into the wall during the day, to maximize living space.**

Right: **Japanese-style screens pull across one end of this loft to make a private, wood-lined sleeping area. The bed is raised on a wide platform to emphasize its status as a special and separate place within the expanse of wooden flooring.**

Below right: **An antique sleigh bed is dressed in ruffle-edged cotton with a canopy of gauzy muslin, for pure romance in an intimate small bedroom.**

Small bedrooms

When we are sleeping we are vulnerable, and our instincts still dictate we sleep most soundly when feeling most secure. Far from being a disadvantage, a small bedroom can increase that sense of security, cocooning us within its walls as if safe in a nest.

A small bedroom, well organized, can be as satisfying aesthetically as it is practical. Bedroom necessities are few: a bed large enough for sprawling, with a mattress relatively hard or soft according to taste; a table or shelf on either side of the bed; lights designed for bedtime reading; cupboards and drawers for clothes; a couple of hooks on the back of the door for dressing gowns. These are the essentials and, with clever planning, they can be fitted into a space not much bigger than the bed itself.

The most efficient way to utilize space is with fitted furniture. Most small bedrooms have at least one wall that can be filled from floor to ceiling with cupboards. In order to maximize every bit of wall space, it is usually worth commissioning bespoke joinery if at all possible. In an old house, for example, wardrobes may fit best on either side of a chimney breast. When planning hanging space, always ensure there is sufficient depth for a wide wood clothes hanger, plus the bulk of the garment hanging on it, to move freely without scraping against the back of the cupboard or the door. Trying to give yourself a few more centimetres of floor space at the expense of the wardrobe is a false economy that will irritate ever after.

Beds can also be built in and designed to incorporate invaluable storage in that dead space underneath, which is otherwise the preserve of fluff and hiding children. A simple wood plinth, extended at the top to provide bedside shelf space and with a mattress laid on top, makes a stylish bed for a modern room. Wall lights, as opposed to table lamps, leave more space for books, alarm clocks and glasses of water.

There are two decorative routes for a small room: one works to create the illusion of space; the other makes a virtue of necessity by emphasizing its inherently cosy, enclosing qualities. The first demands coherence, plain, pale colours and a lack of clutter only possible with ample cupboard, shelf and drawer space. A colour scheme of neutrals and naturals is soothing and not quite as demanding, or potentially dazzling first thing, as brilliant white. Don't forget the power of mirrors – unrivalled for magnifying light and volume as well as being invaluable for checking whether your trousers are the right length. Sliding mirrored doors can look sleek and contemporary while giving the illusion that a room is twice its real size. Using mirrors to panel small areas of wall, alcoves and rebates can make even the most cramped space feel bright and airy.

Fabrics, whether bed linen, curtains or rugs, provide the softness and texture that are essential to the feeling of comfort in a bedroom. Blackout roller or Roman blinds take up less floor and wall space than curtains, and are good for a pared-down look. If, however, you are going for all-out cosiness, there is no better way to promote it than with acres of drapery, be it wafting muslin or heavy folds of linen. Fabric can even be used to line the walls, stretched on battens like a soft, slightly textured wallpaper. A patterned fabric will draw the walls in around you, making you feel thoroughly cocooned and insulated from the outside world. Using the same fabric for walls, curtains and bed-hangings helps to give decorative coherence to a small bedroom which might otherwise be overwhelmed by too much pattern.

Far left: **Foldaway beds used to be ugly, uncomfortable, and needed two people to raise and lower them. Modern versions are elegant in looks and operation.**

Above left: **One solution to sharing living and sleeping space is the bed that can simply be rolled and folded out of the way, like this combination of tatami mats and futons.**

Above centre:
This apartment has been divided into zones by a combination of shelving, cupboards and screen walls, which partially enclose the sleeping area. A cool chain-link curtain provides a hazy view through windows beyond and a modicum of privacy.

Opposite above right: **A big bed, tucked under the eaves, makes a bedroom both snug and welcoming.**

Right: **Skilful use of mirrors, here in the wardrobe and a wall panel to its right, create the illusion of space.**

Above left: **Extra space in a bedroom means you can afford to have pieces of furniture that are more beautiful than useful, like this set of sculptural and decorative steps.**

Left: **Space also means you can accommodate oversized furnishings like this theatrical bed, with its elongated posts, flanked by generous side tables and large lamps to match.**

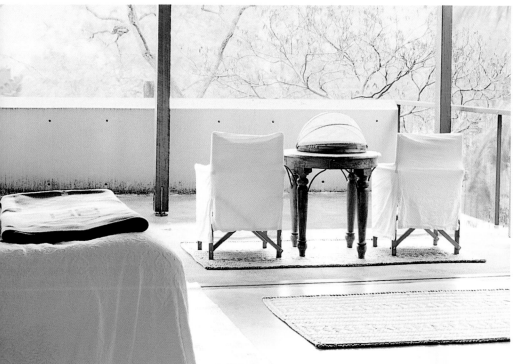

Spacious bedrooms

Space is always a luxury and bedrooms should be luxurious spaces. The joy of a large bedroom can be the opportunity to use it for activities other than just sleeping and dressing. If your rooms are large, but few, you may be tempted to devote a corner of your bedroom to work space. But sharing the place where you sleep with a computer and an in-tray is far from ideal. Most of us prefer to escape from work for the night, even if only from the physical reminders of it. A bedroom should be reserved for quiet, private relaxation – writing letters at a small desk, reclining on a chaise longue to watch television, or reading in a comfortable armchair.

Empty floor space gives you the freedom to play with the arrangement of furniture. Placing a bed in the middle of a room can look very dramatic, for example. Wardrobes can be free-standing and you can indulge in the old-fashioned convenience of a spacious dressing table with three-sided mirror. You could even create a walk-in dressing area with screens or partitions. And, if there is still room to swing a handbag, you can add purely decorative pieces, a screen or a pretty stool, or you could even install a beautiful bath.

The idea of making use of your bedroom during the day is far from new. In the eighteenth century it was polite for society women to entertain friends in their bedrooms. Modern notions of privacy tend to preclude such intimate hospitality, but a large bedroom can still have the feel of a boudoir – a room you can retire to at any time of the day. Your spacious bedroom can become private study, salon, or even reception room, if you choose.

Above: **Space in this airy, modern bedroom just seems to go on and on, through the wall of windows, onto the balcony and into the distance beyond the trees. The pair of chairs, placed to make the most of the view, are an invitation to indulge in leisurely conversation.**

Top far left: **White-painted walls and floorboards maximize the light and volume of a huge bedroom** in a warehouse conversion where you would be tempted to put on your rollerskates to visit the bathroom.

Top centre left: **A handsome antique copper bath on a raised platform at one end of this bright room looks a particularly inviting place for a long soak. Placing a bath within a bedroom can be an elegant solution if you don't have enough space for an en suite bathroom.**

Top centre right:
The unconventional positioning of the bed between two windows, instead of pushed against a wall, gives this room drama and focus.

Top far right: **High ceilings are a licence to go to town with light fittings, whether your taste is for traditional chandeliers or something more unusual, like this futuristic spiky ball.**

Right: **This exotic, oriental-style four-poster with its high mattress has something of the feel of an old-fashioned box bed. However cavernous the surrounding space, lying inside its wooden frame you would feel as snug as a child in a den.**

Opposite above left: **The extra large bed in this spare, modern interior is raised off the ground on hidden legs so that it appears to hover, inviting you to float to sleep as if on a magic carpet.**

Opposite above right: **A four-poster bed without canopy or curtains has instead a mosquito net suspended above. It could be draped over the posts as a diaphanous tent.**

Opposite below left: **A folding wooden screen and a sizeable bedside table help to mark out the territory occupied by the bed in this loft conversion. Table lamps providing low pools of light contribute to the feeling of intimacy.**

Opposite below right: **Although placed against a window, this bed offers a sense of protection thanks to its curved headboard carved from a massive piece of wood.**

Creating intimate spaces

Nowadays a sense of intimacy and privacy is particularly important to us in our bedrooms and, much as we may value the aesthetics of large, open-plan, multi-functional rooms, the territory occupied by our bed demands special attention. The person who can sleep soundly on a mattress in the middle of a ballroom is a rarity. Such exposure makes the rest of us feel a little insecure.

Creating a cosy bedroom space within a larger room need not entail curtains and posts. An ample headboard, a soft rug on floorboards or a piece of furniture, protectively placed, can be enough to provide that sense of safety and enclosure that encourages total relaxation. Movable screens, whether free-standing or incorporated in the design of a larger room, act as flexible walls. Even something as physically insubstantial as a mosquito net can be a sufficient barrier between a sleeper and the outside world.

If there is sufficient ceiling height, a sleeping platform is both an efficient use of space and a way of carving out separate territory within a larger room. Climbing a ladder to bed, like clambering into the top bunk as a child, feels like retreating to a treehouse. And there is the added advantage that no one will notice if you haven't made the bed.

Whatever means you choose to make your bedroom area feel suitably snug, lighting can make or break the effect. Wall lights or table lamps that cast a warm, low pool of light next to your bed can be enough to create an intimate feel.

Bedroom furniture & storage

The bed remains the central feature of any bedroom, its style dictating the feel of the whole room, whether a plain, modern divan or an antique extravaganza. As has always been the case, it is likely to be the most expensive single item of furniture in the room. And, while its looks will dominate the decor, its comfort is equally important. Choosing the right mattress is not simply a question of ensuring a good night's sleep; it can also minimize the problems of back pain. If you prefer a softer mattress, you should choose a bed with a sprung, divan base. Mattresses suitable for laying on wooden slats tend to be much firmer.

Opposite above left:
A bedroom with storage space for non-essentials.

Opposite above right:
Bedside shelf space is cleverly incorporated into this rustic bedhead. Twiggy branches support both tables and shelf in this wood-lined room.

Opposite below left:
Slick bedroom storage with fitted cupboards flanking the bed, linked by a high wooden shelf which frames and shelters it.

Opposite below right:
A fake-fur throw and stacked cushions make this bed inviting. A padded bedhead, plenty of shelf space and the movable bedside table make for convenience and comfort.

Top right: **Sharp lines combine with soft fabrics.**

Above left and left:
Stylish modern storage in a bedroom lined with cupboards and, left, the more old-fashioned solution, a beautiful Arts and Crafts oak linen press.

Antique bedsteads can be very beautiful but apparently impractical, as they are rarely a standard size; Victorian double beds, for example, are often far too narrow to accord with modern ideas of king-size comfort. However, a Victorian double can make a pleasantly generous twenty-first-century single and, even if you cannot find a duvet exactly the right size, there are companies who will make a bespoke mattress to fit an old bed frame for a price that compares very favourably with a good-quality standard mattress.

As discussed at the beginning of this section, the essentials of bedroom furniture are few. Whether or not you choose to expand beyond them is as much a matter of space as personal taste. A small bedroom tends to dictate its layout and contents, which may consist of nothing more than the bed itself and fitted storage, plus that crucial shelf space to put the things you need to reach once you are comfortably ensconced under the duvet.

Unless you enjoy the luxury of a separate dressing room or walk-in wardrobe, storage for clothes, shoes and all the paraphernalia of getting ready to greet the world is the most important bedroom requirement after the bed itself.

Never before have so many people owned so many clothes. Where once a few hooks and a wooden chest would have sufficed, we now require ranks of drawers, tiers of shoe racks, and metres of hanging rail. Fitted cupboards that reach right up to the ceiling, and drawers that slide out from under the bed (good for infrequently used items, like ski gear), are ways to maximize limited storage space. Some companies specialize in storage alone and offer an array of ideas on how to make the most efficient use of available space, from hanging shoe pockets to stacking transparent boxes for shirts and jumpers. Inevitably, some items will be more easily accessible than others. Again, unless you are blessed with a surfeit of cupboards, you will probably find that a certain amount of reorganization is a biannual necessity – moving summer suits to the back in winter and folding away bulky jumpers on top shelves in the summer. Labelling boxes in which you keep things for infrequent use can save a lot of time rifling and rummaging.

Unlike a kitchen or bathroom, where hard, wipe-clean surfaces are desirable and practical, a bedroom needs the

softness offered by fabrics to make it feel comfortable and welcoming. Apart from the obvious and indispensable bed linen, you may want cushions as well as pillows to encourage lounging on, as well as in, the bed. Flooring should feel warm to bare feet in winter, especially that little patch where you first touch down on getting out of bed. This may be the only room in your home where you decide to have fitted carpet. Otherwise, a bedside rug can suffice.

As in all rooms, lighting and the control of light is important. If you like to sleep in perfect darkness, you will require blackout blinds or curtains lined with blackout material. As for artificial lights, remember that bright, overhead lighting is unflattering to you and to the room. Side lights are far more conducive to relaxation and you can use a dimmer to control their intensity. Bedside reading lights should be strong enough to avoid eye strain.

Opposite far left: **A collection of magazines stacked on these bedside shelves leaves just enough room for the alarm clock. The problem of where to position a bedside light has been solved by attaching an adjustable lamp to the side of the shelves.**

Opposite above left and right: **This compact single bedroom makes good use of the space under the built-in bed to provide deep storage drawers for clothes and bed linen. A tiny wall light is placed at the right height for perfectly comfortable reading in bed.**

Opposite centre: **In this room, a long shelf takes the place of a bedhead, making a good opportunity for display and book space combined.**

Opposite below: **Alcoves built into the wall support a grouping of favourite pictures for an unusual, changeable bedhead display. Again, ample extra storage is provided in drawers underneath the bed.**

Below left: **An antique chest of drawers with a pick-and-mix selection of handles doubles as a dressing table in this pretty attic bedroom.**

Right: **The curves of an old wrought-metal bedstead are matched by the shapely lines of an antique armchair in this charming old-fashioned room, complete with its original fireplace. The yellow-gold of the bedstead warms the room's neutral colour scheme.**

Below right: **A double-ended antique bedstead makes a comfortable couch by day with pillows propped at either end. The table lamps have cloths draped over their shades, a lo-tech answer to the dimmer switch for a softer, diffused light.**

Although the bathroom has a practical function, it should also be a place to unwind and relax. In recent years bathrooms have been given sculpted units and hi-tech taps, but the classic roll-top bath is still a perennial favourite, so anything goes. Most sanitary ware is produced in white, in ceramic, enamelled metal or preformed acrylic, so add colour and pattern to your bathroom with accessories and decoration.

bathrooms

Opposite main picture:
A wall-mounted shower over a bath is an easy way of doubling facilities in a small bathroom. The hand-held shower on the bath is useful for washing hair (and ideal if you don't use a shower often).

Above: **Internal windows allow natural light to penetrate through to the centre of this bathroom. These porthole-shaped windows are an attractive and useful feature of the room. Here the bath has been boxed in and faced with** tiles that match the wall finish, to create a contained bathing space with privacy from the main door.

Above left: **Custom-made shower enclosures can be built to fit most spaces.**

Below left: **Spare, simple design schemes are easier to keep looking smart than fussy and frilly finishes. The recessed shelf and stone sink surround provide practical storage and are easy to clean, but still look utterly stylish.**

Planning your bathroom

When planning your bathroom, take it in four stages. First identify your needs and examine the room available. Do you only have space for one bathroom, or could you divide up its functions, thereby taking the pressure off the main bathroom? For example, could you plumb an additional toilet under a staircase or in a deep cupboard in a hall or lobby? Is there an area in a bedroom for a self-contained shower unit and a basin, or have you a spare bedroom that you want to transform from scratch into a spacious and indulgent bathing room?

Second, make a list of your bathroom priorities and think about how you use the bathroom. Is the shower more frequently used than the bath? If you are part of a couple, both getting up and washing at the same time, would it be easier if there were two hand basins? Do you have young children, and if so would a bath with an integral shelf or seat make bathtime easier for everyone?

From this information you should be able to identify and select your bathroom fittings and fixtures, the size and shape of bath you want, and the type of material it is made from. Other considerations are the shape and finish of the taps and spouts, and whether you want a wall-hung or pedestal hand basin or basins.

Finally, the decoration of a bathroom, large or small, needs to be carefully considered. Surfaces must be water-resistant as well as steam and moisture tolerant. Avoid sharp corners and angles, and clad or box in any hot pipes. Floors must be non-slip, especially when wet, and where rugs or mats are used they must have a non-slip backing.

Although the bathroom is primarily a place for cleansing it also needs to be regularly and thoroughly cleansed itself. To make this easy, use smooth, wipeable finishes and keep clutter to a minimum. Good ventilation to expel steam quickly and keep the room fresh should also be a priority.

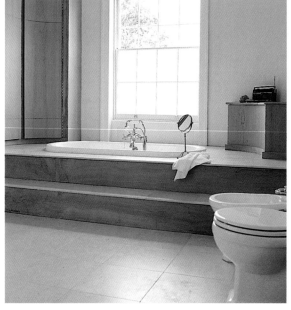

Spacious bathrooms

The spacious bathroom gives good scope for decoration and furnishing. You might want to sacrifice a spare bedroom for the luxury of a larger or en suite bathroom. Sizeable rooms may also incorporate additional functions such as exercise room, dressing room, linen store or laundry space.

A big bathroom can be divided into sections so that one area caters for speedy washing and showering first thing in the morning, with another for calmer, more relaxing bathing. In a bathroom divided like this, or where you want to have a change of mood, choose lighting that is adjustable, either by a dimmer switch or separated on two or three circuits. With different circuits it is possible to switch off bright central lights and leave on only the lower-voltage, peripheral lights, creating an intimate and more low-key atmosphere which can be augmented by scented candles.

The toilet in a large bathroom can be concealed or boxed in so that it is private and can even be used separately while someone else is in the main bathroom, but the enclosure must be fitted with an efficient extractor fan. If a large bathroom is so spacious it lacks intimacy, you can create rooms within the room by putting up glass panels or

Above left: **Tongue-and-groove panelling can be used to help divide up a large wall and bring interest to a plain surface.**

Top centre: **This bath has a broad surround of polished granite, wide enough to make an attractive store for bath oils, books or other requirements.**

Above right: **A raised dais has been created and the bath sunk into it, creating a luxurious focal point to this simple room.**

Opposite above left: **This contemporary style of box bath can be made from pre-cast concrete, specially sealed granite or polished stone panels. The large mirrors are strategically placed for making up and grooming. Natural light is best for this – if you don't have a window in the bathroom, you can buy special lightbulbs that replicate daylight.**

Opposite above right: **Vintage baths, reconditioned or even re-enamelled, make unusual bathtubs.**

Opposite below left: **The roll-top bath is a classic. Old cast-iron designs can be heavy when they are filled with water, so check floor structures and beams before installing one. A good supply of natural light is useful in a bathroom, so leave windows clear if you are not overlooked.**

Opposite below right: **A free-standing frame with waterproof curtains makes a mobile shower enclosure which can be folded up and moved away when you want to use just the bath.**

partitions, or using wood or bamboo screens. These will define specific areas of the room and make them appear cosier and more personal.

Free-standing furniture (including a bath with space all around) is another way of occupying space and making the room feel more comfortable. An easy chair, a padded stool and a small table to hold magazines and towels are all possibilities, but be careful if you use upholstery or cushions. They should be aired frequently so they do not become damp and eventually mouldy. Also plan carefully what other accessories you bring into the room, as books and paintings may suffer in the damp atmosphere. Pictures should be sealed in a frame for protection; if you have a painted feature on a wall, give it a coat of sealant or varnish.

Opposite: **This wall-hung hand basin takes up the minimum of space and leaves the maximum area of wall on show, making the small room feel less cramped. The choice of a flexible fabric shower curtain, rather than a rigid shower panel, also allows the full extent of the room to be seen. The sliding door in the foreground is a great space saver, too, as it does not require room for access – it simply slides back over the existing wall area.**

Left: **A linear floor plan is always an effective and space-saving small-bathroom arrangement. Here the bath is plumbed in at the far end of the room, where headroom is restricted, and the basin, toilet and shower have been installed in a line along the same outer wall. The facilities used most often – the toilet and hand basin – are best positioned nearest the door, whereas the bath, which is used least, can be furthest away.**

Small bathrooms

Advances in technology mean that shower and toilet plumbing can be installed in locations that would previously have been too difficult or expensive to tackle. These developments have been instrumental in the growing trend for dispersing elements from the main bathroom and creating useful, additional, compact washing spaces in other rooms or areas of the home.

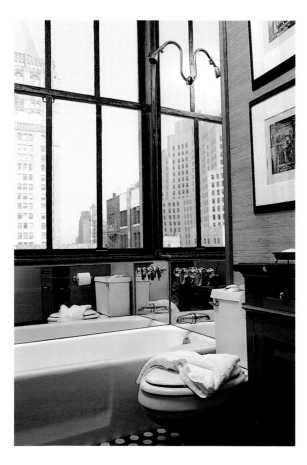

Above: **Folding panels contain the bathroom in this open-plan living and sleeping space. They can be folded back so that the bathroom becomes an integral part of the space. The classic white and off-white scheme is plain but helps to make the overall ambience light and airy.**

Left: **Tall windows and a stunning view reflected in a long mirror exaggerate the size of this small bathroom. Restricting clutter also makes the room seem larger.**

Save space by doubling up facilities, such as plumbing a shower over a bath, or opt for a specialized unit like a self-contained corner shower that will slot neatly into a niche or area of wasted space. Macerator toilets can be plumbed in away from the main soil pipe, but should be regarded as an occasional-use facility rather than a main one. There are also reduced-size hand basins and baths that give adequate washing space without taking up too much room.

Decoration can be used to make a small space feel more spacious. A mirror, which is always useful over a hand basin, can be extended so that it covers a whole wall and reflects the available daylight, view, or the opposite wall. Small does not have to mean dull – as there is less space you could choose more expensive decoration. For example, mosaic is costly, but on a modest scale it could be affordable.

Wet rooms & showers

Showers are energizing and refreshing, and showering is usually quicker and more economical in water use than bathing. Traditionally showers were installed over the bath, but increasingly they are becoming a separate facility. In a wet room – a tiled and completely watertight space with a sloping floor and a central drain – the shower is the primary water source. The great advantage of a wet room is that there are no damp, clinging shower curtains or rigid glazed panels to restrict the bather, and you don't have to climb precariously out of the bath when you have finished.

Modern shower cabinets or cubicles may not only supply a flow of water, but also offer steam or sauna-like facilities. Custom-built shower units can be tailored to fit into most corners or niches; they don't have to be constructed around two parallel walls. You need a single wall into which the plumbing and electrical components can be safely installed, then the other walls or panels can be erected from that.

Preformed shower cubicles come in a complete, sealed unit so that the base, roof and walls are joined, but they are generally available only in standard sizes. This type of product is ideal for steam and sauna options because there is no fear of leakage or seepage, but must be well ventilated in order to prevent mould from forming. These cabinets may also have integral lighting and a preformed seat or bench.

The traditional shower has a single rose, either on a rigid pipe or a flexible hose, but some contemporary designs have a variety of nozzles and sprays at different levels that can be directed at all parts of the body. The heads may also be adjusted to give various strengths and pulses of water, from strong massage to a soft, aerated flow.

There are several options for shower doors. As well as the standard hinged door that opens outwards from the unit, there are bi-fold doors that concertina in the middle. These are useful for showers in restricted spaces. Sliding doors are another space-saving option, as is a pivot door which swings around a fixed, central column.

With wet rooms and custom-built shower cubicles it is vital to ensure that the space is thoroughly tanked or sealed with a polyurethane membrane before any tiles, stone or plaster are applied. As the water is not contained, it will spray in all directions and seep through any unfilled cracks or gaps and may cause wood floorboards or beams to rot.

Glass is a useful material for shower screens and surrounds because it is waterproof and contains the spray

while allowing light to penetrate, but only use glass that is specially finished for the task – in other words, laminated and reinforced safety glass. Another safety feature of modern showers is a preset temperature lever, which maintains the water temperature at body heat and can only be adjusted when the lever or button on the dial has been specifically pressed down and moved.

To prevent a windowless wet room from feeling claustrophobic, you can create 'windows' with mirrors or opaque glass. Set an opaque-glass panel or mirror into the wall with a fine strip light sealed in behind, to create the illusion of space and light beyond. A mirror may also be useful for grooming in the shower. Look for one with an enclosed heating element, which won't fog up.

Left: **These two separate tubular modules, below right and left, contain a shower and a hand basin and toilet. Their opaque surrounds provide privacy but are not so dense that they obstruct the flow of light or form an obstacle in this open-plan living space, above. The round shape is also soft and less obtrusive than a square, pillar-like block.**

Opposite above left: **Subtle lighting behind this opaque glass screen creates a change in mood and makes this enclosure a relaxing and restful environment for a shower.**

Opposite above centre and right: **A custom-built, curving, nautilus-shell-like construction allows the bather to shower in a self-contained niche, with natural light coming in from both sides, while still providing ample space for a hand basin and toilet in the room. Inside, the blue and white mosaic tiles look fresh and light.**

Opposite below left: **In this wet-room arrangement, the window gives ample ventilation while the tiled floor and wall keep spray from damaging the surfaces beneath.**

Opposite below right: **This bath- and shower room is contained within an opaque glass cube. The recessed floor area with a central drainage point makes a generous shower tray, and the shower head fixed on the ceiling is high enough to give ample pressure for a good flow of water.**

Above left: **This rounded bath has been fitted with a contemporary linear hose and lever tap. In this neutral scheme the black fittings are a feature.**

Above: **A sheet of metal provides a splashback to this unusual glass sink and round mirror. The wall-mounted spout and lever taps are plumbed through the panel.**

Left and right: **Jacuzzi and spa baths must be cleaned regularly to avoid stale water from accumulating in the pipes. If the bath has a surround, fittings can be plumbed in at any point around the bath.**

Fixtures & fittings

When choosing your sanitary ware – the basin, toilet, bidet and bath – aim to keep all pieces in a similar style, for example all angular or all rounded, as this will help to give a cohesive appearance to the scheme. If you choose to mix styles, for example by making a special feature of a glass hand basin or a steel bath, it's best to keep the rest of the sanitary ware plain and simple.

Traditional styles can be successfully mixed with new; for instance, a modern monoblock arrangement of a long spout and lever tap can be plumbed in over a roll-top bath, and Victorian-style crossbar taps may be used over a simple modern basin, but the general rule, especially with taps and spouts, is to keep the style and finish the same. If you have chrome accessories for the hand basin, then have the same finish for the bath, shower, bidet and toilet fittings.

Most modern bathroom suites are made from manmade materials such as acrylic resin mixes and plastics. These synthetic materials can be cut, carved, routed, sandblasted and inlaid to form an almost limitless array of shapes. They can also be coloured and textured to look like marble or other stone finishes, and have the advantage of being substantially lighter and warmer and softer to the touch than traditional ceramic ware.

Cast-iron bathtubs have been around since the Victorian hip bath, filled from the kettle and used in front of the stove.

Above: **Wall-mounted fittings make cleaning thoroughly around the sink easier, but be careful not to plumb them in too high above the basin or the water will splash as it hits the surface. This angular sink looks similar to a shower tray. It has been set on top of a table-like surface, as a shallow but ample hand basin.**

Below: **Lever taps are not just stylish but can also be useful for people with impaired grip or hand movement. Some designers search out the sort of lever taps used in hospitals and laboratories.**

Above right: **A roll-top bath can be boxed in or left to stand on raised metal feet. If you choose the second option, the exposed outer surface of the bath can be painted to match or contrast with the overall scheme of the room.**

Below right: **This hand basin has been countersunk into the top of an old console table. The depth of the sink may preclude the use of the drawer beneath, but there is generous space on either side for toiletries and cosmetics.**

Copper is another metal that can be formed into a bath. It conducts heat well, so warms quickly. Modern baths are also made from steel, either polished or with a matt finish. These are often double-skinned, creating an inner vacuum that has an insulating effect. Wood has long been popular in Eastern countries for constructing plunge and hip baths, and has become increasingly popular in other parts of the world. Wood baths need careful maintenance; indeed, most manufacturers advise against using standard shampoos and highly scented bath products in them, as they will damage the surface. Some wood baths also have to be kept damp in order to avoid drying out, shrinking and cracking.

Left above, centre and below:
A heated towel rail will air and dry towels after use, and make them warm and cosy to wrap around you when you step out of a shower or bath. Wall-mounted towel rails take up a minimal amount of space, and some of the more interesting shapes and designs can create a feature on an otherwise bare wall.

Bottom right: **This narrow metal-clad recess above the bath provides just enough storage space for toiletries that are in regular, daily use.**

Below: **Contemporary mirrors may have useful integral lights or a light panel built into their surround. A wall light on an adjustable bracket is another option, as is an adjustable mirror that can be brought to the light source – particularly good if your** bathroom benefits from natural light. A traditional problem of bathroom mirrors has been the obliterating effect of condensation and steam, but modern heated mirrors, backed with a small integral heating element, overcome this.

When fitting the larger bathroom fixtures, especially the bath, check that the floor beneath is solid and firm before you apply sealer or stick tiles to the wall above a rim. This is because, when full of water, a bath or basin may move slightly. This action will be exaggerated on an unstable floor surface, and may cause the gap to widen and so allow water seepage, but the movement may be accommodated with the use of a flexible filler or sealant.

Plugs and waste outlets for baths and basins come in various styles. The traditional option is a metal or rubber disc on the end of a chain with a grid overflow on the wall of the bath. More modern versions are operated by a lever which lowers a round disc over the waste outlet, forming a seal that is almost flush with the bath base. In modern hand basins the pivotal metal disc is popular. The disc simply swings from the open to closed position with a gentle push.

Sinks, toilets and bidets come in a variety of shapes and sizes. Wall-hung units – some of the most contemporary designs – create a clean, spacious look, as well as making it easy for the area around each item to be thoroughly mopped and wiped. The second option is a pedestal fitting, which is secured to the floor with the fitting resting on top. The third choice is a box base: this is a unit, premade or tailored to fit, into or onto which the fitting can be placed. With the first and last systems the fittings can be raised or lowered to a height that is most comfortable for the user, but pedestals usually come in a standard size.

Although under-floor heating was invented by the Romans, a people who also enjoyed the pleasures of bathing, it has recently undergone a renaissance. It is an ideal way to heat a bathroom because there are no exposed pipes for joints accidentally to knock against, and the warm air rises from the floor, creating an equally ambient temperature. With solid floors such as concrete and stone, it also makes the surface more pleasant under bare feet.

All bathroom lighting should be sealed and specifically designed for use in this room, where the combination of water and electricity can be lethal. For areas where close examination takes place, such as dental-flossing or make-up application, a mirror and adjacent light are useful.

Above left: **With wall-mounted fittings such as these, pipes are chased directly into the wall – no need to drill holes in the surround of the bath. Here the only openings in the bath are for the overflow and base, waste outlet.**

Left: **Some shower fittings have a pivoting, single lever which operates the temperature, by moving from left to right, and also the water pressure, which is operated by moving the lever up and down.**

Right: **Traditional fittings such as these Victorian-style metal and ceramic** ones can be bought second-hand and refurbished, although it is wise to check that the old openings are compatible with modern pipework. If they have a brass finish they will need regular cleaning, as the water and temperature variation will cause marks. You can also buy modern reproductions with a non-tarnish sealant, designed to work with modern plumbing.

Above: **For putting on make-up and grooming, a main, general-purpose mirror plus a magnifying one for closer inspection are useful.**

Bathroom storage

Large bathrooms may double as dressing rooms or linen stores, so well-designed and adequate storage is important. Conversely, in a small bathroom you need plenty of storage to keep things neat and contained, so that the appearance of the room is spacious rather than cluttered.

Bathroom storage needs to be tailored to different requirements. Baskets are fine for dry items such as hairbrushes, make-up brushes and cosmetics, but for wet or dripping things – shower gels, shampoos and soaps – containers should be waterproof and made of mesh or some other open-work construction. This prevents water puddling in the base and eventually going stale.

If you keep clothes or linen in the bathroom, it is essential to have good ventilation; otherwise steam and moisture will make the fabrics damp and liable to musty aromas or mould.

A mix of concealed and display storage means that less attractive items such as spare toilet paper can be kept out of sight, while attractive elements such as perfume bottles or shells can be grouped and left on show.

Don't forget those useful accessories which are, in effect, storage items too. Most bathrooms need a towel rail, toilet-paper holder, soap dish, tooth-glasses and laundry basket.

Right: **If you have space, it's logical to have a dressing room en suite to the bathroom, as washing is usually followed or preceded by dressing or undressing. They have practical advantages: dirty clothes can be placed straight in a laundry basket, and collected for washing and delivered back to the same place.**

Left: **A mix of storage styles: a traditional bath rack complements the roll-top bath, while open glass shelves go with the stylish modern basin.**

Opposite top: **Open shelves provide generous storage for stacks of white towels. Mismatched and old towels are best stored behind doors or in covered shelves like those at the back of the room. Items on display should be attractive to look at, or they will detract from the overall appearance.**

Left: **Mirrored panels, flush with the wall, create a smooth finish. Recessed cupboards faced with mirrored panels will have the same effect.**

Right: **These individual compartments, just large enough to accommodate a pair of shoes, form a frame to a dressing table-cum-hand basin area in this multi-purpose bathroom scheme. Towels are neatly stored in a deep basket below the bottom shelf, and cosmetics live in colourful baskets that can easily be lifted to the upper level. The drawers under the basin are ideal for holding smaller items such as jewellery, in trays or individual boxes.**

Left: **This shelf provides dual storage space: bottles and jars can line up on the top surface, while brushes, towels and cloths hang on hooks beneath. Because the products on top are liable to drip or become wet, the upper surface and the front edge need to be covered in a water-resistant finish. It is also advisable to pipe a line of flexible sealant along the edge that butts up to the wall. Facecloths or small towelling mats are useful for resting damp bottles on, as they absorb drips of shampoo or soapy water and can easily be washed and replaced.**

Above centre: **A narrow shelf below a mirror-fronted cabinet provides a useful area for soaps and shampoos that have been decanted into matching chrome dispensers. Using compatible containers removes the jarring mix of colours and contents of standard packaging.**

Above left: **A grid of perspex cubes, here used to display a fossil collection, is visually pleasing but can also be a practical way to store items away from water vapour but still in sight. Keep regularly used items on the lower levels and seldom-used ones above.**

Until the Industrial Revolution turned us into commuters, most people worked at home, living above the shop or workshop, making and mending, buying and selling. Two centuries on, the hi-tech revolution is sending us back home again. Thanks to the microchip, making space in the house for a desk and computer has become a priority.

work spaces

Above left: **The presence of a generous sofa and coffee table suggests that this home office, designed for two, is also a place for conversation and debate.**

Left: **Comfort and good looks meet in a spacious office that has a living-room feel. Combining elegantly stored reference books and files with well-chosen ornaments adds to the sense that this is a room for pleasure as much as for toil.**

Above: **In addition to the functional – chair, desk, computer, filing cabinet and bookshelves – there is space in this bright, light room for the visually appealing.**

Opposite above right: **Separated from the living room by a wall, this essentially open-plan home office can be screened by pulling across the voile curtain to create a symbolic rather than physical barrier. The white**

walls and white desk continue the decorative theme of the room beyond.

Opposite above far right: **The only clue that this richly decorated room (with its painted, throne-like chairs) is also a work space is the computer. Even the shelving is unusually shaped.**

Opposite below left: **An airy workshop full of visual inspiration – ideal for encouraging creativity.**

Opposite below centre: **Compact, tidy, organized and with a place for everything, plus the bonus of a view. Box files stacked on simple shelves provide convenient, accessible storage, and the built-in desk which spans one wall of this small, sunny room makes the most of limited space.**

Opposite below right: **Looking through the dining area to an office which has been separated by a screen wall in the vast volume of this New York conversion.**

Dedicated work spaces

The long list of advantages of working from home is balanced for most people by a shorter list of disadvantages. Top of this list is likely to be the lack of a clear boundary between work and home, between your public self and your private one, between pressure and relaxation. If your house is also your office, you may miss the sense of arriving back home after a long day, shutting the front door behind you and heaving a sigh of relief and release.

When your commute consists of a trip down the stairs and across the hall (or upstairs into what used to be a spare bedroom), having a room in your home that you use only for work is one way to achieve that distinction. Commuting down the path to an office in the garden is even better, especially if it has a phone line and modem. Apart from

the psychological benefits of being able to close the door on a dedicated work space, there are obvious practical advantages, too: privacy, peace and freedom from distraction; the opportunity to be as messy or as organized as you please; the freedom to create a selfish environment best suited to your own working practices.

Combining working from home with bringing up a family can be a very satisfying compromise between the conflicting demands of career and childcare. However, convincing a child that your deadline is more important than their dead snail can take considerable powers of persuasion. Demarcating your dedicated work territory within the house is crucial here – sticking a large 'Do not disturb' sign on the door of your office is one way out.

Work spaces in other rooms

A shortage of rooms may mean that the only possible place to create work space is within another room that has another use, or you may not require a full-time, dedicated work area. In these cases, the choice is usually between sharing your living areas with working space, or sleeping with working space. Parents with children at home may prefer to work in the relative quiet of their bedroom, often the only room in a busy house, apart from the bathroom, where you can escape from the activity and bustle of television, homework and play. Single people and those without children may prefer to reserve the bedroom for pure relaxation and, instead, find a corner of the living room where they can install themselves to work. In this case, you might consider a 'galley' office, which can disappear behind closed doors at the end of the working day.

In either case there are issues to resolve, both of decorative aesthetics and of practical organization. Office furniture can be ugly and ungainly, and its machinery – the bland beige plastic of computers with accompanying scanners, printers, speakers and bird's nest of cabling – is far from good-looking and can be difficult to accommodate on and under even the most generously proportioned desk. Only recently have computer designers caught on to the

Right: **Working, eating and relaxing are accommodated elegantly in a single, stylish room. The desk, lamp and chair (below) all share an unusual delicacy of design.**

Below: **Custom-made fitted furniture makes the most of space in a bedroom where wardrobes, shelving, desk and drawers are all of a piece. Take away the computer and box files, and the desk would work equally well as a dressing table.**

Opposite above left:
One way of creating a sense of separation in an open-plan space is to build another floor on a platform – here used as an office. Not acoustically, or even visually, separated from the other areas, the different level marks this area as new territory.

Opposite above right:
A wall of this bedroom has been devoted to desk and office storage, to create a compact work station.

Opposite below: **A raised platform and change of flooring mark this office within a much larger room. The desk is placed to make the most of natural light, and ample shelf space keeps it tidy.**

importance of looks as well as performance. The resulting trend for smaller and more stylish hardware is a bonus for anyone attempting to work from home and unable to hide away their assortment of electronic office trappings.

The issue of organization is also an aesthetic one. While a separate office allows you to shut the door on a desk piled with files and a floor spread with assorted papers, this level of chaos – however essential to your mental processes – is less acceptable in a bedroom or living room. Tidying away at the end of a working day is an essential discipline in a room that you also use for relaxing and escaping from work.

Right: **A wall of shelving provides ample space for reference books, but also incorporates drawers of different sizes for storing small items and stationery. This is a convenient and efficient way of combining different types of storage within a single unit.**

Far right: **These simple metal shelves, often used as shop fittings, are fully adjustable. Here they are used to store labelled boxes of different sizes.**

Below left: **Here antiques, including a metal-framed garden chair and an old document chest, are commandeered to make a bright, attractive office. Wicker baskets store files, and even the laptop is unobtrusive in pale grey.**

Below right: **This curved, two-tier desk makes particularly good use of available space, with everything within arm's reach of the chair.**

Work space furniture & storage

One of the less obvious, but significant, advantages of working from home is the opportunity to choose your own furnishings and design your own surroundings exactly to suit yourself. For example, there is no one design of office chair, however adjustable in all dimensions, that suits every size, shape and personal preference. Some people like armrests, some like a footrest. Others feel horribly stuck in a chair without castors.

For any sedentary work, the comfort of chair and desk combined is important: the chair must be supportive and should encourage a good working posture; the desk should be the right height so that your legs can move freely underneath it and your arms are not straining unnecessarily to reach a keyboard. It should be big enough to allow room for more than the minimum equipment of telephone, computer, keyboard and lamp. It should be solid enough not to wobble. These issues are more important than looks or style and are worth spending time and effort getting right.

Lighting is equally important for comfort. Siting a desk beneath or next to a window makes the most of natural light, with the added benefit of a view, somewhere to rest the gaze and something to interest tired eyes. However, bright

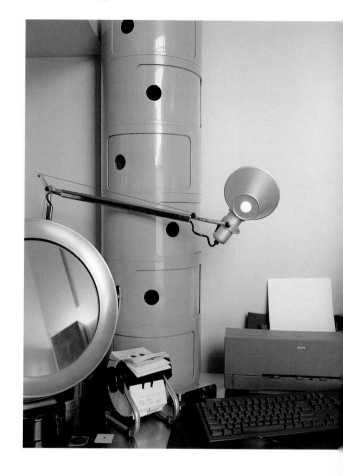

Above right: **Aesthetics and efficiency can go hand in hand, as this slightly eccentric desk arrangement shows. The tower of white plastic drawers is like a small piece of table sculpture, its round finger holes echoed by the lamp and mirror. Even the roller address file has curves in all the right places.**

Right: **An interesting use of materials makes this slim desk stand out from the crowd, its one wooden drawer balanced by a wrap of punched metal. The chair matches its marriage of wood and metal but uses them in a more conventional way. This stylish 'office' would not look out of place in a modern bedroom.**

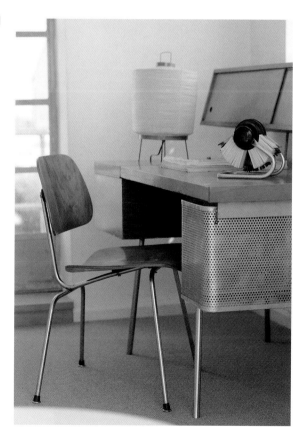

sunlight can be hot, glaring and cause distracting reflections on a computer screen. Ideally, your computer screen should be at a ninety-degree angle to the source of light. Blinds to control the intensity of light are usually necessary. Likewise, artificial light should be strong enough to avoid eye strain without dazzling, and its source should be adjustable. The classic anglepoise remains an excellent design of desk lamp.

Just as you can never have too much wardrobe space, you can never have too much shelf, drawer and filing space in an office; better to have empty shelving (it will eventually fill up) than nowhere to put things other than in piles on your desk or on the floor. Tools and the sources of information you use most frequently should ideally be easy to reach from your chair. How you choose to store the remainder of documents, computer disks and loose papers associated with your work will, again, be a matter of personal preference. The more you can enclose in drawers, filing cabinets and boxes, the less dust your work space will gather. Providing a place for everything, even if you don't always put it there, makes an office look and feel organized, a quality that you hope will be reflected in the work itself.

children's rooms

Plan the children's spaces with practicality and a sense of fun. Designs should be flexible, because kids' needs and tastes change even faster than our own. It's perfectly possible to integrate a cool play space into a design-conscious home – plenty of good-looking storage is the key.

Above: **Children appreciate scaled-down furniture. Search junk shops for quirky period styles or investigate mini versions of classic chairs. Painted Swedish styles, bright plastics and wipe-clean laminates are all options.**

Above right and centre: **The vast floor spaces of lofts and open-plan homes are a boon to active kids, who can race around in all weathers. A structure like a mini maze contains mess and is great fun. Relish the planes of colour and hard surfaces found in contemporary interiors – they provide the perfect backdrop for children's bright art and playthings.**

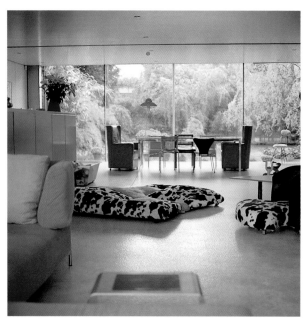

Right: **A comprehensive storage system is the key to kids and adults happily sharing a space. Built-in cupboards are neater than open shelves. Experiment with unusual doors such as perspex, painted MDF with fretted patterns, or stainless steel.**

Main picture: **At one end of the house, a conservatory play space affords good noise control, and means kids benefit from natural light all through the year.**

Play spaces

The best play zones boast sufficient space to run around, a quiet lounging area and tables for concentrated activities. Few of us can devote a separate room to the kids, and with the trend towards open-plan living it makes sense to integrate play space. There's no need to compromise your style. Adapt what furniture and surfaces you have to cater for the children's safety and freedom, and your own sanity!

Consider the available space – along with human traffic through it – then exploit it for the kids' needs. Can dining furniture be moved to one side, allowing a free run from kitchen to back door, or a sofa swapped for a window seat to free up floor space? Think about safety. Is the runabout zone well away from the kitchen? Are trailing wires or rugs securely in place? A play space with direct access to outdoors is a boon; so, too, is proximity to a downstairs loo.

Practical surfaces are essential. Plain painted walls touch up well, and laminate or wood kitchen cupboard doors wipe down easily. Children spend lots of time on the floor, so choose hard-wearing, comfortable flooring. Laminate or real wood floorboards, colourful rubber or lino, or limestone (with under-floor heating) are great options. Add a soft rug if possible. If the dining table is precious, protect it with a PVC tablecloth. If buying a new table, bright laminate, zinc, stainless steel, or painted MDF all scrub up well. Rethink upholstery: a set of loose covers will protect a smart sofa, which would otherwise be ruined by sticky fingers. Strong, washable fabrics include cotton duck, denim and ticking.

Storage is paramount, not just for toys but for bulkier items like musical instruments. Plan it minutely, with a home for everything. Fill fitted open shelves with identical containers – wicker baskets or plastic crates are good – as this looks smarter and makes categorizing toys easier. Locate favourite toys and books on the bottom shelves so kids can help themselves. Within wall cupboards – always a neat option – provide different-sized boxes, from small containers for tiny toys to lidded crates for craft activities. Tailor-made alcoves, for videos or books, are also helpful. Storage needn't be fitted. Free-standing options include traditional plan chests, a sideboard, or school-style lockers.

Don't forget a chill-out zone for watching videos or taking a nap. If there's no space for a sofa, children will find beanbags, seating cubes or floor cushions just as fun. Locate the video player and videos low down, so kids can access them, and wall-mount the TV to save space.

Babies' & toddlers' rooms

In the early years, babies and toddlers need little in their rooms. Concentrate on buying the basic furniture – a cot, clothes storage, nappy-changing table and feeding chair – and choose surfaces that are practical and comfortable. The prime aim is to create a tranquil environment for you and your child, so that feeding, sleeping and nappy changing – at whatever time of day or night – is reasonably stress-free.

The cot is the most important buy, and these days there's a good choice of models in white-painted and colourful finishes, retro metal styles, as well as the traditional cherry or pine. Consider if it's a better investment to buy a cot-bed, which will grow with the child until he or she is four or five. Don't waste money on a nappy-changing unit, which will be redundant within two years. Provided there is nappy storage close by, a padded changing mat on top of a low chest of drawers will suffice. Babies and small children don't need a designated wardrobe. Store clothes instead in wicker baskets on shelves, hanging from hooks or in a conventional chest of drawers that will grow up with the child.

Try to steer clear of traditional 'baby' motifs on wallpapers or fabrics: within a couple of years, your child will have outgrown them. A fresher, more contemporary approach is to pick plain, painted walls in soft pastels or clear primaries, teamed with lots of white. Contrast the plains with funky abstracts which little ones will appreciate – freehand painted stripes on one wall, perhaps, or a spotty dotty fabric on a roller blind. Flooring should be neutral and easy-care. Carpet is softest, but a jolly rug laid over floorboards or lino is equally good.

Rather than buying coordinating bed linen, go for a mix-and-match selection. Basics include cotton sheets, blankets, a cot bumper and a quilt; after one year, you can add a pillow and baby duvet. These days there's a huge selection on the high street, from sheets in hot colours and pastels to contemporary fleece blankets and appliqué quilts.

Control of natural and artificial lighting is essential. Simple curtains – choose plains, checks or an abstract nursery design – should be teamed with a white blackout

Top and above left:
Bright primaries and acid shades stimulate children and fit well into a modern home. Either team one painted wall with white, or contrast blocks of colour using a mix of modern furniture. Polypropylene drawer units, plastic chairs and contemporary blinds all offer splashes of brights, yet are supremely child-friendly.

Above: **If the dominating style at home dictates a softer colour scheme, choose knocked-back pastels in preference to fondant pinks and blues, which run the risk of looking twee in a child's room. Muted shades also create a better background for the inevitable primary-coloured toys.**

Above left and right:
Little eyes need bright colours for stimulation. Consider bold stripes, bunting, a hand-painted frieze or giant dots on the ceiling. Babies spend a great deal of time on their backs, so give them something to focus on.

Left and right:
Storage should be practical and simple. Neatly stacked purpose-built shelves make for easy access, as do hooks, small alcoves or a row of baskets.

blind to cut out the sun for daytime naps. Other simple window options include American-style shutters, Roman blinds or Venetian blinds. Fit a dimmer switch to an overhead light, and add an entertaining plug-in nightlight. A string of twinkling fairy lights is also fun.

Don't go overboard with nursery decorations in a baby's room. It's much nicer to start a personal collection of treasures – christening presents, perhaps, or family snapshots – that can be added to over the years. Yet every baby needs stimulating things to look at. Twirling mobiles, a string of bunting, an older sibling's paintings or a shelf full of favourite stuffed animals have great visual appeal.

Girls' rooms

Most girls have a finely tuned sense of what they like. Ask your daughter about her colour preferences, then steer a tactful course between hers and yours. Children's tastes change fast, so avoid frilly fads and provide neutral decor with lots of scope for change. White walls may be teamed with a single wall of colour – repainted lime one year, scarlet the next. A curtain pole with curtain clips allows unusual drapes to be swapped, from sparkly saris to floral cottons.

Make the bed the focus of the room. The bed is a child's relaxation zone, so make it cosy. While little girls will enjoy

Opposite and left: **Children love theme rooms, but don't restrict girls to a fairy grotto. Boat, castle or treehouse murals are much more exciting, though keep painting simple with bold shapes and bright colours.**

Above right: **Treat older girls to the grown-up options of a double bed, four-poster, or a romantic hanging such as a flower-studded mosquito net. All will cross the boundaries between girlhood and the teenage years.**

Clockwise, from above: **Little girls love pretty colours, but that doesn't have to mean pink. Soft grey-blues, lilac, pale sherbet yellow or grass green are all equally good alternatives. Give a girl's room a fresher, more contemporary edge by substituting traditional floral prints for leaves or butterflies, and mix with checks, whitewashed wooden floors or tongue-and-groove boards.**

high-sided Goldilocks-style or alcove beds, older children find bunk or platform beds more fun. A divan with another bed underneath is handy for sleepovers. For the boudoir look, consider a four-poster, from which everything from curtains to fairy lights may be hung. Let little girls create their own looks with bed linen. Floral or gingham styles, embroidery and blocks of plain colour create a good mix.

If space permits, add a low table for quiet activities such as drawing, and a display shelf. All little girls have special treasures to show – make the display area accessible so they can add to their collections. A giant pinboard will also delight them. Cover cork with a bright fabric, or try powder-coated steel and magnets for a contemporary look.

Boys' rooms

Given their natural energy levels, boys need ample play space, furniture they can climb on and robust surfaces that improve with wear. Those are the basics, yet boys are also sensitive to style, so ask about their favourite colours, too.

The bed is the mainstay of any boy's room, but try to make it as exciting as possible. For a little boy, commission a creative carpenter to turn a plain divan into a spaceship or car made from MDF panels (spray-painting gives a more robust finish). Even better, choose a bunk bed, or platform bed with desk and computer area beneath. Ladders, ropes or mini slides all add play opportunities. Older boys may prefer a classic bed style from a wooden sleigh bed to an iron school-style bedstead, or an army canvas camp bed.

Keep remaining furniture to a minimum, so even a small room has play space. Wall-mounted shelves and hooks for clothes will take the place of a wardrobe, or add castors to chests of drawers so furniture can be pushed back for play. While a hard floor, from wood boards to rubber, makes a better surface than carpet for toy cars, it's also useful to provide a low table on which complex Lego structures can be kept. Robust surfaces include zinc, stainless steel and MDF.

Boys need decent storage to make clothes and toy-tidying easy. Help them to sort out myriad tiny toys by compartmentalizing storage first. Choices might include: oxo-style open shelves, furnished with mini crates; apothecary-style chests of drawers, with many little drawers; or – for older boys – stainless-steel office drawer units on castors. Wicker baskets on the floor make great instant

Above and right: **Try to avoid busy-patterned wallpapers which kids and parents will tire of. Instead, use plain painted walls as a canvas that will endure fads and fancies. Walls may be painted in a bold shade or simply in white. It's more fun (and easier to ring the changes) using patterned bed linen, floor cushions, curtains or an upholstered chair.**

Clockwise, from above: **These days, there's a huge choice of bed style. Don't just look at what is available on the high street: consider antique or reconditioned junk-shop buys, or commission a carpenter to custom-make a design. For a contemporary look, opt for built-in styles with under-bed storage in painted MDF, plywood or tongue-and-groove panelling. Older boys will be happier with a classic design in wood, or MDF that can be repainted in different colours over the years. The beauty of providing plain walls is that jolly items, from a punchbag to a football table, space hopper to a giant flag, become decorative, colourful accessories in their own right.**

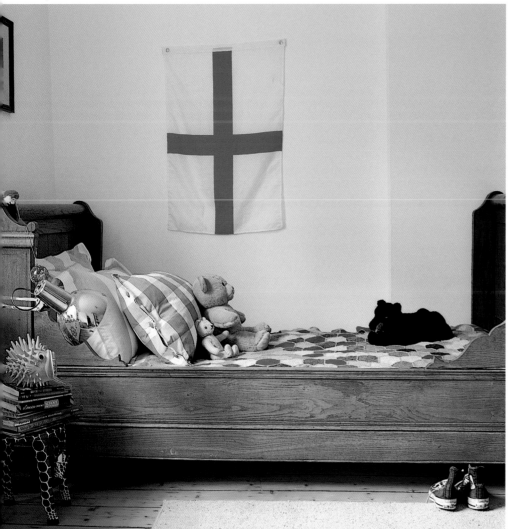

storage for bulkier clothing items such as sweaters and shoes. If there is no space for cupboards, look at shallow toy crates on castors that can hide underneath the bed.

Don't be swayed into decorating a boy's room in the latest cartoon craze as he'll grow out of Batman very fast. Help your son to choose appropriate paint colours, and indulge the cartoon phase with a framed poster instead. A generic theme can endure for several years and will please younger boys – perhaps porthole-painted circles and ship's decking for would-be sailors. Don't spend much money, and you won't mind decorative changes when the time comes.

Left, top to bottom:
When very young or same-sex children share, the easiest decorative choice is to pick identical bedsteads, lamps, chests of drawers and display shelves, which stops arguments and makes life simpler all round. Subtle ways to personalize special things include an embroidered initial on a cushion or laundry bag, colour-coding for duvets and towels, or wooden letters spelling the child's name above each bed.

Above: **If two or more kids share, it can be fun to pick a dormitory or holiday-camp theme. Choose reconditioned metal-framed school beds, old sports lockers, utility-style chairs and a trunk for each** **child's toys, emblazoned with their initials. Allow individuality, too. Their own choice of cartoon duvet cover, a set of framed sports certificates or a car collection displayed on a shelf near to the bed gives each sleeping area a real sense of personality.**

Above right and right:
Avoid arguments when a boy and a girl share by picking identical contemporary-style furniture and allowing each to dress his or her space with personal colours, bedding and picture displays. For girls, the ideal colour combinations are bright, pretty shades, from pink to orange, and, for boys, strong neutrals from khaki to dark grey. Such tones combine well together, so everyone is happy.

Shared rooms

Most children enjoy sharing a bedroom, but parents need to employ rigorous space-planning and a modicum of tact to create successful shared spaces. Demarcation of territory is crucially important. Even a young child needs to know he has his or her own space. Whether you divide a room down the middle or employ other criteria – one child gets the door, the other the window – make the division fun but fair. Little ones will enjoy colour-coding to delineate each side (red for one, pink for another) or a painted, dotted line on the floor; older children may prefer a physical division between beds. A plasterboard wall with cut-out portholes, sliding MDF panels or mobile screens on castors are possibilities.

Arrange the beds to suit the personalities and ages of the children. Younger ones might prefer identical bedsteads sharing a bedside table, or cosily placed at a right angle. Bunk beds or a shared, raised platform bed – with a mattress at either end – are amusing options. Older children might prefer a single bed on either side of the room.

Aim to pick decoration that pleases everyone. Provided colours tone, each child might pick their own paint shade for one wall. Choice of pattern may be a thorny issue if boys and girls are sharing, and the safest bets are checks, spots or abstracts. If tastes differ, concentrate pattern on the bed linen, in toning colours if possible. For younger children, a fantasy mural is an excellent compromise. Devoting an entire wall to a woodland grotto or cityscape with cars and shops will entertain everyone and arguments will cease.

Left and right: **The ideal storage combination combines wardrobes for clothes and bulkier toys; open shelves for books; and a low chest of drawers. Furnishing a bedroom is much more fun if you look beyond the high street. Retro pieces often come in primary shades, and may already be a little worn. Distressed, painted furniture, likewise, will take plenty of hard wear without showing its age!**

halls & awkward
spaces

Make awkward spaces work for you, decoratively and as practical areas. Designed with subtle simplicity, you will find these are places you return to again and again for their unpretentious charm. On sunny days, the rooftops glimpsed from the attic window might inspire your day's work. Even narrow halls and landings can be converted into libraries or a home for your collections.

It is the entrances, hallways and landings of a house that create its atmosphere, not the set-piece living rooms or kitchens on which so much care is lavished. The instant you arrive in a house, through the front door into the staircase hall, you can spot what the whole place will be like and you can find out quite a lot about the owner, too.

Therefore, these difficult spaces – often narrow, full of odd corners or vistas and sparsely lit – are very important. Not only that, but they have to be practical enough to take the constant pounding of feet, the arrival of boxes, bags and paraphernalia – anything from groceries to mountain bikes – and also to give a great welcome.

The answer is to make these areas an extract of your overall style – minimalist, authentically period, shabby chic or whatever you fancy – while keeping clutter to a minimum. Stairways can also be used to adapt the feeling of the rooms as you go upward – paintings on the walls changing gradually from black-and-white eighteenth-century prints, say, to very twenty-first-century modern abstracts.

It's also worth remembering that entrances are also exits and have to look inviting whether you are arriving or leaving. So make sure that areas above doors which lead outside are taken into account, too.

Entrances, hallways & landings

Above: **Leaving your home should be as interesting as arriving. Seen from the stairs, this elegant hall combines soft neutral colours with a practical floor mat and basket for sticks. The urns on the hall table make a classical statement, while leaving enough room for the post.**

Above right: **Plants, strictly symmetrical, are echoed in the mirror, increasing the feeling of space.**

Below right: **Even a tiny space can be cheered with pale walls and furniture – plus welcoming plants.**

Far right: **This hall reveals its owner's interests, from old doors to exotic lanterns. Hydrangeas add a touch of colour.**

Above: **Halls and landings needn't be wasted spaces: shelves are a smart way to add interest. Cleverly lit, they are ideal for pictures and other collections.**

Above right: **This exotic hallway is an extension of the library beyond – not only housing extra books but encouraging you onward. The hall shelves are painted a dark shade, in contrast to the inviting white ones beyond.**

Left: **Mirrors, carefully positioned, always create a feeling of space.**

Right: **An upstairs landing becomes a hideaway with old furniture, a crammed bookshelf and a daybed – a perfect place to relax.**

Those awkward spaces which seem to need such ingenuity to get right are very rewarding. These are the places where you show your bravura, colour sense and style. What's more, they offer small havens, unexpected views and privacy, plus the sense that you have created something from nothing.

For years, people have thought garrets are romantic, artists' eyries. The top of the house offers the best light, the best views and complete privacy. Add to that the sloping ceilings, the unfussy detailing in what architects have often seen as merely utilitarian spaces, and the criss-cross of

Attics, under stairs & awkward spaces

unplastered beams, and you can easily recognize the charm of an attic, whatever the period of the building.

Like under the stairs and boxrooms – unconsidered extras – attics are best kept simple. Materials should also be kept natural – sanded, waxed wood floors or boards painted pale grey or stone, brushed steel for joists or stairs left bare, and fabrics as neutral and uncluttered as you can make them. Let the complex spaces speak for themselves.

Attics, in particular, lend themselves to modern treatment. Even if the main house is full of eighteenth-century furniture, up at the top you can burst into Bauhaus or Sixties Italian – both styles where shape is crucial – and abstract expressionism. Or you can suddenly turn rustic after all the elegance of the floors below. Alternatively, use these rooms to house prized but bulky collections, from fossil dinosaur parts to miniature railways.

Below left: **Someone has had fun creating a garret with cane chairs, carefully arranged treasures and colourful old books. Note the neutral background.**

Below: **Louvre blinds create patterns, and control the light from the many windows in this narrow corridor. The room beyond is much brighter – this and the carefully placed rocking chair make the whole scheme inviting.**

Bottom: **Pure white paint and fabrics exaggerate the angles and textures of this loft bedroom and add light.**

Under stairs and other awkward spaces need a bit more control – they must conform to the rooms around them – but they can be both useful and inviting. Small spaces benefit from generous treatment – building in shelves or including large bits of furniture can actually make them seem bigger. Finally, you can turn a forgotten space into a practical one: a home office, ironing or sewing area, plunge sink for flowers.

Practical areas really don't need to look scruffy. Modern tools and equipment mean that you can buy colour-coordinated computers, paint a cheap desk to match and team with desk accessories; flower-arranging equipment always looks charming; while sewing kept in pretty baskets around a comfortable Victorian chair is both cosily domestic and a reminder of diligence. And, yes, even ironing has its own charm as the picture below demonstrates. Think of the bliss of never having to fold up that ironing board again...

Above left: **A large, squashy sofa is swathed in a quilt which matches the banisters above.**

Above right: **Wood and metal are the only colours in this cool kitchen-dining space with its plain ladder leading to a gallery above. Kitchen equipment and tableware should be kept metallic or white too.**

Left: **Ironing as an art. The pretty yellow cupboard and wood board tone with the stairs. Hide violently coloured laundry here.**

Right: **The simplicity of white and wood is cosy and cool in this attic eyrie.**

essential elements

colour

Choosing the right colour is at once the most exciting and the most daunting of decisions. It is also one of the least expensive ways to achieve a near-instant effect. Paint a room spotless white and you have light and space. Paint the same room plum red and its walls will wrap around you. The difference is dramatic, and all you need is a pot of paint.

Above: **The colours here might appear to break the rules, mixing dark red with deep pink and purple. But rather than clashing, these warm, rosy hues work in harmony because they are similar in tone. No single shade dominates.**

Left: **A quiet combination of white walls, bleached floorboards and the cool, soft green of paintwork in this timeless kitchen is clean, fresh and calm.**

Right: **The bright, strong forget-me-not blue walls of this period living room make a perfect foil for the marble and gilt of picture frames and fireplace.**

Colour principles

Colour is light, as discovered by Newton and revealed in the rainbow. The human eye is astonishingly sensitive to light, able to detect the presence of light equivalent to one candle ten miles away, and capable of discerning between several million colours of varying hue. Some colours make you smile, others make you cringe, but they might have a completely different effect on someone else. Little wonder that poring over colour charts can be a fraught business.

If we arrange colours in a colour wheel (left), putting the three primaries – red, blue and yellow – at equal distances and filling the gaps between them with secondary colours mixed from them, and the gaps between these by mixing secondary to make tertiary colours and so on, some general principles are easy to see. Colours on the blue and green side, for example, are thought of as 'cool' and 'receding', while colours on the red and orange side are 'warm' and 'advancing'. Greens and blues are calm and contemplative, hence the 'green rooms' of theatres and television studios. At the other end of the spectrum, bright red is the colour of danger, of traffic and brake lights, of warning and of passion.

The colour wheel can be enlarged almost ad infinitum but, even so, it only shows one dimension of colour, known as the hue. Colour has two further areas of differentiation: saturation, which refers to the vividness of a hue, and lightness, which refers to the amount of white or black mixed in with it. This is one of the reasons that some of the basic 'rules' about colour have so many exceptions. While a pure yellow hue is generally thought of as warm and welcoming, there are just as many shades of yellow that are sharp, acidic and decidedly cool. Likewise there are icy blues and sunny blues, harsh whites and gentle whites. And, just to complicate matters even further, the same colour can look quite different at different times of day, on different walls of the same room, placed against another colour, matt or shiny, in daylight or under electric light.

Colour charts offer a great choice, but they only give an indication of what a paint will look like on a wall or door. This is why sample pots are so invaluable. Paint as large a patch as possible of any colour you are considering, ideally on more than one wall, and live with it for several days. Look at it in bright sunlight and by the light of a table lamp and, if you still like it, it is probably a good choice. Remember, mistakes can usually be rectified. Get it right, and your colourful room will be a source of intense visual pleasure.

Above: **The colour wheel puts the primary colours – red, blue and yellow – at equal distances and fills the gaps with secondary colours mixed from the primaries on either side of them. More colours can be introduced by filling the gaps between secondary colours with tertiary colours mixed from the secondaries, and so on until the gradations of colour are very small. The colour wheel is useful to decorators because it can be divided into the warm colours, here on the right, and the cool colours on the left. 'Complementary' colours are found opposite one another on the wheel.**

Left: **This period dining room owes its theatrical effect to the use of complementary colours, here red and green.**

Paint finishes

By the end of the last century paint finishes had got a bad name for themselves. Thanks partly to the Eighties vogue for authentic period interiors, and encouraged by do-it-yourself paint finish books, it seemed that no kitchen was complete without a coating of dragged yellow paintwork, no bedroom finished until it had a stencilled border or two, no fire surround sufficiently grand until it had been marbled. Suddenly everyone was experimenting with rag-rolling, stippling and sponging. Paint finishes became victims of their own success, used indiscriminately, executed badly and just too commonplace to be interesting.

Twenty years on, there is still a place for paint finishes in fashionable interiors. Used with restraint and applied with appropriate skill, paint finishes offer ways of manipulating and playing with colour, treating a wall like an artist's canvas, achieving illusions of depth and texture on a flat surface with thin layers of paint or glaze.

Not all paint finishes require professional skills; sponging, stippling, dragging and rag-rolling are self-explanatory paint effects which demand practice but, happily, not a particularly high level of skill. You will get best results if you make sure the background colour and applied broken colour are a close match. Too much contrast between the two tends to look clumsy unless applied by a professional. You can also have fun with different textures in paint: try blackboard paint, metallics or lime washes.

The decorative effect of all these techniques should not be to call attention to the effect itself but to achieve a softer, 'distressed' colour which looks gently aged. For this reason these paint effects are particularly appropriate for traditional and period interiors, where the uniformity of modern paint can look too flat and unforgiving.

More testing types of paint finish include those designed to imitate another material such as stone, wood, marble or even tortoiseshell. These are not effects to attempt yourself. However, done well, they are a relatively inexpensive way

to achieve a rich and exotic interior finish. *Trompe l'oeil* can also be used to emphasize and highlight existing panelling, for example by using a lighter shade for the raised border of a fielded panel and a slightly darker one for the panel itself. Or, more ambitiously, you can add instant period glamour to plain walls by painting your own panelling using lines of diluted emulsion to imitate mouldings. And don't forget floors. Even the most dreary chipboard can be transformed by a simple painted design.

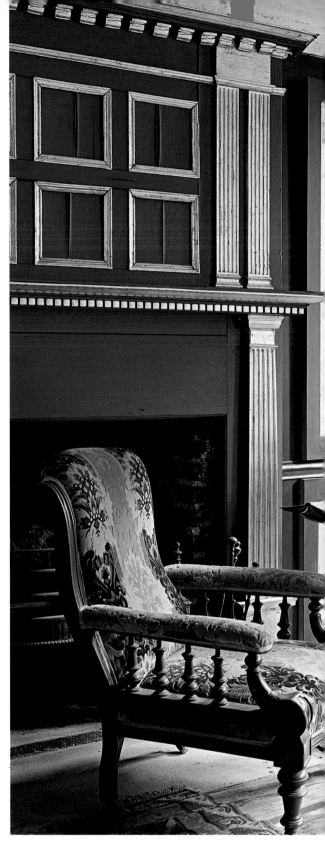

Above left: **A mottled paint finish using three shades of antique yellow makes a continuum of walls and door. The effect is parchment like, adding depth and textural interest to a featureless surface.**

Below left: **The fielded panelling of these doors is accentuated by the use of three different colours and paint effects. The central panel has been painted pink and combed to imitate watered silk.**

Left: **A detail of the silver and gold leaf on the Georgian panelling, far left. Laid directly onto the dark blue paint, the metal leaf has been gently buffed with wire wool for a softer, distressed look. The same technique can be applied to any paint finish for an appearance of instant ageing.**

Above: **This Georgian interior with original panelling has been given a glitzy face-lift with a bold combination of dark blue paint and reflective silver leaf. Gold leaf is used for luxurious highlights.**

Right: **Paint effects can add atmosphere and warmth to spaces that might otherwise feel too hard-edged and industrial. The concrete pillars of this old factory have been painted to look like heavily textured stone.**

Neutrals

Some of the most stylish and sophisticated contemporary interiors are those that confine themselves to a palette of the gentle, natural colours we term neutral. In between the extremes of black and white, these are the tones of stone, sand, wood, fur and earth; browns, greys and creams and all their subtle variations.

Accepting the discipline of a palette that excludes the bright and the primary has many aesthetic advantages. Like the woman who only wears black, thereby side-stepping the problems of matching shoes and handbags, a room decorated in neutral colours will never look vulgar. Neutrals, unlike stronger colours, don't clash or fight each other for the eye's attention. This is why neutral colour schemes are so often described as harmonious. Traditional Japanese interiors, with their reliance on the soft tones of self-coloured materials such as rush, wood and unbleached paper, have a quiet beauty that has long inspired many Western designers.

Since the Eighties, when decorative interiors – with patterned fabrics and rugs, busy wallpapers and fussy paint finishes – were the height of fashion, the trend in interior design has been a steady move away from pattern and clutter

Right: **Neutrals can create interiors of surprising warmth, as well as sophistication. In this sleek sitting room the walls are mid-grey. Far from being cold, this is a gentle, welcoming shade. Contrasts of texture are provided by the ribbed rug and pale tan upholstery, while the shiny, reflective whites of the coffee table and the satin cushions also provide colour contrasts.**

Left: **Deep, chocolate brown and white is a classic combination of colours, as chic as black and white but not quite so hard-edged. In a living room dominated by the pale gold of wood, there are browns from honey to nearly black, while white walls maximize the light flooding in through the huge window. Tactile fabrics including luxurious heavy velvet curtains and thick-ribbed corduroy upholstery make the room cosy and homely.**

Left and top right:
Two views of an ultra-smart New York living room in a disciplined palette of black, brown and white. The hard and soft, and the shiny and matt, contrast and complement one another, while the bold, bright scarlet of the ranunculus stands out as if under a spotlight.

Right centre and above: **Pale, creamy browns, greys and ivories are cool and classy, but high maintenance – not for dogs or toddlers.**

towards a look that is much more simple, empty and plain. Natural materials have come into their own; wood floors are stained or polished, left bare of rugs; pale limestone has ousted tiles or lino as the kitchen flooring of choice; cream calico or taupe linen has replaced chintz, and seagrass and sisal the fitted carpet. Instead of painted bookshelves and dragged kitchen cupboards, wood is being left bare, oiled or lightly waxed, celebrated for its own colour and grain. Basing a neutral colour scheme around the warm shades of these natural materials is one way to ensure that they are shown off to best advantage.

This might imply that creating a neutral colour scheme is easy. In fact – even though matching the different colours in a room may be less of a juggling act – neutrals are demanding in other ways. Choosing the right shades of paint, carpet and upholstery can be just as taxing as if you are using a cocktail of blues, reds and greens. White, the basis of so many neutral colour schemes, sounds straightforward enough until you start to explore its myriad possibilities.

There are dozens of shades of white available to bewildered householders, including 'historical' whites that aren't white at all: do you want bright white or old white, grey-white or brown-white, white with a hint of peach or white with a hint of periwinkle? John Fowler, perhaps the greatest twentieth-century interior decorator, always softened white by adding a touch of raw umber (very dark brown). A less artistic solution is to choose a cheap brand of brilliant white and wait for it to fade. Taupe is another notoriously difficult colour to find in a perfect shade – some are too pink, some are too blue, some are too yellow. As with any other colour, a neutral should be tried out and tested, however minute the variations between shades of beige appear to be.

While the eye may find a neutral colour scheme pleasantly restful, there is conversely a danger that lack of colour and contrast will result in a boring blandness. In order to avoid this you need to take extra care with form and texture. Just as bone structure and skin quality show up more in a black-and-white photograph than in colour, the eye will concentrate more on shape, arrangement and the effects of light and shade in a space where colour is not a distraction. For this reason neutral colour schemes are particularly effective in rooms of real architectural merit, allowing you to concentrate on the beauties of proportion and focus on features such as windows and fireplaces.

Your eye enjoys contrast and, when this is not provided by colour, differences in texture between the smooth and the rough, the soft and the hard, the hairy and the silky, can be just as satisfying. A room with a shiny wood floor, glossy leather upholstery and smooth plastered walls offers no variety for the sense of touch. Add some big grey velvet cushions, a thick, creamy sheepskin rug and a lamp with a parchment shade, and it is transformed from the clinically sleek to somewhere welcoming and tactile. Textiles play a particularly important role in these pared-down interiors; thick corduroys with slippery satins, coarse linens with supple suede, rough tweed with flat, matt felt – the opportunities for mixing and matching fabrics by feel as opposed to by colour are endless.

A successful scheme of neutrals looks smart, timeless and expensive. And, if you tire of the perfect good taste of your sepia-toned interior landscape, you can make a dramatic statement with a mere splash of colour, whether a vase of poppies or a pair of beaded slippers.

Left: **In this open-plan space the kitchen area is loosely defined by chunky, natural oak shelving. Its warm honey colour and strong, straight grain unify the whole room, as it is also used for the kitchen cupboards and the floor. Touches of fresh green enhance the organic, natural feel, while the pale walls and rug and cream crockery reflect an abundance of light.**

Below: **The discipline of a limited palette is key to the perfect elegance of this room. Black, deep blue and two browns make a stark contrast with white paintwork and the pale putty of the bedspread. In between these extremes of light and dark are balancing mid tones of the wood floor and grey walls.**

Opposite left: **The glow of auburn cherrywood dominates in a room without strong colours. Cream upholstery looks cool and contemporary but is practical only as washable loose covers.**

Above: **A poised, modern living room. Natural materials are a strong element, in colour and texture – the wood of the staircase, antique ladder and the modular coffee table – and in the pale sand of the limestone floor. Other gentle colours of similar tone include soft green and the smoky blue of the striped upholstery.**

Cool colours

Cool colours are whites, greys and those pale, watery blues and greens that remind us of glassy pools and icy streams and the bleached dawn of winter mornings. Their effect in an interior can be cold or even bleak but, used with care, these pretty, pure shades have a delicate beauty.

Bright white, the colour of snow, frost and cloud, must be the most enduringly popular of all interior paint colours, whether it is the whitewash of a simple country cottage or the flat white emulsion used to accentuate the soaring classical architecture of a Robert Adam entrance hall. White is almost as effective a reflector of light as mirrors are, and it not only reflects light, but also expands space. White walls seem to recede and white ceilings lift, which is why we almost always choose it for a ceiling, whatever other colours we have used in a room. Small, dark spaces, low-ceilinged basements, cramped attics, internal bathrooms – all can be transformed to give an illusion of light and increased volume by the simple application of white paint.

Even in homes that are otherwise a riot of colour, white is often first choice for the bathroom. Plain white sanitary ware has long been classic bathroom style, but when first introduced at the beginning of the twentieth century it was the relatively recent importance of hygiene that made white the fashionable choice. A white bathroom feels clean; indeed it demands to be cleaned. Just as crisp white linen sheets, laundered white shirts and fluffy white towels are ruined by the smallest stain, a white interior is high maintenance. However, if looked after and kept free of grubby fingermarks and smears, the all-white room is reassuringly fresh.

Some of the most successful interiors which use white harmoniously, together with other cool colours, are the Swedish interiors of the late eighteenth century (the style known as Gustavian). Enlivened by touches of gilt and the milky gleam of white-tiled stoves, the appeal of these homes relies on the brightness of a pale palette combined with the inherent warmth of scrubbed

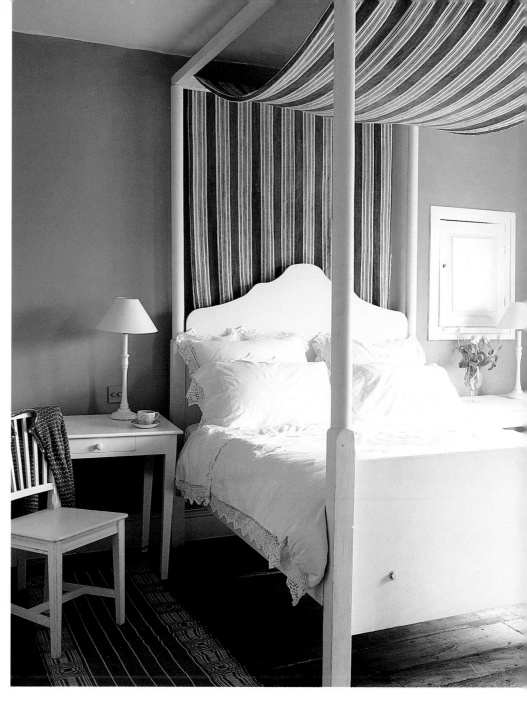

wood floors, flat-weave rugs and the faded patina of old painted furniture. Complemented by fabrics in simple stripes and checks, this is a look that combines the restrained simplicity of modernism with a homely, traditional feel.

A more contemporary effect can be achieved by using the same range of cool colours with modern furnishings in pale wood, graceful metal or even perspex. Black-and-white photographs, pencil and pen-and-ink sketches, or engravings will all fit well into this type of scheme.

Top left: **Soft, fondant blue woodwork and faint yellowy walls maximize light and space in this airy hall. Even the floorboards reflect light, stained white with a thin coat of emulsion.**

Above left: **Old blue and white china looks well in a sunny kitchen which is largely white. A paler blue links the dresser with the tables.**

Opposite: **The greens, blues and whites of this room are refreshing and light, rather than cold.**

Above: **Different blues, from the dark navy of the striped bed canopy to the smoky blue of the runner, are contrasted in this pristinely pretty bedroom with the dazzling white paint of the furniture and other woodwork.**

Left: **White, the colour of purity and cleanliness, always seems very appropriate in the bathroom. White towels, like white shirts, have an air of luxury – largely because they demand regular laundering.**

Hot colours

Opposite above left: **This living room glows. While the walls are a relatively subdued primrose yellow, the sofas buzz with fruity oranges and pinks.**

Opposite above right: **A saturated imperial yellow is a bold colour for a kitchen. Framed by white tiles and the warm toffee of the wood floor, cupboards and walls strike the eye like slices of bright sunshine.**

Opposite below: **Red is good for night-time rooms because it is warm and enclosing. Here, raspberry-red makes a womb-like library and sitting area.**

Right: **Orange and black is a classic combination. Here the effect is lightened by pale wood cupboards and furnishings.**

Below: **Bright colours with this much punch are only for the brave.**

At the red, yellow and orange end of the spectrum are the bold, vibrant hot colours. These are colours to make you smile; cheerful, extrovert colours, impossible to ignore. Because they are so strong, they are not to everyone's taste, but given sufficient confidence and panache they can create the illusion of sunshine on the greyest day and make the most unprepossessing space cosy.

Of all the hot colours, yellow is probably the most approachable. However, it is also one of those colours that can go horribly wrong; a warm buttercup or imperial yellow is uplifting, but there are other shades of bright yellow which are so acidic as to be nauseating. Yellows

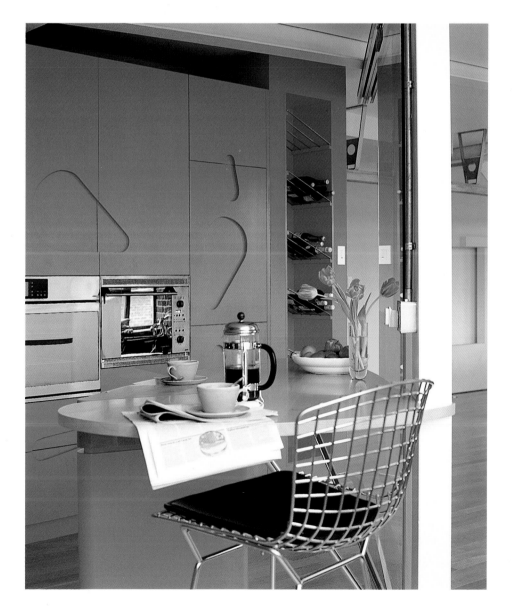

containing even the tiniest hint of blue or green are generally to be avoided but, as with all elusive shades, the only way to be certain you have found the right one is to paint some on your wall.

Yellow's nearest colour cousin is orange, a particular shade of which, combined with dark brown, was a favourite kitchen colour scheme of the Seventies. Subsequently outcast as irredeemably naff, orange has recently seen a revival thanks to the resurgence of interest in Seventies style. In fact orange is an easier colour to use than yellow. While its yellower, neon varieties might be a bit too dazzling, there are dozens of more subtle shades of orange, ranging from the safely traditional terracotta to clear mid-oranges, which work well with wood and stone.

Which brings us to red, the most versatile of all the hot colours and one which can soothe or excite in equal measure depending on its hue, saturation or lightness. Bright pillarbox red is such a forceful colour it is rarely used in interior decoration; add white and yellow, however, and you have pink, which is always popular, whether for sophisticated drawing rooms or little girls' bedrooms. Pink may be pretty, but in its darker hues red seems to glow with a warmth that can seem almost as comforting as a crackling log fire.

Contrasts of colour, texture and even styles of furnishing make for interiors that are lively and visually engrossing. It can seem much simpler to give yourself rules: only cutting-edge modern furniture; only eighteenth-century English antiques; only shades of white or only shades of blue. While even the strictest rules don't make decorating easy, you can at least achieve a certain coherence. Going for a mix is always more of a challenge, and combining colours is a challenge many don't feel equal to.

However, there are some tried and trusted colour combinations which never seem to go out of fashion. Yellow, blue and white, as used by Monet in his house at Giverny, or green and red, as used by the architect Sir John Soane in his London dining room (and by all of us at Christmas), are two examples. But it would help if there were some guidelines to apply to combining colours. 'Blue and green should never be seen', 'pink and orange always clash', or 'never use primary colours and pastels in the same room', perhaps. But we can all think of glorious exceptions that prove these rules meaningless. As with any aspect of interior design, the key is balance. This is something you can learn through experience, by looking at rooms you admire and living with schemes of your own devising, by experimenting and tweaking and being prepared to start again.

Mixing gentle, faded colours in one room is more straightforward than mixing more vibrant shades. Bleached or tea-stained shades of almost

Combining colours

Above: **Mixing subdued colours in similar tones is easier than combining vibrant shades and can look charming. Areas of broken colour, such as stripes and checks, incorporate some of the more dominant hues and cohere the scheme.**

Left: **Primary colours make a surprisingly sophisticated Shaker-style dining room.**

any colour will blend with one another without fighting for attention. This is the effect achieved in the crowded drawing rooms of well-worn English stately homes. There is no obvious colour scheme, just a motley collection of sun-washed damasks and tapestries, subdued chintzes and sober rugs. A modern version to try yourself might be to use a selection of pastel shades. To avoid a sugary, baby-sweet effect, choose stronger, purer versions of these pale colours – forget-me-not blue rather than duck-egg blue, pale yellow with a hint of ochre rather than primrose yellow, for example – and introduce small amounts of deeper colour, perhaps in soft furnishings, to add depth.

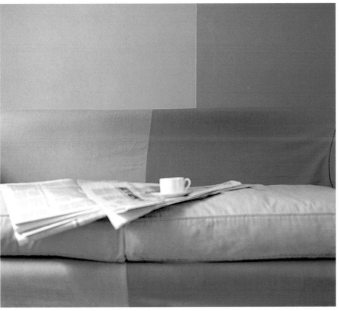

Above: **Powerful, jewel-bright colours from the hottest section of the colour wheel contrast with the cool, reflective aquamarine of glass screens and wall panels. In a converted home with a sharp industrial edge, the warmth of red, orange and yellow is very welcome.**

Left: **Subdued checks on this sofa are echoed in panels of brighter colour on the wall behind, for an effect that is as subtle as it is arresting.**

Faded colours work well together because they tend to share the same tonal values; if you screw up your eyes to look at them they all appear to have a similar level of brightness. This balance can also be achieved with stronger colours by deliberately paying attention to tone, thereby ensuring that no single colour will grab all the attention to the detriment of the rest.

When combining forceful colours, you might find it useful to return to the colour wheel to consider the effect of complementary colours, found opposite one another on the wheel. They are often used by decorators to provide maximum contrast and definition. (A good way to darken a shade is to add a little of its darker

Above: **Mixing hues that are close on the colour wheel looks harmonious. In this appealing period dining room, everything seems to have a patina of age. Bright peacock blue is complemented by the softer blue-grey of the woodwork, painted chairs and the large fruit bowl.**

Right: **A dining room in rich shades of purple and blue, its regal feel enhanced by a crown-like chandelier.**

Above right:
This funky kitchen-diner seems to mix colour with abandon – clover pink, orange, royal blue, turquoise and powder blue. Handled with less skill the effect could be messy. Instead, strong shapes and a careful balance of areas of dark and light colour give the room the poise of an abstract painting.

complementary colour. This gives a softer result than adding black.) Purple and yellow, red and green, and blue and orange are all pairs of complementary colours. Placed together they intensify each other, so if the effect you seek is drama, you might choose to scatter your navy sofa with orange cushions or to lay your table with yellow crockery on a purple tablecloth. Used together over large areas these are not colour combinations for the faint-hearted. However, they can be deployed more subtly, for piping on upholstery or as a statement vase of flowers.

Such pointed contrasts may not be to your taste, but you can be sure that complementary colours will not detract from the vividness of each other. This is not true for other colour combinations – something to bear in mind when putting colours together. Light shades next to very dark ones have the effect of deepening the darker shade. Shell-pink cushions on a deep-red sofa will enrich the red and make it appear to recede from the eye. Replace the shell pink with black velvet, however, and the red of the sofa will seem lighter. To make matters more difficult, reds tend to look as if they are closer than they really are, while blues tend to look further away.

Giving equal weight to more than two or three colours in an interior is always a difficult decorating trick to pull off. However, as these illustrations show, the reward can be a room full of life and unexpected harmonies.

Opposite below:
Complementary colours – red and green – used to dramatic effect.

Below left:
Colours combine between rooms, too. Looking into this bathroom, with its vibrant red walls and dark marble floor, you also see a blue door and outside wall.

Below: **The dominant colour in this daring scheme is a deep, bright, saturated cobalt blue, to which stripes and slices of even stronger colour have been added.**

Light adds shape and form to our world. It defines colour and texture and has a powerful influence over our moods. Electricity has given us the opportunity to design with artificial light. As well as providing practical illumination so we can navigate spaces, artificial light can enhance interiors, highlighting beautiful objects and details, opening up or closing off spaces, sculpting rooms and providing ways of enjoying our homes to the full.

lighting

Lighting principles

Lighting is a powerful interior design tool. Well-planned lighting can add enormously to the quality of a space: poorly planned, it can spoil a room, so it's worth careful thought.

When planning lighting, take into account the size, shape and decoration of the room, how it is to be used, what effects you'd like to achieve and the size of your budget. As a general rule, the larger the room, the more light sources you'll need. Many older homes have a central pendant lamp. This is useful, but should be supported by a range of other fittings and lights at different levels. Remember that darker decorative schemes require more light sources than pale ones, because dark walls and fabrics absorb light.

Having a clear idea of a room's use is vital to planning a good scheme – a family kitchen, for example, is used from

Opposite: **This is clearly a carefully considered scheme, with its trio of pendant lamps over the dining table, good task lighting in the kitchen, recessed fittings up the lower stairs, soft reading light by the upstairs sofa and natural light cascading downstairs and through the skylight.**

Above right: **This scheme makes the most of decorative lighting. To complement the modern interior there are intriguing Seventies-style table and pendant lamps with multi-coloured glass shades. Here lighting is one of the room's main features.**

Centre right: **Dimmer switches give you maximum control. In this hallway, lights are turned up full to spotlight details such as the beautiful bunch of flowers sitting in its alcove.**

Below right: **This flight of stairs is given extra visual interest, and is safer to climb, with the addition of recessed fittings at the base of the wall. Light washes across the stairs, making it easy to see the outline of the steps, and also makes the staircase a sculptural feature.**

morning to night and may include lights for the dining area, the work surfaces, and inside the cupboards. The scheme will be quite different for a guest bedroom where you may need just a central light or wall lights and a reading lamp. With the use in mind, you can also start to build in subtleties such as different moods. For example, in the family kitchen you'll probably want plenty of bright light to get people up and going in the morning, but you may also want to tone down the atmosphere for grown-up suppers. Dimmer controls are a good idea here: there is only one thing more disturbing than too little light, and that is too much.

And then there is your budget. Essentially the sky is the limit for any lighting scheme. The most lavish might include recessed light fittings, expensive classic designer lamps and a computer-controlled system board. However, you can still achieve great results with a modest array of stylish free-standing floor and table lamps, found on the high street, mixed with some built-in wall and pendant fittings.

To create a basic lighting scheme, consider starting with a central pendant for a general wash of light, and adding interest to the room with wall lights, table lamps and tall floor-standing lamps. Remember that the quality, intensity and spread of this illumination will react with your room's colour scheme. Once the space is filled with a fairly even spread of light, add in points of interest. For real drama, spotlight architectural details or focus on paintings. While beams of light are at their most intense on a subject, at their edges are the dense shadows which give form to objects and underline a scheme's dramatic tension.

Far left: **A white decorative scheme is given a crisp edge with sparkling halogen lighting. Tungsten bulbs would give a softer, yellower light.**

Left: **Tranquil, period-style lighting to enhance a room's traditional style of furnishings and colours. The glass pendant lantern over the table produces a soft wash of ambient light. Below it, the splendid candlesticks bear fat candles for some gentle tabletop illumination.**

Below left: **A lighting plan which turns the beautiful cantilevered stair into a stunning sculptural element. The simple table lamp creates a sunburst of light under the stair that falls on the tabletop below and reaches across the objects on display. To balance this table lamp, there is a softer wall light casting its beam of light from top right.**

Armed with the basics of how to plan your scheme, you can then use light to create different moods. Because our ancestors relied heavily on the natural rhythms of sunlight and moonlight, we respond well to bright sunlight or electric light when we need to get up in the morning and, as darkness draws in, our bodies begin to slow down for sleep. Of course electric light has artificially extended our days, but we remain sensitive to light levels. We know instinctively that bright light means action and soft light is restful.

A knowledge of the types of light available is useful for creating moods. There are three main sources – tungsten, halogen and fluorescent.

The familiar domestic lightbulb is tungsten. It is the world's most ubiquitous electric light source. The inexpensive tungsten bulb has a filament housed in a glass dome which glows

Creating moods with lighting

when charged with electricity, producing the soft, creamy light found in most homes. This type of bulb is now made in a variety of shapes and sizes, including slim tubes. In recent years, the most significant competitor to arrive on the scene is the halogen bulb, available in low-voltage and mains-voltage varieties. This light source was first used to add sparkle to shop window displays. It gives a hard, crisp, white light. Halogen fittings are small, but provide a powerful beam of crystalline light. However, they are difficult to fit into the ceilings of older properties, the low-voltage variety requires the use of hefty transformers, and they are still relatively expensive. Completing the trio is fluorescent lighting, now much kinder on the eye than the flickering bleak light most people have experienced in kitchens or garages.

When you create moods with lighting, remember that the calmer and more laid-back the scheme, the lower you should set the light levels; for a lively, upbeat atmosphere, turn up the brightness. This versatility is best achieved by having a series of lights on different circuits – for example, ceiling lights on one, wall lights on another, and plug-in floor and table lamps on a third. And make full use of dimmer controls.

Main picture:
This room has many light sources, with a mixture of tungsten and halogen bulbs. Each lamp is turned to a low setting, to create a restful, laid-back feeling in the space.

Above: **A quiet corner is created with a soft sofa, a fake-fur throw, plenty of cushions and a low table lamp with an ordinary tungsten bulb and cream shade – the ideal place to curl up and read.**

Top: **Simple drama. A single spotlight just above and left of this intriguingly shaped vase draws attention to it and enhances its shape. The vase and shelf shadows create a dramatic effect.**

Above: **Lighting is key in making small room settings. Here three sources make a cosy corner: a small picture light, glowing table lamp, and a floor lamp with movable arm ideal for reading.**

Task lighting

As its name suggests, task lighting is the type of illumination we need for carrying out everyday tasks. As a general rule, task lighting needs to be brighter than the surrounding room lighting; tungsten or halogen bulbs are both suitable sources. We need greater levels of illumination to work efficiently and safely and be able to see important details. Brighter light also keeps us sharper and more alert, it is stimulating, and it helps to prevent eye strain and headaches when doing close work like writing, sewing or using a computer. And as we grow older our eyesight becomes weaker, and we need more light for any close activity – including reading the newspaper.

In a well-lit home, there is task lighting in every room. In the kitchen it is needed primarily for the work surfaces but also for any other work area, including the sink and hob. The very best sort of task lighting here is a series of good strong lights, tungsten or halogen, suspended over the work area just above and in front of you. It is important that the light is cast directly downwards without any interruptions, which may cause shadows.

In the bedroom and bathroom, task lighting for dressing and make-up is usually fitted around mirrors – the best light is that cast from both sides of a mirror, giving even illumination across your face. Lights fitted above or below can produce unflattering shadows. In the bedroom, task lighting also includes reading lights. Table lamps provide just enough light for reading, but lamps with articulated stems that allow you to manipulate the beam of light to the page are far better. Among the best types of reading light for double beds are those fitted on the wall between the sleepers – this way you can angle the light away from a partner who may want to sleep without being disturbed by bright light.

The last main category of task light is for the home office or workroom. The best solution for these areas is to buy one or two desk lamps which can be focused on the work surface. For those using a computer, the light should be placed at an angle to the screen to minimize glare.

Above: **This simple, beautiful and practical scheme incorporates a pair of large pendant lamps with industrial-style aluminium shades for the dining area, plus a track of smaller task lamps, also given aluminium shades, over the work surface. The track system is based on sturdy metal tubing suspended from the very high ceiling.**

Right: **Concealed and recessed task lamps are fitted here into the extractor hood above the hob; a very useful type of task light. Most modern extractor hoods have integral lighting, but it is worth checking before you buy.**

Above: **Wall-fixed reading lamps are a good idea for bedrooms because they are space-efficient and can't be knocked over in the dark. This design has a useful movable arm.**

Left: **This home office area in a converted industrial building has large windows either side, so benefits from plenty of natural light. However, it is always a good idea to have an adjustable lamp actually on the desk. This will provide high levels of targeted illumination for your work area.**

Right: **Bathroom lighting needs to be kind – this is where you see yourself first and last thing. For lighting around mirrors, two side lights are always better than one, because they cast an even light across the face without creating shadows.**

Right: **This small area of tabletop is made into an interesting tableau with two stylish lamps.**

Centre right: **The clever positioning of this sequence of fish pictures – following the arc of a fishing line – is given extra emphasis by the lighting, which highlights the lowest-level picture. Positioning an uplighter on the floor at the start of the sequence helps the eye read the pictures correctly, from the bottom upwards.**

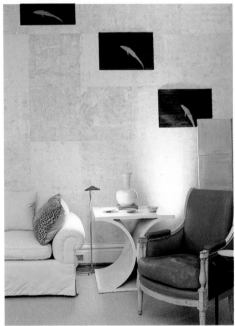

Below: **Light fittings set into shelving units provide really exciting illumination. Borrowing from the techniques of shop-lighting designers, these tiny recessed lamps cast a sparkling light downwards onto the items displayed beneath them.**

Above: **Ceiling-recessed lights come in several varieties, including fittings with an 'eyeball' at their centre, seen here. The lights wash down the walls across these exquisite screens.**

Right: **This disc of light shows off the textures and details of the surrounding objects.**

Opposite above: **Unusual illumination for a large picture. Rather than providing an even wash of light, different areas of the canvas have been highlighted.**

Opposite below: **In large, open-plan homes, accent lights (like this clip-on design) create little moments of intimacy.**

Accent lighting

When you are designing a basic lighting scheme for any room, try to think like a painter. Be aware of adding washes or layers of light – then finishing with highlights. Accent lighting has a crucially important role to play in bringing out the best of your carefully planned, decorated and furnished home. You can add interest, drama and the highlights to complete the overall picture. Finally, shadows and low lights will modulate the scheme.

Accent lighting is a hard-working element that needs to be added to your plan. With your ambient lighting in place and the task lighting set up, accents work to draw the eye through a space. This lighting category is very broad and includes table lamps, uplighters, downlighters and spotlights. A useful definition of an accent light is that it should draw attention to the object or area to be lit, rather than the light fitting itself.

Table lamps are the odd man out of accent lighting. They are not directional, but they cast a fairly contained pool of light, which can be deployed to add drama to the corner of a room, a table or a chest of drawers. They have the ability to add life to a whole area of room which may be out of reach of the rest of the lighting scheme. Table lamps also cross over into decorative lighting (see page 170 for more).

Other accent lights are all directed to illuminate their subject. Uplighters and downlighters are fairly self-explanatory. Probably the most common type of uplighter is the wall-fixed light with a solid shade, which prevents light flooding out below and instead concentrates the lightfall upwards, perhaps to illuminate a pretty decorative cornice. Another type of uplighter is a fitting set into the floor, or a floor-standing lamp, both of which have the job of sending light upwards. A final design to mention here is the big, industrial-style flood lamp, often seen in loft-style apartments, fitted on beams and blasting light upwards to show off the rafters, or, in a conversion, old factory pipe- and ductwork.

As you might expect, the reverse is true of downlighters. These include ceiling-recessed fittings with 'eyeball' centres, which enable the light beam to be used as a spotlight and can therefore be focused on objects around the room. These can be directed at paintings or architectural features. Contemporary standard lamps can also be used as downlighters, as their main purpose is to focus a beam of light downwards. Accent downlighters include those small light fittings, many of which often started life destined for use in shop displays, which are built into cupboards and shelving units to add an extra glow or sparkle to the objects on show.

Spotlights are also true accent lights. They can be deployed anywhere in the home to add some extra interest or definition and liven up any space. They are also extremely versatile, available in various widths of beam.

Finally, don't forget your visitors. When looking at a building from outside, accent lights by windows or lining the path to the front door will make your home look warm and inviting.

Ceiling lighting

The ceiling-mounted light is essentially a substitute for the sun inside the home. It is a poor imitation of the real thing, but most interiors do benefit from light cascading from above.

When electric lighting was first introduced, the standard lighting scheme was based around a central pendant lamp fixed to the ceiling. These tend to cast a rather gloomy light, with a pool of illumination in the middle, leaving the corners in shadow. Today's schemes are a great deal more sophisticated and pleasing to the eye, although the main type of ceiling lighting is still the traditional pendant – a light suspended from the ceiling (usually its centre) from a cable. There are also fittings which are recessed into the ceiling, and tracks which are mounted on its surface.

The pendant lamp has a long and glamorous history: in its heyday, chandeliers adorned the world's most prestigious buildings, all illuminated with candles. Now it is electric light which makes the crystals twinkle. Since these days of glory, the pendant lamp has become a rather prosaic lighting element and has spent decades in the doldrums of dreary design. The Sixties and Seventies saw the invention of the pendant light on a spring or cable mechanism, which allowed it to be raised or lowered over the dining table, and there are signs that the pendant lamp could once again be reborn as a thing of beauty. Lighting designers are now bringing plenty of new pendant lights, which successfully lift the spirits, to the market.

Meanwhile, the recessed ceiling fitting has become extremely popular. This type of light, whether it features a tungsten bulb (usually a fairly large fitting) or a halogen bulb (much neater fittings), has been used in just about every setting. It is extremely useful in bathrooms, where sealed units can be fitted flush with the ceiling and remain protected from damp or accidental knocks. They are much used in kitchens and living rooms, where the wide-beam versions provide good ambient light, dispensing with the need for hanging lights. And they are particularly

Left: In circulation areas such as corridors and passageways, a ceiling studded with recessed lamps marks out the route. In this very modern apartment the use of so many lights is not just practical, but also decorative.

Above right: The traditional-style chandelier still has strong appeal. While only purists would insist on using real candles, most of us are happy to install a design suitable for electric light.

Centre right: This ceiling uplighter is one way of using a traditional light source, the central ceiling fitting.

Right: The elegance of this cream hallway, with its panelled doors and polished dark wood floor, is enhanced by the large metal-framed glass feature lamps. The glass lamp covers diffuse the light, which fills the entire space with a soft, inviting glow.

Lighting fixed to the walls of a room usually provides a very sympathetic quality of light. For those evenings when a restful atmosphere is required, turn off the main, central light and keep on wall lights for a soft, laid-back glow.

Most wall lights are a permanent part of the lighting design scheme, so it is important to make sure they are in the right position, at the right height on the wall and in an appropriate style for the room. It is also common sense to make sure these are in place before you redecorate.

In most rooms, wall lights look best when seen in pairs; for example, either side of a fireplace or window. If you are using them to flank a picture, make sure you are happy to live with it in the same place for a long time. The electrical cable will be chased into the wall and then plastered over so that no trace of it remains. Note where these cables run, so that there are no accidents later when you are driving in nails to hang pictures.

The shops are now bursting with stunning designs for wall lights – anything from the most traditional designs to truly modern, abstract shapes. Plenty of contemporary designs make use of recesses dug into the wall where the back of the light is let into the wall and then the front panel sits flush with the wall surface.

Wall lighting

Opposite top row:
Decorative sconces, left, and unusual wall lamps.

Opposite centre right:
Low-level recessed wall lamps act as guide lights along a corridor.

Opposite below left:
A wall light with an articulated arm can be swung over a sofa for reading, or moved back against the wall to provide general light.

Opposite below right:
A soft, warm glow is provided by a wall light, left; a neat, modern low-voltage halogen lamp which can be angled to cast light where it is required, right.

Left: **An unusual wall light which climbs, plant like, up the wall between these two large windows. The yellow shade produces a warm, light tone.**

Right: **Providing extra light in a stairway, this wall-recessed lamp is a welcome departure from the usual ceiling-suspended fittings.**

Wall lighting is particularly well suited to living rooms, but it is also increasingly found in other areas of the home. It looks very effective when used to line and illuminate corridors and stairs – also making it a useful safety feature – and is a handsome addition close to the dining table or even in the bedroom. It is worth carefully considering at what height to fix wall lights in dining rooms and bedrooms. Think about setting them at a lower level on the wall than you might in other rooms because, in the dining room, people spend most of their time sitting down and, in the bedroom, lying down. Lights fixed at a lower level here will provide more useful illumination.

Floor lamps

There was a time when the traditional standard lamp was virtually the only type of floor-based lighting in common use. However, in recent years there has been an explosion of interesting new designs and innovative ways of using these highly versatile lights.

Floor lighting can incorporate a vast spectrum of design ideas and functions. There are tall designs based on the traditional standard lamp, intended to provide a three-quarter-height downward light in the corner of a room or close to a seat for reading. Standard lamps are a handsome addition to many lighting schemes. Another version of this is the free-standing uplighter – a light which

casts its beam to wash upwards across a wall or ceiling, reflecting soft, diffused light back into the room. There are also floor lights that provide light halfway up a room and which are intended mostly for reading. All these types of lamp look great when used in pairs. They look especially grand at either end of a large sofa or standing sentry either side of a doorway, window or fireplace.

The other main category of floor lights are those which are intended to cast their illumination around the lower part of the room. These fittings are often highly sculptural, with a lovely brooding presence. As well as providing an interesting

Far left: **Lighting as sculpture: a floor-standing column of light, in a corrugated paper design.**

Left: **Reading lights are always welcome by chairs and sofas – here a classic floor lamp can be angled to where light is required.**

Below far left: **Providing a warm glow in the lower level of the room is this fabulous Glo-ball lamp by Jasper Morrison, also made as a table lamp.**

Below left: **Standard lamps are a handsome addition to the lighting of any room, and are particularly attractive used in pairs.**

Above right: **Arco, a design classic by the Castiglioni brothers. This great arched floor lamp is a sculptural feature.**

Right: **This egg-shaped lamp looks stunning in a contemporary setting.**

Right: **This wild-looking, tree-like standard lamp has three light sources, which can be angled where needed. The conical lampshades give this design the look of a large plant.**

Below right: **Standing guard by this distinctive metal bookshelf is a floor-standing uplighter which casts its illumination upwards to wash the walls.**

Below far right: **Glowing light globes make a stunning addition to any room and look particularly striking in simple modern settings.**

Below: **This tripod lamp features an unusual loose-fitting cloth shade.**

glow at the base of the room, they can also be positioned behind furniture such as sofas, from where they will cast light up across the lower part of the wall. Used at floor level they add a welcome wash of light up the wall, but are not a glaring intrusion into the room.

Floor-standing lights are incredibly versatile. They don't need to be fixed permanently in one position, so can be moved around the room or indeed the house. And of course you can take them with you when you move home.

Like wall lights, floor lights are most often associated with use in the living room, but they also make useful additions to lighting schemes elsewhere in the home. Both the high- and low-level versions can look extremely good in a bedroom or a dining room. You might also consider powerful, free-standing lamps, originally

intended for use in commercial offices, as part of the artificial lighting of a home office.

Lighting can help to mould our perception of space, and floor-standing lamps are helpful for manipulating large areas. For example, if a room is very tall and you want to accentuate its height, build in floor-standing uplighters to wash the ceilings. To achieve the opposite effect of lowering a high ceiling, use floor-standing lamps fixed at a lower level in the room, add pendant lamps which cast a downward light, and perhaps also paint the ceiling a darker shade. To make a low ceiling appear higher than it is, remove pendant lamps, fit ceiling-recessed light fittings and keep floor lamps at a low level (at or below half the wall height) in the room.

Above far left: **This utterly charming lamp – Lucellino, by Ingo Maurer – features a standard tungsten lightbulb flanked by a pair of wings made of real goose feathers. The name is a play on words, from the Italian** *luce* **for 'light' and** *uccellino* **for 'little bird'.**

Above left: **This multi-faceted metal and glass lamp sits on the polished tabletop like a glowing crystal or starburst.**

Centre left: **A distinctive tower of light has been created with this stack of cubes which climbs up the wall. Some of the cubes glow more brightly than others.**

Left: **Frank Lloyd Wright's sculptural Taliesin lamp resembles an architectural model.**

Far left: **Vertical strings of light can be incredibly beautiful and highly decorative. Here the tall space features two very different designs, one string with round shades and another with dozens of tiny illuminated cubes.**

Above: **Tom Dixon's polyethylene Jack light looks great on the floor or on a large tabletop. It comes in different colours, doubles as a seat and can be stacked into tall towers.**

Above centre: **A classic of the Seventies, the lava lamp contains coloured liquids which move slowly when the light is switched on.**

Above right: **A dome-shaped fibre-optic lamp, also dating from the Seventies. A sheaf of fibre-optic threads is held vertically at the centre of the lamp, and splays out to make this perfect dome of tiny points of light.**

Below left: **An Art Nouveau-inspired double lamp with flower-head glass shades.**

Below centre left: **A table lamp to complement the ethnic style of this room, with a dark-wood base and a two-tiered, neutral circular shade.**

Below centre right: **This boulder-shaped, moulded all-in-one lamp glows subtly to illuminate a corner.**

Below right: **Rows of small, coloured pointed lightbulbs make an unusual 'picture' of light.**

Decorative lights

The world of decorative lighting embraces all lamp designs and fittings that you choose for the sheer joy of their presence. Decorative lighting is not compelled to perform any particular practical function; it is there by the merit of its design (although many examples are invaluable light sources, too). It demonstrates that artificial lighting can add poetry to a space.

It is not surprising, then, that decorative lighting can encompass a huge variety of lamps and light fittings. Pretty table lamps can be chosen to enhance and complement the overall design and decor of a room. Others, like the classic retro lava lamp or the fibre-optic lamp, can be included for their novelty value. Floor lamps, such as Tom Dixon's Jack light, and even table lamps such as Ingo Maurer's Lucellino (both featured here) can be intriguing sculptural presences in a room – just as beautiful switched off as they are when they're switched on. Even in the simplest of spaces, one glorious light fitting can add real magic. In recent years many independent design studios have started to provide the market with stunning, sometimes highly idiosyncratic, lamps.

When you set out to buy decorative lighting, always make sure you see what each light looks like when it is switched on. And instead of opting for the safer, more staid designs, consider lamps or fittings with real presence. A single room can't withstand too much eccentricity, unless it is in tune with the room's theme, but one or two unusual pieces of lighting design can have the impact of an artwork. And consider lights featuring coloured bulbs. They can add points of interest even in the most neglected corners.

flooring

Flooring is a prominent element in any home.
As the foundation of a decorative scheme,
it helps to set the tone of the entire room.
It must be attractive and practical, so your
choice should balance looks with function.
Flooring can easily devour a large portion
of your decorating budget, so take care
to research well and choose wisely.

Above: **Rugs can help to define spaces. Here a pair of pebble-coloured rugs is used as the base for the dining table and also for the sitting area. The dark-stained timber flooring underneath provides a colour and texture contrast.**

Above left: **Ceramic tiles have long been used in high-traffic areas like halls because they can withstand heavy wear and tear. The threshold marks the divide between hallway, finished in black and white ceramic tiles, and a rich timber floor.**

Left: **A terrazzo hallway. This durable stone composite is made of small stone, marble or coloured glass chips set in concrete and then cut and polished to produce a shiny, smooth surface.**

Main picture: **The simple modern furniture in this room is echoed in the** plain, short-pile, stone-coloured rug. The colour theme of stone and dark brown, seen in the furniture, is repeated on the floor in the large rug placed over a dark parquet flooring.

Right: **This open-plan space is clearly split into the circulation area and dining area. The gleaming polished wood boards are solid oak, giving a warm honey-coloured glow. This hard wood makes a very durable surface for a key circulation area.**

Above right: **A satisfying pairing of materials where neat, narrow-plank timber flooring meets a sisal rug. The tones of the stained wood work beautifully with the woven sisal.**

Centre right: **This floor demonstrates how you can give a classic design a fresh new edge. Here, instead of the more usual square tiles, rectangular white floor tiles are laid in a pattern with contrasting tiny square black tiles.**

Below right: **To delineate areas in this compact apartment, wood is used for the main circulation routes and soft carpet is inset for other areas.**

Below: **The luxurious and supple quality of leather, seen to good effect in the safari chairs, is echoed in the unusual leather floor rug composed of neat squares. Leather, although expensive, is a particularly hard-wearing and beautiful flooring material.**

Flooring principles

Flooring finishes and materials range from the plain and understated, such as sleek polished timber, to the most flamboyant mosaics or wild-patterned rugs. Today's choice is very extensive.

The main considerations when planning new flooring are what sort of finish is in place already, how the room or area is to be used in future, how it is to be decorated and the size of your budget. Think too about your room's dimensions. It is possible for a flooring material to alter the way a room is perceived – for example, long rectangular stone tiles will have the optical effect of lengthening a space.

Essential to the success of any flooring is what lies underneath, an ideal base being level and sound. For best results, you need to know how that base has been constructed. A solid concrete floor gives the greatest scope, as just about any flooring can be laid on top. Even if the floor is in an upper part of a building in an apartment block or converted industrial building, reinforced concrete should have the structural strength to carry the additional weight of heavy materials such as ceramic or stone tiles.

However, in most homes, particularly those which have been traditionally built, the floor substructure is made of long timber joists finished with softwood (usually pine) floorboards. This type of construction is not usually strong enough to bear the weight of stone slabs or tiles. One option here is to salvage and clean up the existing boards, if they are not too badly damaged by wear and tear and the disturbance caused by plumbers and electricians fitting wires and pipes underneath. Alternatively, remove the old boards and replace them with new wood, or consider any of the lighter flooring options such as cork, vinyl or linoleum, wall-to-wall carpet or natural grass coverings such as sisal. On the ground level of a traditionally built house, the old wood floor can usually be replaced with concrete, which then provides a base for stone or ceramic tiles. If you are in any doubt ask the advice of an architect or structural engineer.

Hard floors

Hard floors – made of stone, ceramic or brick – provide a glorious palette of texture and colour and look equally good in period or contemporary settings (first check that your subfloor can carry the additional weight of a hard floor).

Hard flooring is traditionally used in areas with high traffic, such as hallways and corridors, or in wet areas such as kitchens and bathrooms. Flagstones and terracotta quarry tiles are kitchen classics; stone flagstones or encaustic and black-and-white ceramic tiles are often found in halls; and marble always adds a splash of luxury to the bathroom. Recently stone, particularly creamy-coloured limestone, has been very popular for dining areas, living rooms and even bedrooms.

The secret of a long-lasting, good-looking hard floor is to start with a solid base and then make sure the material is laid correctly. A stone floor is expensive, so budget for a professional to lay it. This is not a job for the inexperienced, especially where floors need to be levelled and stones or tiles cut to fit a room's shape.

When choosing a material, think about your room's decorative scheme. You can buy stone, marble or slate in just about any colour, so choose with your general colour scheme in mind. Do you want a (dark or pale) neutral base, a floor with a subtle pattern or a heavily veined marble? Perhaps a composite material will answer your needs. Composites include terrazzo, made of large or small stone chips suspended in cement; poured concrete, which can be mixed with an aggregate to produce a flecked but smooth finish; and marble chips suspended in resin, for a textured finish. The last type of flooring (used in car showrooms) is unusual and less expensive than other solid stone floors.

All stone is porous to some extent. During your research it's useful to ask how the floor can be sealed so that it can repel stains and spills.

Similar advice also applies to ceramic tiles and bricks. These are available in a huge range of colours, textures, shapes and sizes. Ceramic can be as tough and long lasting as stone, and where

Above: **Square white tiles make a neat grid on this professional-style kitchen floor. Glazed ceramic tiles are easy to clean, hard-wearing and can withstand kitchen spills.**

Details, clockwise from top left: **Large white stone tiles with a diamond-shaped black slate inset; handmade Spanish terracotta tiles; a grey, yellow and white floor of tile fragments; outdoor courtyard tiles sporting a star design; non-slip tiles for a shower floor, featuring a fish design; a subtle bathroom floor in small dark and light blue tiles.**

Opposite above left: **A combination of cream and brick-red tiles is unusual, but looks stunning in this kitchen.**

Opposite above right: **This modern island unit divides a kitchen and dining area. Its white marble continues on the floor and in the steps down to the table. Either side is a wide ribbon of long, red-brick pavoirs.**

Opposite below left: **A wild-looking crazy paving effect created by combining a spectrum of different-coloured marbles to make an abstract pattern.**

Opposite below right: **Huge, creamy limestone tiles have been laid in this bathroom. As the tiles are so large, they look considerably more exciting than their regular-sized cousins. The limestone complements the marble used on the wall and bath panel.**

it is glazed, the surface is impervious to stains. Terracotta tiles are made from a variety of clays and have a glazed or unglazed finish. Very hard-baked quarry tiles have a densely textured, matt surface which repels most stains. Glazed terracotta will act in the same way. Unglazed terracotta is softer and can be finished with brushed-on linseed oil or floor wax for a matt finish. Gloss floor varnish will give shine. With tiled flooring, especially in the kitchen and bathroom, always pay special attention to grouting. While the tiles may be glazed, grouting is often porous and will absorb spills; waterproof varieties are available. It's also a good idea to choose a colour that won't show every mark.

Flooring bricks usually require some sort of finishing because they are porous and produce lots of dust for months after being laid. Again linseed oil or wax can be used as a gentle sealant which maintains a natural look. More drastic treatments include polyurethane-based varnish and sealant, but they can look artificial. Suppliers should offer advice on finishes and maintenance.

Finally, stone, ceramic and brick flooring is expensive. Even finding what you want in a salvage yard is no guarantee of a bargain. However, investment in a beautiful floor, expertly laid, will give years of pleasure, withstand plenty of wear and tear, and should improve with age.

Opposite above left: **This unusual but extremely elegant floor is made of poured concrete coloured with yellow pigment and then inset with lines of tiny pebbles to make a simple diamond pattern.**

Opposite above right: **The same floor shown in context. The pebble pattern stops short of the edges of the room, making a 'rug' for the centre of the floor.**

Opposite below: **In warm climates, a stone or ceramic floor is a cooler option than carpet. In this period house the scheme is classically simple with pale limewashed walls, well-worn terracotta-tiled floor and comfortable furniture upholstered in white linen – just the place to escape the sun.**

Details, clockwise from top left: **The smooth, shiny surface of well-worn rectangular Cotswold flagstones; a minimal interior set off by extra large, pale honey-coloured stone pavers; black-and-white speckled terrazzo tiles; a stunning tiling scheme using small pieces of coloured stone set in a cement base.**

Right: **A dark-tiled floor gives a solid base to a design scheme. The rich colour 'anchors' the white walls hung with abstract pictures and the modern furniture.**

Left: **Small terrazzo tiles are laid with contrasting dark border strips. The two-tone colours of the speckled tiles are found again in the woven stool seats.**

Above right: **An unusual form of parquet flooring, using recycled hardwood to make a large herringbone pattern. It captures the feeling of American Colonial buildings.**

Centre right:
Bleached teak gives this unusual silvery finish, complemented by silvery upholstery fabric and Venetian blinds made of cedar.

Below right: **Flooring as beautiful as the best cabinetwork. Here the handsome solid oak parquet is finished with a stunning border featuring fine lines of dark hardwood inlay.**

Above far right:
This subtle finish is achieved with small, square wood tiles laid in a diamond pattern. The slight variations in the wood colour create a lovely dappled effect in a floor which extends throughout this home.

Below far right:
Where the original boards are good enough quality, as in this period building, they can be sanded, finished and simply left bare.

Opposite: **An all-white modern interior is complemented by pale wood floorboards. You can achieve this light finish in several ways, including painting with a diluted pastel-pale or white paint before varnishing, or rubbing a lime paste into the wood grain with a cloth.**

Wood floors

Wood is perhaps the most versatile of all flooring materials and can be used in just about any setting. It is warm and welcoming, hard-wearing and almost always stunning to look at.

In its most elemental form, wood is used as simple planking or boarding. During the twentieth century decorative wood flooring achieved mass popularity laid in block or parquet form. Hardwood blocks or 'tiles' were laid in tight geometric designs, often in a herringbone pattern, to make a decorative and hard-wearing floor covering. Among the most recent innovations in the use of wood for flooring has been laminate, where slim wood veneers are stuck to a backing board and given a protective coating, usually clear PVC. These are then formed into panels or tongue-and-groove boards.

Because it is so versatile, wood flooring can be used just about anywhere in the home, with the possible exception of areas where exposure to water may produce stains, warping and rot. Wood is not always the best choice in a family kitchen or bathroom, where spills are inevitable.

If you are considering wood flooring, think about your decorative scheme – old pine floorboards which have been sanded and stained will probably not suit an interior which is highly finished, sophisticated and furnished with state-of-the-art contemporary furniture. In this case a thoroughly machined new hardwood floor with a sheer, flawless finish might be a better option.

Also take into account the existing floor. A solid, stable concrete slab is the perfect base for wood flooring. The usual process is to lay battens and then fix boards across these. This allows air to circulate between the concrete and the wood, preventing rot. Another option for a concrete base is to use wood blocks which can be fixed in place with an appropriate adhesive.

Where there is an existing boarded floor, first decide whether it is in good enough condition to be saved and revived. Consider whether any damaged boards can be repaired (and try to imagine whether the final result will be what you had in mind). Be aware that plenty of old pine boards, when sanded, reveal themselves to be an unattractive orangey colour – this can be obscured with dark stainer, or painted over, but is unlikely to improve with just a coat of varnish. Laminate flooring can be laid directly onto a base, whether it is concrete or old floorboards, as long as the base is stable.

Laying wood floors takes time, patience and skill, but the surface finishing is often key to making sure that the floor looks its best. Most laminate flooring comes pre-finished, saving the extra work of staining or varnishing. However, with solid blocks and boards the finish is usually added after laying. Remember to try out your stains, paints and varnishes on spare offcuts of the timber, especially if you are new to the techniques. While a particular stain might look quite wonderful on pale oak, it can produce an altogether different result when applied to pine or ash. Varnish is a good all-round finish – it is tough, hard-wearing and easy to clean – but it is unlikely to improve with age. Wax-polished wood does improve with age, but this requires regular, time-consuming maintenance.

Like all flooring materials, wood is expensive, but prices vary enormously between different materials. Prices also vary between suppliers, so it is always worth shopping around. You may even

Above: **In this converted warehouse the wood boards have been restored – sanded, stained and varnished. They bear the knocks and scrapes of use, retaining something of an industrial quality.**

Right: **Neat, slim boards, stained and glossily varnished, make this room gleam beautifully.**

Left: **Perfectly smooth, finely finished boards – the hallmark of a brand new floor. The high-quality finish makes a wonderful dark base for white-painted rooms.**

be lucky and find just what you want in an architectural salvage yard, but don't expect rock-bottom prices even there. When calculating the cost of the whole floor, take account of how time-consuming and tricky the wood will be to lay and to finish, as this may add considerably to the overall price. For example, some architectural salvage yards sell block flooring in its freshly reclaimed state still coated with sticky, black, tar-like adhesive. The prices may seem a bargain, but it can take days to chip off the glue and clean up these blocks before they are usable. They will also need to be fully sanded and finished once laid, so that, too, adds to the bill.

Finally, when buying timber for flooring, check its provenance. Make sure your wood comes only from sustainable and managed sources.

Above: **Original broad floorboards, sanded and finished but retaining a worn look to contrast with elegant furniture.**

Above right: **This highly unusual floor is just one of many factory-made wood finishes available.**

Below right: **A marquetry border. Coloured woods – here, cherry – are inlaid into contrasting wood to make complex geometrical patterns.**

Far right: **Narrow strip flooring, sophisticated and markedly different from wide floorboards.**

Left above and below: **New pale floorboards make a simple, crisp base in this contemporary home. Non-slip textured vinyl in a deep cherry red covers the stairs.**

Opposite above: **In this comfortable, old-style kitchen the floor has been covered in a chequerboard of blue and white linoleum tiles. Linoleum is popular because it is extremely hard-wearing and composed largely of non-irritant ingredients.**

Soft sheet & tiled floors

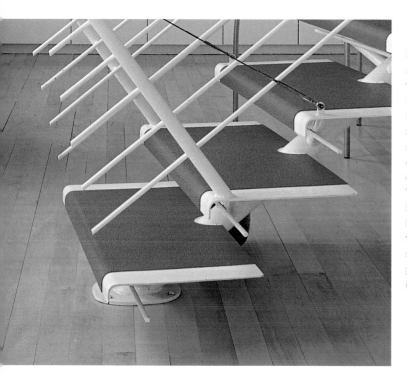

Opposite below left and right: **Soft tiles are incredibly versatile and are easy to cut to fit. Vinyl and linoleum (shown here) were once used only in bathrooms and kitchens, but they are now found in all corners of the home – even in home offices. These patterns have been made using the latest linoleum-cutting technology, which makes it possible to produce quite finely detailed designs.**

The recent fashion for wood and stone floors has left soft sheet and tile finishes rather in the shade. However, manufacturers of soft flooring are fighting back with new products in great colours and interesting, subtle patterns.

This category of flooring includes four main groups – linoleum, vinyl, cork and rubber. After a couple of decades as an unfashionable outcast, linoleum is now recognized as a warm, tough, attractive material which has found favour with many, including those who suffer from asthma or allergies. Linoleum is a composite material made with natural ingredients including linseed oil, chalk, cork and wood powder. Many asthma and allergy sufferers find it one of the few flooring materials they can tolerate. It is also fairly easy to lay, and very easy to keep clean. As demand has increased, so has the range of colours and patterns, and hi-tech cutting equipment makes complex floor patterns possible.

Like linoleum, vinyl can be cut to form patterns, and is sold in sheets and tiles. Vinyl can also be solid or cushioned. It is a plastic-based material which is warm to the touch, strong and stain resistant. Vinyl is sold in many different grades, from very thin and easy to manipulate cheap sheeting to incredibly tough, high-grade material which commands substantial prices.

Cork enjoyed huge popularity in the Sixties and Seventies. It is sold mostly in tiles – pre-finished with a tough transparent PVC coating, or left in its natural state for finishing once it is fitted. It can be stained and varnished to make a resilient surface. The appeal of cork is that it is warm, natural, characterful, acts as a fairly efficient soundproofing material and is inexpensive, easy to cut and very hard-wearing.

Finally, there is rubber. Sold in sheet and tile form, this material enjoyed huge popularity in the Eighties, when it made the transition from commercial use in hospitals, warehouses and factories to the home. Rubber is a very tough material, also warm to the touch, fairly pliable, easy to lay and available in a great range of colours and textured finishes.

The very good news about these materials is that they are virtually maintenance free and can be forgiving of slightly uneven floors. Before you lay the tiles or sheet, prepare the area by fixing a base layer of plywood or hardboard sheeting. The soft flooring can then be stuck to this surface; always use the adhesive recommended by the manufacturer.

Laying sheeting (once you have manoeuvred the material into the space) is usually straightforward, although the thicker the material, the more difficult it is to manipulate. Where the floor to be covered is an unusual shape or involves cutting around doors or cupboards, make a card or thick paper template. Cut the sheet material outside the room, then bring it back in when you are ready to lay it.

Left and far left:
Textured sheet and tile materials like these rubber sheets were developed for high-traffic areas in commercial buildings such as hospitals and warehouses. Their excellent track record for withstanding heavy wear and tear can be transferred usefully to the average kitchen. Now they have entered the domestic market, they are available in extensive ranges of interesting textures and colours.

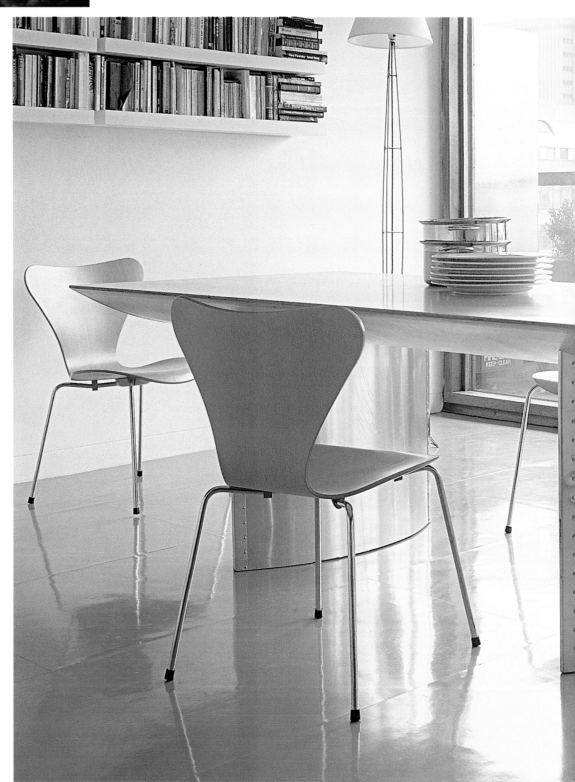

The secret of success in laying soft tiles is to measure the room and mark a cross at the exact centre of the floor, place four tiles in a square with its centre at this cross, and continue laying tiles outwards. The logic behind working this way is that the lines of joins run absolutely straight and parallel to each other across the centre of the room. The eye reads these straight lines and doesn't notice that the walls may be out of true.

Leather floor tiles are luxury items in this category. They are obviously expensive, but leather is warm and hard-wearing and, like wood, it tends to improve with age. Leather tiles are available naturally coloured or dyed in a variety of dark shades.

The latest type of sheet flooring to enter the home is metal. This is a fairly recent innovation and has found favour in contemporary-style interiors. The success of the finish is dependent, as ever, on careful fitting. Metal flooring is sold in large sheets or tiles. Like all flooring, it requires a solid, level base. Metal flooring can be stuck directly onto a concrete base. If the subfloor is wood, it is advisable to create a hardboard base, then the tiles can be stuck or screwed to this. Always make sure metal flooring is isolated from any electrical source.

Sheet and soft tile products are good news for anyone on a tight budget, as they tend to be considerably cheaper than stone or wood floors.

Below: In this refurbished Sixties apartment a thoroughly modern style has been adopted. The industrial look of the pale wood and stainless-steel dining table and shaped plywood chairs is echoed in the smooth rubber tiling used on the floor.

Sitting under the expanse of glass, the bright yellow is a sunny addition.

Above right: Leather flooring might seem impractical, but it has a long life and can improve with age. It should be treated like

a timber floor, cleaned regularly, and waxed and polished about every three to six months.

Below right: Luxurious leather in the bedroom. Its soft, matt surface feels great under bare feet.

Left: In this landing and corridor, perfectly plain walls and a generous amount of wood sit on a neutral carpet base. The plain carpet means that attention is focused on the fine detailing of the space, the lighting and objects on display.

Below: Pale timber flooring as the backdrop to an abstract-patterned rug. In carefully controlled interiors featuring pale colours and plain upholstery, rugs and carpets in dynamic patterns can add drama.

Right: The all-white theme of this contemporary home is broken only by the chequered throw and collection of pottery. The backdrop is entirely white – including the wall-to-wall fitted carpet. A plain backdrop gives objects on display increased prominence.

Below right: Recreating period interiors includes finding suitable furnishings. Here an understated cream rug adds a perfectly authentic note to this Sixties-style living room.

Above left and right:
Pattern in carpet can be purely decorative, as in the rug (left), with its neat graphic design in black. Pattern can also be used to emphasize architecture and define a route (right).

Left: **Real presence: the ponyskin rug takes pride of place in a white room.**

Far left: **The geometric pattern in this tufted wool rug complements the modern sofas.**

Carpets & rugs

There is something undeniably warm and cosy about soft flooring. The choice is awesome, from the finest, close-weave wool carpets, to jewel-bright stitched rugs, inexpensive cotton runners and humble rag rugs.

The perennially popular wall-to-wall fitted carpet dipped out of view when stripped wood floors and stone came to dominate fashion underfoot. However, it is now back in favour. And rugs have never diminished in their popularity, because they are available in such a vast range of colours, shapes, sizes and patterns – and portable from home to home.

Recent decades have also seen the rise in popularity of natural, woven-fibre flooring such as seagrass, sisal, coir, jute and even paper. These tough, neutral-coloured materials are stuck in place. Among the toughest wearing is sisal, sold either as a wall-to-wall finish or in the form of rugs.

Top row, left to right:
A grey-and-cream-striped woven cotton rug looks good with pale natural wood.

In a room with plain furnishings, pattern is added in the rug.

Sisal floor covering is tough and hard-wearing.

The pattern of the striped red wool stair carpet is complemented by the Venetian flat-weave wool runner on the hall floor.

Left: **In this light, sunny room furnished with natural wood and pale, plain upholstery, the seating area is defined by the addition of a neutral flat-weave rug over the plain, neutral carpet. The restrained colour palette means this slight variation of texture is enough to delineate an area.**

Above right: **Real drama is added here with these bold stripes in red, black and cream. The rug is a heavy flat-weave material and its red stripe is picked up in the throw over the sofa and the pictures on the wall. In contrast, the rest of the room is simply furnished.**

Right: **Here the emphasis is on layers, with piles of books and cushions. On the timber floor is a creamy stone-coloured rug. On top is a pale grey-green rug, made of squares of heavy felted wool.**

Consider a room's decoration and use when selecting carpet. Fitted carpet is suitable for most areas except kitchens and perhaps bathrooms – excessive water spills will cause rot. Pale carpet is best reserved for child-free rooms to avoid the inevitable sticky fingermarks. Natural-fibre carpets, except sisal, are slightly slippery so they are not recommended for use on stairs, and will not withstand damp conditions. Meanwhile, rugs look great just about anywhere in the home – they can add softness to a timber floor, and look smart laid over wool or natural-fibre carpets.

When it comes to budgeting for soft flooring, the sky is the limit. The best rugs and wool carpets can cost as much as a family car, but it is possible to pick up flat-weave cotton rugs for a very modest outlay.

storage & display

Well-considered storage solutions can change your life. Imagine – no more frantic searching for a belt, a book or a bag of flour, and cupboards which look as good inside as out. Indeed, there's only a fine line between storage and display – bags of flour can look as good as books on open shelves. Smart solutions come with patience and practice and a willingness to work out what you want in advance. Careful storage planning can make all the difference between a home that works and one that doesn't.

The theory behind successful storage and display is that ugly or pedestrian objects should be hidden and beautiful ones shown to their best advantage. It's not an easy thing to get right – and storage is generally harder than display.

The point about good storage is that it not only conceals things but also makes best use of available space and keeps anything from hoisin sauce to hundred-pound hats in the best possible condition and, of course, easy to find. Apart from the disciplined control freaks among us, very few people can honestly say that they have solved their storage problems.

The principles behind successful storage are to keep like with like (all keys together, all biscuit tins, all plimsolls) and to have special places to which objects are always returned after use. Thus, a larder can be both attractive and useful if all Italian foods are kept separate from Chinese ones and jams are kept apart from chutneys. Clothes look better in wardrobes and on shelves if organized by colour, ranging from, say, black to white via deep blue, pink and cream. Shoes should be arranged by height of heel and use, preferably with their own trees and on special racks. It may involve fuss and expense but knowing that – behind closed doors – order reigns is very satisfying. It also saves time – imagine waking up knowing just where your black mac is, or calmly cooking with ingredients immediately to hand.

While storage is complex, display is simpler. You are trying to improve the look of a room by showing off the objects you love, whether beautiful, curious, funny or valuable. People who are really skilled at display tend to work instinctively. Too much thought creates contrivance. But do not despair; instinct is honed by practice and lots of observation. Look at displays around

Storage & display principles

you, consider what you like and try to analyse why. Analyse, too, what you want to display. Don't be conventional – a pyramid of Heinz baked bean tins looks terrific and so do piles of old boxes and exercise books. Both are cheap and are useful, too. You can also display your storage,

Above far left: **Storage can also be display. These old cases are good homes for unwieldy belts or bags.**

Centre far left: **There is plenty of good-looking storage – even for tricky items. It pays for itself in saved time and temper.**

Below far left: **One way to display is to theme objects. Lighthouse, bottle boat and lantern recall maritime holidays.**

Left: **The best storage, like these open shelves, is custom-made.**

Right: **Much clever display is instinctive. Uniting factors here are blue (pictures and walls) and gold colours.**

Below right: **This library combines working books, set at eye level and lower, with elegant bindings, set above. The higher books are for display, the lower in use.**

from huge black and gilded Chinese chests stuffed with ugly work files to rows of identical rosewater bottles with old-fashioned labels. Foods stored in identical glass jars are always interesting and colourful.

Objects can be grouped by common colours: a brilliant red stamp in a painting can be echoed in a red lacquer box below; blue-and-white china can be matched with indigo hangings and a glass vase of cornflowers; ebony and silver have an affinity. Other groups may have a theme: model lighthouses made of Cornish serpentine beside marine pictures; lots of animals in prints, fabrics and carvings; books about mushrooms along with botanical illustrations of fungi; sepia family photographs hung in huge groups.

Make jokes. Mess about with scale: set a large pigeon next to a small elephant, have pottery dogs beadily eyeing painted foxes, or hang a delicate kimono by a rack of wellies.

We're talking about adorning walls here. Though pictures can be propped on shelves and textiles spread on beds and chairs, the best way both to see a picture or an embroidery and to conserve it from damage and wear is to hang it up.

Before you get into the enjoyable part of making patterns on the walls, make sure that each item is kept in the best possible conditions you can give it: no direct sun on fragile pastels, watercolours or tapestries; no damp seeping into oil paintings on chimney breasts or causing rot

Displaying pictures & textiles

behind impermeable plastics; no old string or wonky nails to break and let pictures fall.

Then you need to decide what to put together, how good a light you want on any object (bad pictures can look good in a gloomy corner) and whether to hang in large or small groups or singly. Pictures can be teamed with textiles – a fine old damask behind an old master (or a reproduction of one) – but, generally, they are best separated.

When grouping pictures which are all of a set – same size, similar subject – the best solution is to give them matching frames and hang them a few centimetres apart. Each picture has a pattern and the group makes a second pattern. Diverse shapes and sizes need different frames, but they should have something in common. It's no good putting flat aluminium frames beside ornate gilded versions. Pictures don't need to conform to a period or style, but do need a point of contact: any black-and-white etchings may well suit, as will dashed-off charcoal sketches – eighteenth century or twenty-first.

Before you hang them, experiment by arranging the intended group on the floor. Here you will spot obvious mistakes – wrong colours, wrong subjects, the fact that you'll run out of wall. You can also adjust the space designated for each and spot whether the best picture in the group has enough prominence. For instance, you may have one genuine Piranesi and eight cheap copies – make sure the real thing is centre stage.

Hanging is best done by eye, not spirit level. Walls are not perfect rectangles and old ones will

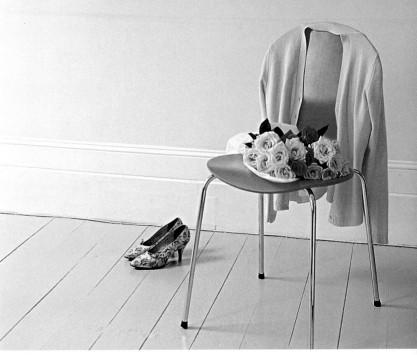

Above: **Floral fabrics include a beautiful tapestry and rose-strewn shoes, set off by a bright pink chair.**

Above left: **Black-and-white photos, identically framed, are close hung above a heavily carved Eastern cabinet. The simplicity of the pictures points up the complexity of the cupboard.**

Main picture: **This decor is deliberately simple – white walls, sisal floor – to show off the shapes of the objects and metal sculpture (which follows the black abstract).**

often defy the stoutest drill, which means that the spirit-level-and-ruler approach will never work. The look of the whole is more important.

Textiles, being generally bigger, lighter and floppier, need fewer load-bearing nails but will often require loops sewn on at the top and threaded through a rod (bamboo from garden shops is good) to hold them flat. Never put nails through the fabric itself – they may rust and damage the cloth permanently.

Finally, work out the lighting: a table lamp for soft focus, concealed ceiling lights angled down on the display or spots mounted on walls and ceilings are all good. But, unless your pieces are museum standard, don't bother with picture strip lights or those cunning devices which illumine only the area of the picture. It's too elaborate.

Far left: **A collection of beautiful vintage shoes, carefully racked and colour themed.**

Left: **The forms of these wood skittles recall natural seaweeds and underwater growth. They are grouped on a display cabinet of similar tone.**

Centre left: **This collector has made a virtue of security by giving each valuable fossil a stand in its own perspex cubicle. The whole display becomes a wall of objects.**

Right: **Holes have been made in the wall to display specific objects; only do this if you are confident in your choice.**

Below left: **Throw away convention and put your old knives and forks in matching black frames. In this instance, the frames probably cost more than the cutlery.**

Below: **A low Indian table is the perfect foil for a group of dark, interesting shapes. The whole is echoed by the pots in the background on chunky cupboards.**

The first rule in displaying objects is never to think of them as ornaments. Ornaments are tiddly little things you've been given by various relations and, really, would like to consign to the bin. Objects, on the other hand, are pieces you love and cherish, maybe collect in all their forms, and which have at least one thing in common: your own taste. Be true to yourself and toss out auntie's Copenhagen blue bird (or put it in a drawer until next time she visits) and make the most of your favourite things.

In deciding how far to go with the display, remember that you'll probably buy new things and discard old ones, so any really expensive shelving, lighting and stands should be adaptable. By allowing plenty of space around each piece, you are also showing it to best advantage, in that every beautiful pot, sculpture or shell will have an interesting silhouette. You can decide whether this shape should be emphasized by back lighting or its patterns and textures made focal by side lights or raking light. You can also decide whether the object looks at its best standing alone or whether it is enhanced by being part of a group of similar pieces.

Another consideration is the fragility and value of each piece. You will never enjoy your Tang horse if, every time your eye rests on it, you worry about it falling off the mantelpiece. Instead, construct secure cupboards with glass doors or deep shelves which protect the piece from accidents. If you have children, even visiting ones, you may need locked doors for security.

Displaying objects

Above and left:
It takes skill to arrange these colourful twentieth-century glass vases, and discipline to allow their tones to be the main colour in the room. Those in the picture above all have lips and similar shapes and autumnal colours. They are divided from the flat bowls below. The three (left) recall the shape of onions and are in citrus colours.

The best displays, however, are not necessarily the most valuable ones. A bowl full of mah-jong counters, a line of jars filled with dried chillies, a pile of sea-washed glass – all are beautiful, as are seed heads arrayed in tiny boxes or old buttons still sewn onto their cards.

The skill is to spot the varieties of shape, form, texture, rarity and age in what you collect and then team them together. Fossils and modern stoneware pottery have much in common, as do modern sculpture and Tang figures. Have confidence in your own eye, see beauty in the unexpected – and your displays will be full of vigour and charm.

Displaying books

Above left: **If your shelves are too generous to fill, hide the empty space with a carefully sited picture. But never hang a picture over shelves that are in full use.**

Above: **Books of many different colours are given cohesion by a few similarly coloured box files, chosen to match the office chairs.**

Left: **A working library may need closed shelves for filing cuttings, thin paperbacks and ugly magazines, and an adjustable ladder to reach higher shelves.**

Main picture: **These cube shelves impose control by preventing books from flopping to one side. Yellow on the shelves is picked up in cushions.**

Opposite right: **This all-white room makes bright books a focal point. Tan archive boxes and art emphasize their colours.**

The purpose of books is to be read and the purpose of a book collection, if you're lucky enough to have room for a library, is to have all your books about you, each in its proper place. In a display of books, therefore, content is more important than appearance.

That being said – and there's nothing more obvious and sterile than a library collected for its looks alone – there are a number of things you can do to display books to best advantage. One is to go to a good bookbinder and have all your books bound in a similar colour buckram with gold lettering on their spines. Wildly expensive, of course. Next, you can repair only those which are falling apart, again in matching bindings. Third, you can give your books new dustcovers in stout paper of your choice (there's a good deep turquoise which builders use with insulation) and, fourth, you can buy books of similar bindings and put them together. Old Penguins, book club choices, and collections of reprints are all valid, as are runs of the *Encyclopaedia Britannica* (well worth reading), auction catalogues or magazines. It is these groups which will provide the backbone for the shelves. Your books are not – should not be – all identical, but a few feet here and there look good and solid.

When you have an idea of what will be on your shelves – small paperbacks, large illustrated books, hefty reference works – design their height and depth accordingly, because books look best if they fit neatly. Allow a good inch above the book height to fit your questing finger. If you have lots of tall, floppy books, make the shelf length shorter, though this will reduce the number you can fit in. Then graduate the shelf height so the largest books are at the bottom and the shortest at the top – making sure the top shelf is tall enough for paperbacks. If you have some extra-deep books, you may need a breakfront section.

While most books look good on open shelves, you may have some which are very thin, floppy or dog-eared. These can be hidden behind doors or even slung in files. Elsewhere, if you have the space, books can be interspersed with propped pictures and photographs, sculptures or heavy objects like fossils, stones or old brass weights.

It is important to be able to find the reference book of the moment. You may want to arrange books together for their looks – runs of similar bindings are obvious – but keep an eye out for theme as well. It's as easy to search through books arranged by subject as through those classified alphabetically.

But the best thing of all about libraries and serious bookshelves is that they should never be too neat. Use your books well and let it show.

Above: **Despite apparent disorder, the shelves of this kitchen hold objects in only a few neutral colours – white, ochre, tan, blue and silver – which calms the whole.**

Left: **Curvy cubes stack up to display modern glass (note how the cupboard doors echo their colours). Books and records live in the rest.**

Right: **This shelving scheme uses black for coherence: black book spines, drawer knobs, and a dark focal vase.**

Opposite: **Children's toys, especially well-loved and worn ones, have a charm of their own. Here they are well spaced on plain white shelves.**

Shelves

Shelves are for both display and storage, and the way to get the best out of them is to unite the two purposes. But the objects, rather than the shelves themselves, should be the attraction.

Shelves, therefore, should be seen but not scream. They should be neat, workmanlike, carefully designed to do their job but not obtrusive or so over-designed that they become more important than what they hold. The more shelves are used for display – especially of collections – the more they should be custom-designed. Equally, the more their purpose is to house kitchen equipment, box files, piles of sweaters or garden tools, the simpler they should be.

Ideally, shelves should be wide enough to house only one layer of objects. This almost never happens, but in a perfect world we'd have all our tinned tomatoes lined up on tin-deep shelves and never have to rummage in the depths of a dark cupboard again. At the same time, a row of tinned tomatoes would look extravagantly Andy Warhol and thus a display in its own right.

The most mundane objects take on attraction when well grouped. Huge aluminium pots and pans, set on a white shelf, have interesting silhouettes, as do children's toys; piles of matching cheap archive boxes are as good as a sculpture, and collections of modern blue-and-white plates, used every day, will give a dresser as much presence as old Staffordshire.

The shelves should complement the collection. Thus, if you are going for eighteenth-century pottery, design a built-in dresser to suit the period; if you want a modernist kitchen, hide all but a few shelves of stainless-steel equipment. A rustic kitchen lets it all hang out with lots of woven willow baskets, bread crocks and bowls of fruit on the shelves. Children's toys need deep, deep chests to keep the primary-coloured plastics at bay, with just a few matching pieces on open shelves, while old toys from your own childhood deserve a good show.

Keep looking at your shelf life carefully, edit and rearrange. Otherwise it will get out of hand.

Left: **Stores of tins, boxes and bags of food should ideally be visible from all sides. This clever system of metal racks within sliding doors is a perfect answer.**

Main picture: **The perfect wardrobe for a well-organized man has areas for hanging ties and suits and open shelves for shirts. There are deep drawers and a mirror too.**

Below far left: **Mundane objects such as older hi-fi equipment can still be housed in interesting cupboards.**

Below left: **Hi-fi systems are more attractively designed today. This one is on shelves behind sliding doors so you can conceal – or admire – it.**

Below right: **Even large, chunky cupboards can be made to vanish – or nearly – by painting them like the room walls and reducing their handles to a minimum.**

Opposite below left: **Ranks of useful drawers are given small but obtrusive knobs in a Shaker-inspired scheme. They are painted the same colour as the door and hanging rack.**

Opposite right: **The whole wall of this bedroom is cupboards, made to blend with the wall. The upper ones are for rarely used luggage, hats and so on.**

Opposite far right: **A series of cupboards with internal shelves stands above drawers of all shapes and sizes made for specific items.**

Cupboards & drawers

If most of us were asked unexpectedly to open up our cupboards, there would be a small avalanche as objects stuffed away to create the illusion of tidiness cascaded around us. Ideally, of course, the proud owner would open the doors to a fanfare of applause for neatness.

Yes, neatness is achievable and desirable, even if we all slip back on bad days. The secret is to use all the devices that clever designers are inventing to hold such disparate shapes as shoes, hats, fish kettles and Pokémon cards. Look at catalogues and spend money on buying sock separators and pan-hanging racks, because it will save time and stress in the end.

Cupboards and drawers are designed not just to hide the unwieldy, the bad and the ugly; they are intended to reduce dirt and dust, to keep moths and cooking grease at bay and to allow easy access to books, disks, files and soy sauce. An important by-product (because no one puts up cupboards for their looks alone) is that they give interest and variety to a plain wall with their panels, handles and planking. They also provide insulation against

cold and noise. It's true that cupboards may reduce the size of a room, but the reduction in clutter will make the lack of space less evident.

Cupboards should be designed to suit the style of a room. Minimalists may want the doors to match the walls and have no handles (hidden magnets hold the doors shut), while classical rooms often look good with a giant free-standing mahogany wardrobe complete with camphor-lined drawers. Rural rooms can go the Shaker route or use built-in cupboards constructed from old panelled doors, while hard-working areas, like work spaces, bathrooms and kitchens, can benefit from neat metal cabinets with sliding, pull-out shelves.

Once you get the design right and work out how to use the hidden space – remembering that even an antique cupboard can benefit from up-to-date wheezes for socks and CDs – your life will be transformed. Honest.

Free-form storage

Storage needn't cost a mint. Of course, it's nice to have spacious walk-in wardrobes and larders with cool slate shelves, but there's satisfaction, too, in using your ingenuity and a sure eye to achieve the same effects.

There are some surprisingly good-value unstructured storage solutions in the catalogues of office equipment firms. Flat-packed archive boxes made of strong cardboard are very cheap but are excellent for shirts and sweaters, children's toys and newspaper cuttings, as well as for real archives and files. Pick solid, handsome ones, make sure they are all identical and pile them high. Antique black tin boxes are even better looking, and also inexpensive.

Real baskets are another excellent source, and there are craftsman basket-makers around who will weave to your exact measurements. Cheaper, however, are ready-made baskets – especially Eastern ones – which can be found to fit onto your shelves (unless you make the shelves to fit the baskets). Baskets also have an advantage over drawers – you can pull them right out to see what lurks at the back.

If you are tidy by nature, you can find trolleys to wheel under worktops – from the archetypal Twenties trolley of fumed oak to modern versions of steel and aluminium and office designs with lots of pockets and shelves. Trolleys are excellent in the office. Pile them with your current work, then wheel them under a shelf at the end of the day.

Shallower mobile boxes and baskets are ideal when space is tight: shove them under the bed – often a forgotten area – or pile them up in cupboards under the stairs, carefully marked with attractive labels. Pack them up with completed projects – again well labelled – and put them in the attic or garage in neat towers. If you throw important papers away, you are bound to regret it.

In these days of cramped houses, space is valuable. Do you have objects to store, and furniture that is empty? Not just drawers and cupboards, but decorative chests and elegant boxes. They can be filled with market finds such

Above right: **The space under a bed may be wasted. There are modern boxes and good-looking bags designed specifically to take advantage of this area.**

Below right: **Heavy-duty cardboard, or light laminated wood as here, makes attractively neutral and surprisingly strong drawers and boxes. They are very cheap, and stackable.**

Main picture: **Old cases, in graduated piles, are a fashionable way to store anything from photos to sweaters. Search out those with funny old labels and don't worry if they are battered.**

Opposite above: **Baskets are an attractive alternative to drawers. They can be made to measure, as can the shelves. Free-standing baskets are more adaptable than conventional drawers.**

as old quilts, bits of antique fabric waiting for a use, and photographs and negatives, carefully sorted.

Luggage also tends to lie empty after the holidays. Why not use it all year round? Modern suitcases are an excellent place for clothes, sponge bags or shoes which are only ever used on holidays. Pile them in the bottom of cupboards, out of sight. But old-fashioned luggage – the sort with brass locks and handles which needs a porter's trolley to move – is now put on display.

It's still possible to find nice pieces in junk stores or flea markets, especially if you don't mind that the locks have burst and the handle has snapped. Buy them when you see them and pile them in graduated heaps – perhaps with old labels describing what they hold.

Opposite below left: **Attractive piles of matching crockery, spices and kitchen equipment look good on open steel shelves – making your everyday equipment act as a display while it is neatly in storage.**

Opposite below right: **Baskets are very adaptable. They can fit under a bed as easily as in the kitchen and are also attractive piled on the floor. Use them for office work as well as vegetables and towels.**

window treatments

Windows are one of the most important architectural features, whether you look at a house from outside or in. Thus it is important to treat them right. There's a huge choice of styles, from authentic eighteenth-century curtains with all the trimmings to minimalist translucent blinds. With attention to detail and a clear idea of the style you want to achieve, dressing up your windows can be great fun.

Window treatment principles

Windows are the most visible parts of a room. Because they are the main light source during the day, it is to them that the eye first travels. Get the look of your windows right and you are well on the way to getting the rest of the room right, too.

The first thing to consider when you are deciding how to dress your windows is whether you want to go along with the immutable style of the window itself, whether you are somehow going to obscure its shape, frame and glazing bars, or whether you will impose a foreign style upon it. If, for instance, you have a large and beautiful Georgian window which looks out on an unfortunate view, will you let it be itself or, in trying to hide the view, impose a casbah-type fret or Louisiana louvres over its surface?

It is, of course, always best to let the window be itself. In this way you will make few period or design errors. But if this is impossible, try to impose as sympathetic a solution as you can. The Louisiana louvres are a much better answer than the casbah fret because real Louisiana windows approximate to Georgian ones, while Moroccan ones do not.

A second principle in window dressing is to work out how to change the window space by night. The beautiful daytime light source becomes a cold black space after dark. What's more, uncovered, who knows who's watching you.

If you are lucky enough to have shutters, curtains may not be necessary and will, anyway, detract from the architectural features. If there are none but the window is beautiful, try the plainest blinds possible. They will disappear by day and simply block the window glass by night. Another minimal solution, good for any style of house (as are blinds), is to have the plainest available white cotton or linen curtains. No pelmet, no fancy hangings, but a sheer sheet of fabric to pull across by night.

If, however, the windows are ugly or you want a cosier approach, then curtains are the better option. The shape of the opening can easily be hidden by voluminous curtains which disguise the window area, and other ugly features minimized by making the curtain more important than the window. An equally good solution is to have a dramatic fake curtain covering up the window surround with, behind it, another, simpler curtain or blind to draw at night.

When you take the trouble to think hard about windows, solutions come easily. Consider the pros and cons in your home, decide what would be ideal, copy other people's ideas – then add your own style to the mix.

Clockwise from right:
Sheer voile curtains, toned with walls and floor, will hide an ugly view or difficult window shape, yet allow in muted light.

Detailed heavy curtains in a strong colour distract the eye from a dull view.

Deep windows are made important by three treatments: shutters and louvres minimize the light and outside noise, while a single dramatic curtain is swept to one side. The mirror between adds light and space.

Only a glimpse of the window and a garden outside is allowed through a white Venetian blind. A perfect solution on a hot day.

A half-drawn blind controls both the light in the room and the shape of the window behind it. The dark frame adds a modern, geometric touch.

Blinds can be as sheer or thick as you need. Here a pleated blind minimizes outside noise. A pink curtain softens the scheme.

Three beautiful floor-to-ceiling windows have been given extra prominence by the white furniture and surrounds. The blinds, pulled to different levels, emphasize their shape, as do the bookshelves between.

Right: **Three lovely arched windows are unimpeded by either curtains or blinds, but the soft sheen of the shutters draws attention to them.**

Clockwise from top left: **This window is emphasized with painted glazing bars to match the boldly checked curtains.**

Here, everything from the position of the furniture to the stark window treatment points up the view.

Plain gingham curtains, simply made, are perfect for this leaded window. The checks and the diamond panes are cleverly contrasted.

This room shows the American Colonial style of painting windows in a darker shade than their surrounding walls.

Louvred blinds work where curtains are less practical, as in damp bathrooms.

Window seats with inviting cushions are perfect for windows with stunning views.

The arch, set in front of a large window, acts as a second set of curtains in a theatrical display.

This window is virtually a headboard for the bed, which is subordinated to the view beyond.

Large areas of glass can be alienating. Here translucent blinds are a solution.

Window styles

The shapes and materials used for windows are one of the most important aspects of house design – whether they are seen from inside or out. In the past, window styles were dictated by the cost of glass, its technology (large areas of glass became possible when the Victorians invented rolled plate glass), the need for warmth or cool and the available materials for the surrounds.

Curiously, countries with extremely high or low temperatures opted for very small windows. In the tropics windows were pierced and shaded to keep heat out but allow breezes in, while in the far north they were shuttered both inside and out to conserve what warmth there was.

Today, with the increasing use of central heating and air-conditioning, it's possible to have huge areas of glass where the view is exciting. But we still need the solace of heavy curtains and shutters in winter, or louvres and voiles to keep blinding sun out in summer. If you do have huge areas of plate glass in your house, remember that they can be unpleasant in climatic extremes.

Small windows, by contrast, need to be opened out. If you can, make a vista to stretch beyond the glass so the small area seems to widen into a view. Ensure maximum light penetration by keeping curtains, blinds and ornaments from encroaching into the glass area. Paint sills, surrounds and reveals as light a shade as you can to enhance the incoming light. In Mediterranean climates, consider different curtains for summer and winter: hot summers need light voiles, but it gets cold enough in winter to warrant fabrics heavy enough to be unmoved by draughts.

If your windows' shapes are interesting or elegant, don't disguise them with fussy curtains or fabrics. Most of us have rather dull, rectangular windows or, worse still, positively ugly ones. If you are lucky enough to have round arches or Gothic points, Corbusier-type wraparounds with metal frames (increasingly fashionable), stone mullions or Shaker panes, celebrate your luck. This means subordinating the window treatment to the window. If need be, do without curtains and rely on interior or exterior shutters. Paint the window in a strong colour to contrast with pale or neutral walls, or draw attention to the window by placing the furniture around it.

Curtains

There was a time – and the fabric manufacturers must have thrown their hats in the air with glee – when curtains seemed about to take over the world. No designer could look at a window without seeing gilded dolphins disporting over curtain poles and tassels big enough for a state visit. Everybody got the bug just as, at one time, every woman had shoulder pads big enough for an American footballer. Today, we're in reaction against these excesses and, generally, curtains are as slimmed down as our jacket shoulders. Indeed, many people now live without any curtains at all, relying on built-in shutters or blinds so neutral as to be practically invisible. It has done wonders for our bank balances.

So, window treatments are as much the creatures of fashion as hemlines and hats – the only difference being that they change more slowly. It is possible to ignore the trends, but this requires the willingness to stick with what you have until it becomes fashionably retro.

Curtains today are very understated. You will see that many of those illustrated here are

unpatterned and many have no strong colour. Most are translucent enough to let light through and fine enough to blow in the wind. The inspiration for this trend came from Sweden, where light is precious. As can be seen in the nineteenth-century paintings of Swedish interiors, curtains were even then intended to let in any light available, while closed shutters provided insulation at night.

Of course, translucent curtains are not a good choice in bedrooms, where darkness is essential, but curtains can be backed with blinds and still retain their fragility. An alternative is to have two sets of curtains – the inner ones light and airy and the outer ones heavy and shady (or vice versa). Other areas of the house are less complex. These gauzy styles can be left drawn all day where the view is poor and tranquillity important, or partly drawn to admit as much of a view as you want.

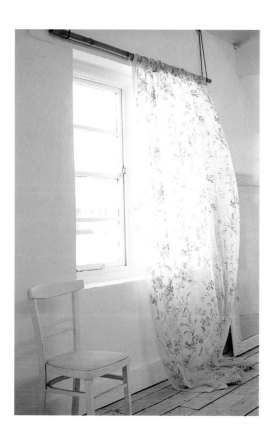

Far left: **A Swedish-inspired curtain – soft, billowing, pale and translucent. Ideal for lightness and privacy.**

Left: **These curtains, made of contrasting sheer fabric sewn in wide vertical stripes,** **are a dramatic feature. The lightness of the fabric encourages them to billow in the breeze.**

Above: **More translucent curtains serve to screen the bathroom without loss of light. Everything else is in pale shades.**

Above: **Curtains don't have to cover all the glass. This neat scheme leaves the top of the windows free, giving the impression that only a small part of the glazed wall is actually window. Pure white, slightly** scrimped curtains cover two smaller side windows. Only enough of the third, larger window is revealed to show an interesting garden view.

Above right: **Very plain – preferably washable –** curtains suit kitchens, which will inevitably become untidy at times. These semi-translucent curtains are an unassuming backdrop, and screen the room from passers-by. They run smoothly on a concealed track.

Right: **French-style windows can open fully to reveal balconies and gardens beyond, so curtains have to be able to hang inside the window frame as well as out. They can push right back before the windows are opened.**

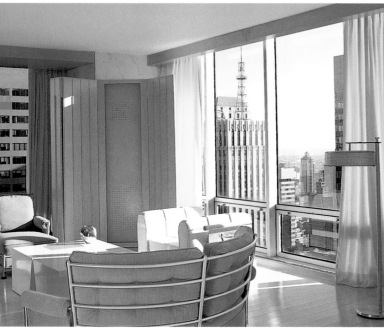

Opposite above left:
The light streaming in from this generous window gives definition to an exotic antique lantern by showing off its colours and lines. Its ornate shape cleverly echoes that of the balcony outside.

Opposite right: **If this were the Eighties, these complex curtains would be shiny, trimmed and multi-coloured. Today's treatment of swags and folds is just as romantic but the use of a plain off-white fabric adds a touch of bedsit chic.**

While the current trend is for plain and pale, it's still possible to admit a little colour in your curtains. Pure white is lovely, especially in an all-white room or one painted a slightly darker pale grey. It contrasts well, too, with primary colours and touches of black. Otherwise, neutrals can veer to cream for a warmer effect, or to pretty lime greens and old rose pinks, once again teamed with whites and greys. Because simplicity is important in this style, keep pelmets and curtain poles to a minimum. Black iron, brushed steel and painted metal rods are good, as are built-in pelmets, which disguise the hooks and other gubbins while being painted in with the room.

If you love patterns, don't despair. Patterns haven't vanished entirely, but are more restrained. Stripes, checks, tickings and self-coloured patterns are perfectly in keeping with twenty-first-century simplicity, but all used with a tweak of difference. Gingham need not be confined to the country – imagine it with full-length eighteenth-century town-house windows backed by a matching plain lining. Urban damasks turn up in country farmhouses and toiles have been revived in overscaled form, every detail of the print

Top: **Strong and overscaled scallops in dark fabric edge these pale neutral curtains in order to give them shape and form. They also serve to draw attention to the window's shape and the view beyond.**

Above: **This Thirties-style living room high in the city is composed of blond woods, leathers, fabrics and wall. The curtains, just a shade lighter, are hung from an integral pelmet for maximum translucency.**

Top right: **Eighteenth-century windows adapt beautifully to modern living. These have been treated with the utmost simplicity, yet the room's restraint means that they and the view beyond become the focal point.**

Opposite below left:
The designer of these subtle lime-green curtains has allowed a hint of floor creep but allied it with very narrow, simple hangings. Plain blinds, knotted at the base for weight, diffuse the light.

enlarged. The traditional country-house look lives on, with modern chintz bleached to look worn or its background tea-stained to seem aged. And authentic window treatments are always acceptable, so these chintzes can be lined with pretty cottons patterned with tiny all-over floral designs as were used in the eighteenth century.

Authenticity has, however, less power than before. Once, purists would suck in their cheeks if you dared to deck your period window with something incongruous, but that's now a valid choice. As a result, all sorts of unconventional fabrics are being used, helped by the fact that, when the treatment of the material is simple, the fabric itself can be unconventional. Don't do both

– fake leopardskin is lovely, but not when ruched. Designers are now looking at crossovers between fashion fabrics and soft furnishings. Yards of men's suiting – grey flannel, chalk and pinstriped worsted, even cavalry twill – make fine curtains because the cloth is simple, strong and fluid when hung in long lengths (don't try it for cottage windows, though). Designers also love checked tattersalls, Viyella shirtings and denim. Cashmeres and silks can be very expensive, but sari silks, beautifully embroidered, can sometimes be picked up cheaply when you are on holiday or in ethnic neighbourhoods. Likewise, beautiful batik cottons can be bought by the cheap bolt load. Every market stall, at home or abroad, has exciting and cheap fabrics on offer.

The best way to spot them is simply to look at other people's windows, clothes and curtains when you are abroad. In India it will be fine and fiery silks, in Sweden stripes and checks in subtle shades, while Italy has narrow white appliquéd strips intended for glazed cupboard doors. West Africa offers stylized portraits of important politicians and the United States is big on flags. What you see around the place can usually be found in the markets and local shops.

Then, of course, you can put your nous and your needle to the job. Plain fabrics can be cut into overscaled checks and stripes, quilted, or blanket-stitched around the edges with contrast thread. Pedestrian materials such as dishcloths, linen tea towels, sailcloth or terry towelling can be stitched together and mixed and matched. Borders can be added, top or bottom, around the edges or even in the centre, the fabric fringed by removing the warp or weft, or appliquéd with matching or contrasting motifs. Fine cloth can be pleated or tucked, horizontally or vertically, to make darker bands against the light, or it can be hung halfway down the window or folded at the top to create a self-pelmet.

Once you start to assess the possibilities – helped, perhaps, by pictures in magazines which start the imagination flowing – you can come up with window treatments which are not just elegant, subtle and clever but ones that are entirely your own invention.

Use your ingenuity. You'll find it's fun.

Above: **A mix of patterns adds weight and grandeur. The curtain fabric here complements the two French chairs.**

Left: **In this pleasant, French-inspired living room, the wallpaper pattern is repeated as a curtain border. But the curtains themselves are quite plain.**

Opposite below left: **Checks are really only doubled stripes. In this bedroom, a striped wall dilutes the impact of heavy checks. A pelmet border adds form.**

Left: Though this room contains busy patterns, control is exerted by the use of few colours. The curtains are a strong element – the stripes are more assertive than the other patterns.

Above right: If you find antique hangings or needlework to fit a window or door, snap them up. Deficiencies in the width can always be made up with secondary curtains or blinds.

Right: A window of maximum theatricality. The translucent dark curtains against a sombre wall pull back to reveal the glass framed by bright contrast lining.

Below centre: Here's a clever mix of scarlet geraniums and checked red gingham.

Below right: Note how even the curtain pole matches this neat soft pink treatment.

Above left:
Huge expanses of windows can be tamed by plain blinds. Some of these are pulled down, allowing only a few panels of glass to remain visible.

Far left:
Roman blinds are sympathetic to many fabrics. Here a busy paisley is let down at varying levels. The colours are echoed in the furnishings.

Blinds

Don't even think about ruched blinds. They should have been consigned to the pages of history long ago. Into the same black hole throw any blind with itsy-bitsy frills around the edge, blinds made of net-curtain material and, unless you insist on retro kitsch, all plastic Venetian blinds. Despite this wholesale slaughter, there are plenty more blinds that are not only useful and good-looking but also smart. The tendency here is towards simplicity – minimalism has finally been adopted and adapted by the mainstream – camouflage and lack of pattern.

Virtually all blinds are better professionally made. Don't think about making your own sprung roller blinds, for you will spend your life winding them back and forth by hand or leaving them hanging at half-mast or wherever they decide to stop. Properly made, however, roller blinds are unobtrusive when rolled up, can be fixed onto the window surround and do not deprive the room of any light. Thus, they are excellent for dark rooms where every ray of light is needed. Rollers are good, too, when you want a neutral blind. A roller in a plain white or off-white fabric, teamed with the colour of the room or in a dull dark material, is the most recessive blind possible. No strings, pleats, loops or hangings. Just a stretch of material. Some years ago, there was a fashion for making roller blinds into rectangles of jolly scenery or faux stained-glass windows. Drop these into history's trash can, too.

Roman blinds are a mite easier to make and easier, too, to rescue when things go wrong. But all those strings which ensure that the blinds ascend and descend in their required pleats need something of a mathematical genius to make, so a professional job is a good idea here as well.

Romans are one step away from plainness. If the fabric is translucent, the pleats will double up the colour intensity; if opaque, the lines of the pleats are pleasingly visible. They look more like blinds than the rollers do and they shut out a bit more light by hanging over the top of the window. They do, however, allow for a pattern (overscaled

Above: **Most blinds are calming. These Roman blinds are made of a neutral fabric but are given form by red borders. The wider blind has a border a few centimetres in from the edge, making the three widths appear less varied.**

Left: **Floppy fabric works well in Roman blinds, allowing a casual note in a formal dining room.**

Above: **Roman blinds are excellent for noisy rooms as the fabric can be heavily padded to keep out both draughts and the roar of traffic. This all-white scheme emphasizes the comfort of the blind and cushions.**

Left: **These blinds have doubled fabric to make borders around their edges. Their plainness sets off the artwork below.**

ones look startling) and contrast fabric as a lining. And, unlike roller blinds, they can be made in virtually any fabric.

Roman blinds are also good for reducing noise levels since they can be lined and interlined, padded or even quilted. These blinds can also be given extra touches by adding contrast borders, sewn lines of contrast fabric at the point of the pleat and irregular bamboo poles at the back to give interesting silhouettes.

While plastic Venetian blinds are definitely Fifties (except in pure white, when they are acceptable), slatted blinds in various natural fabrics are very much of today. These include wooden louvred blinds, which are sometimes used on cupboard doors, and exotic slatted versions made from oriental grasses, split bamboos and rattans. These work very well if carefully sited, because they have all the subtle variations of natural stems. They may be uneven, blotched or veined in subtle browns and beiges.

The caveat is that such blinds are quite definitely oriental. They work well in a scheme that has oriental qualities, be it a Manhattan loft sparsely decorated with Chinese furniture or a garden room filled with exotic orchids. You may even get away with them in a French farmhouse if the fabrics are Provençal (these were originally imported from India) or a stark modern home dedicated to the grains of wood and sheen of metal, but they are not suitable in every room.

Wooden louvres are an easier choice because they have been used extensively all over the American south and Caribbean. Thus they work in period buildings in warm climates. They even add to old farmhouses and manor houses, especially if the idea is to keep them shut and allow the light to make patterns on corridor walls.

All such blinds can happily be teamed with curtains. The blind does the work of keeping the light at an acceptable level while the curtains add colour, folds and a certain cosiness. This is also a good solution to using incredibly expensive curtain fabric – cut the amount to a minimum and never draw the curtain. However, in all cases, the blind and curtain should have something in common – colour, pattern, trimming, texture – or a good strong contrast.

Opposite below left: **Very thin strips of cane (as used in cheap beach mats) make delightfully cool, textured blinds, fragile enough to blow in the wind.**

Opposite below right: **A rough form of hemp in strips makes these unusual blinds. They let the light through but are strong enough to withstand constant rolling. The** edges are bound in white and the whole is raised from a single central cord and pulley. It is an ideal complement to the timbered walls.

Opposite above: **Roller blinds, in a fabric just a shade darker than the walls and table, are hung at half mast to give low light levels and, just maybe, hide something nasty higher up.**

Top left: **An all-white scheme with a deep window has plastic shutters which mimic the lines of wooden ones. They are translucent enough to glow in the sun.**

Above left: **Plain white Venetian blinds make a virtue of narrow windows in a calm living area. Dark spaces between slats emphasize the black patterns of the cushions and lamp.**

Above: **The virtue of louvred blinds is that they keep out the heat of strong sunlight but, even when closed, tiny slivers of light creep in to create shadows on the walls.**

Right: **White Venetian blinds create rays and patterns both on the walls and on their own slats. The shade they offer is far less than the louvres, above.**

Trimmings

One of life's pleasures is to find old trimmings and impedimenta for curtains in flea markets, French *brocantes* and antique shops. French ones are rich sources because the French have made an art of dressing up curtains, blinds and other fabrics.

Tie-backs of gilded tin, brass or iron are common sights and are an excellent way of controlling heavy curtains with style; punched lines of brass can be discovered to tack together into pelmets, while the range and exuberance of passementerie is immense. Keen trufflers will also find ancient, curvy pelmets of quilted *toile de Jouy*, once intended for four-poster beds but just as good for curtain pelmets.

French manufacturers still make both passementerie and metalwork curtain trimmings today, and these are sold worldwide, with other producers following suit. It's now possible to find whole ranges of colourful bobbles, tassels, bullion fringes and embroidered borders to complement your curtains, along with little brass clips, Victorian-style wood and metal rings on curtain poles and curly iron tie-backs and poles.

All these are intended to disguise the boring fact that curtains and blinds have to hang above the window and behave themselves as they drop to the floor. The ruches and hooks at the top of the curtain, all those white tapes and strings, need to be hidden and, frankly, the old pleated pelmet in a matching fabric is very old hat.

This page: **A complex window treatment with dramatic detailing. Contrasted with the brilliant white cornices, which are a focal point, the curtains and blinds make a border for each window, then divide it. The curtain fabric hides the space between the windows, and the hangings of the blinds imitate the geometrics of the glazing bars (echoed in the striped mat on the table). The curtains are lush and very full, encroaching on the floor, which softens the stark effect of the window treatment itself.**

Opposite main picture: **This very feminine window combines soft colours, translucency and a swagged, trimmed pelmet. It is saved from over-sweetness by the window's formality and the view of the garden.**

Details, clockwise from top left: **From a distance, this smart curtain looks like muslin, but it is in fact a dimpled plastic fabric. Decorative dark ties keep the carefully formed pleats tidy.**

This curtain is a fringed throw whose tassels have been tied over the curtain pole – a trick which works as long as the curtains are not drawn too often. The back lighting exposes the throw's texture.

This rich, ornamental scheme combines a painted ceiling detail above the cornice

with heavy satin curtains, hung with gilded wood rings on a gilded curtain pole.

A heavy red pattern and matching tassels make a dramatic pelmet.

Roman blinds are, at once, formal and casual in their folds. This one tends to formality with its rich silky grey fabric and contrast backing.

Fragile-looking netted material forms a striped blind. A deep but insubstantial fringe belongs to curtains of the same material which hang in front of it.

Top: **Curly iron tie-backs work best with simple fabrics, either as a contrast or toning in.**

Above: **The ruched pelmet made of the same fabric as the curtain is now obsolete. A much tidier version is to use the curtain fabric attached to a stiff backing, with not a pleat in sight. You could also trim the edges to define the border.**

Trimmings should be chosen to suit the decorative scheme. Thus iron poles and tie-backs work both in ancient houses with small windows and in modern schemes where ornament is reduced to a minimum. Gilded pelmets and tie-backs are for grandeur – though they can be modern as well as classical – while fabric trimmings can be found to suit virtually everything but a cottage. Silk tassels and bobbles are best suited to classical rooms filled with antiques, while hessian and velvet versions are excellent in more contemporary settings. That's not to say you can't have fun going against convention – imagine brilliantly mixed primary-colour bobbles *à la* Damien Hirst on a modern blind, for instance, or brushed-steel poles in a medieval hall. Both, with care, will work well.

With a few basic rules, trimming curtains and blinds isn't difficult. The first rule is to determine your style and stick with it – don't be seduced by the charm of the passementerie. Second is to be disciplined and keep trimmings under control (the price will help you to do this). Third is to consider the options for some days before you take the plunge. There's lots of choice out there and you need time to make wise decisions.

Genius is in the detail. It is just as important to put a final effort into the last tweak of a curtain or blind as it is to pick the fabric in the first place.

Working with fabrics is like dressing up. It's the fun part of creating a room, where you can allow your fantasies full rein. Rooms can be completely altered by different soft furnishings – and changed for summer and winter – while clever use of colour and contrast will highlight good points and disguise bad. If furniture is the underpinning of a design scheme, then soft furnishings provide the fashionable touches.

soft furnishings

Soft furnishing principles

It is a rare house or flat which completely ignores soft furnishings. And it will be one which is poorer for doing so. We've all been in those minimalist restaurants where the walls and floors are concrete and the tables metal. What is the result? It is brutal cacophony as sound waves caused by noisy conversation meet hard surfaces to bounce and echo back. As the ornate interiors of the Vienna Opera House prove, large areas of matt fabric make for a great acoustic.

Soft furnishings are also the most adaptable, the most frequently altered and the most variable element of any decorative scheme. If you were to take a plain white cube, with the simple use of fabrics – gingham, French toile, cut velvet brocade or hazy voile – you could change its style to anything from English country to Provençal, from palazzo to Gustavian Swedish. Equally, with the misuse of clashing colours, overactive or inappropriate patterns and a wild assortment of textures, even the most perfectly proportioned room and the best furniture are overwhelmed.

It's important not to try so hard that your cleverness is more apparent than the room itself. The flouncing Eighties are a dire example of what can happen when too much money meets too much design. Yards of ornate fabrics writhed and twisted around curtain poles and oozed, lava-like, across the floors. Edges were bobbled, trimmed and ruffled – a truly overplayed style.

Below: **Remainder bins or obsolete swatch books are good places for fabric finds. This generous throw of squares of soft tweed in browns, beiges and greys has been sewn together with a luxurious velvet border. The cushions – not an economy suggestion – are covered in cashmere. Their neutral tones perfectly complement the natural dyes of the tweed and the stone fireplace.**

Above: **Clever ideas often spring from necessary economy. Designers search for scraps of expensive fabric and eke them out with appliqué work. This cushion is covered with glowing silk sari fabric embroidered and bordered in gold, the whole contrasted with a wide central band of black. It is cunningly teamed with a neutral silk cushion as backing.**

Fashion, even in interior design, is a fickle beast and it's pretty certain that, after today's spare and neutral themes, we will return again to something a bit fussier. Thus, if you still love your Eighties curtains and can keep your nerve, you may well find you have a delightfully authentic interior forty years on. But expect lots of sniggers before that.

Just like designer clothes, well-thought-out interiors, however neutral, need touches of colour, texture and even eccentricity to be enjoyable. The new trimmed-down curtain, so much cheaper than before, can be changed for winter or summer, entirely altering a room according to season. Winter demands wool, tweed or velvet; summer, light linen, silk or cotton. If you decide to have a seasonal look, the two fabrics can obviously be more extreme both in weight and colour.

Similarly, covers, throws and cushions are infinitely variable. Suppose your winter curtains are grey flannel and summer ones French cream linen. In winter, chunky tweed cushions with grey among the colourful threads can be

Above: **The cushions are the only spot of colour in a neutral living room where every other shade is monochrome, from black and dark brown to stone, string and bone. Their effect is startling.**

Above right: **This drawing room is coloured in exotic shades of red and gold. Yet the only element of pattern is in the cushions and curtains. Their colours draw together the room's various shades.**

Right: **Eastern patterns and rough silks are very smart, and their subtle shades rewarding.**

tossed over grey cashmere throws, while as the days draw out the French linen drapes will be complemented with bright green-and-white gingham loose covers arrayed with leafy-patterned cotton cushions. And, if that finally bores you, add shocking-pink velvets to your grey flannel scheme and gilded Indian silks for the summer.

Fabrics are equally adept at creating a mood. Bedrooms should be the most heavily clothed areas, and kitchens, where smells and grease are attracted to fabrics, the least. Bedrooms do need to be comfort zones, and the colder the climate, the more you need fabrics. In the north, cashmere, silk, muslin and chintz are all contenders – even a man's bedroom looks fine with dark-brown silks and tobacco-dyed toiles. Warmer climates encourage bedrooms with floating curtains, plain blinds and pale-covered chairs – all creating a sense of breezy cool. It's always a good idea to take colours from the landscape: brilliant blue by the Mediterranean, terracotta in the Tuscan hills, ice and pine in the frozen north and brilliant primaries on the streets of New York.

Above and below left:
Using soft furnishings in a room isn't necessarily all about colour and fabric; it's about texture and surface, too. These details show how neutral shades can contrast with each other by taking advantage of the variations of surface and how the light reacts to them. Suede and leather are perfect examples of the use of light: suede, with its brushed matt appearance, tends to recede and add comfort, while leather is shiny, glamorous and assertively hard-edged. Neutrals such as slubbed silk, sheeny satin and matt velvet can also be combined with the skins.

Patterns often conjure up visions of chintz. But they can be exotic and abstract, too. The cotton fabric *(above left)* **is printed in modern blocks of neutrals, while a brilliant painted wall** *(above right)* **makes a dramatic foil for the purple and pink easy chair and cushions. The leopard-print stool** *(left)* **would be quite happy in a traditional setting.**

Left: **What is it that makes this room so effective? The idea of teaming a sofa covered in a soft, flowery chintz with another in a strong mix of leather and velvet would seem wrong. Yet here it works. The first reason must be the way white has been used for walls, floor, railings and furniture. The next is that the dark sofa's presence is picked up by the black-and-white pictures. Finally, the cushions on the dark sofa refer back to the pretty chintz. This room has been created by a great eye.**

Below: **If working with fabrics in a room is like dressing up, then someone has had a great deal of fun here with the costume box. Note first that the whole scheme is in variations of a single colour and the fun is in the textures. The geometric lines of floorboards and tabletop lead the eye to the wildly appliquéd oatmeal and cream throw, tossed over a plain cover on the sofa and emphasized with pretty cushions. Even the position of the crystal globes is intended to reflect the whole.**

Choosing fabrics

Never let anyone tell you that choosing fabrics for a room is easy. You simply need to look at the photographs of posh houses for sale in upmarket magazines to see the many pitfalls. Sitting rooms are abuzz with chintz, oriental carpets and fancy cushions; dining-room chairs are dressed up like milkmaids and everywhere curtains are too short, too grotesque, or look ready for a garden party.

In deciding which fabrics to pick, it's a good idea to approach the whole as you would an outfit. Would you wear matching hat, bag and gloves? No, you wouldn't – so don't team your curtains with the wallpaper *and* the cushions. Would you add a cotton printed with roses to a touch of chinoiserie with gingham? Not unless you were very experienced at mix and match.

Thus, when you approach the soft fabrics in a room – and you can do this first or last, before or after picking the furniture – the secret is simplicity and relaxation. Decide on the kind of room that you want, whether it has to work all year round, morning and night, or whether it can focus on a particular season or lighting pattern. Simplicity means keeping patterns under control – no more than two for the fabrics unless you're an expert, and nothing too dramatic. If you do want to mix patterns, keep them to a theme. This can be the type of fabric – gingham, say, or toile – or it can be the colour. Indigo batik fabrics from Africa may team happily with denim or Swedish navy stripes. If in doubt, watch what experienced decorators do and adapt their ideas to suit your home.

Relaxation in picking fabrics means not over-straining. Should you decide on a chintz with a white background covered in purple fuchsias with green leaves, steer clear of designing the rest of the room with matching plain white, purple and green touches. It's just too contrived. You could, however, pick just the fuchsia shade and play games with it in different tones and textures.

If caution is good in choosing fabrics, so too is the unconventional. Soft furnishings need not be made only from furnishing fabrics. Curiously, it's often cheaper, as well as more effective, to buy

Top: **The secret here is simplicity. When using fabrics, stick with a very limited colour palette and be disciplined about pattern. Here, the charming patterned chair cushions are given centre stage against the restrained background.**

Above: **A single colour choice allows you to mix the patterns on fabrics. A variety of checks, stripes and plain rose-and-white fabrics has been joined by a single floral, while the rest of the room – even the chair and books – is simply a soft white.**

Top: **Mixing textures – here a leather sofa, velvet cushions and a mohair and satin throw – is simple if you keep to a colour scheme. All are in tones of brown and cream, but vary from shiny to matt.**

Above left: **Plain wool blankets often have a shiny satin edge; an idea to copy for hand-sewn throws and cushions.**

Above right: **If you cover cushions in shiny silk, cover the furniture in wool. The contrast helps both – and cushions won't slide about.**

Top right: **A very feminine scheme which relies on one colour. The femininity comes in textures: a gold-trimmed sari is draped over the gilded sofa, while the cushions are velvet.**

tailoring or dressmaking fabrics. Grey flannel, for instance, looks stunning as long curtains in period windows because it hangs so fluidly; it also works for cushions and chair covers. Tweed is another men's fabric to watch out for. It may be expensive but it wears extremely well and is full of subtle colourways which will pick out objects in a room. African fabrics from markets around the world are often in restrained, if colourful, combinations and some make you laugh out loud – you can't say that for many cushions. Antique cloths are another wonderful source, from those characterful old French linen sheets, often with cross-stitched monograms, to scraps of tapestry and embroidery which can be used as collage.

It's important when choosing fabrics that each room should not be seen in isolation. People will walk from one to another, so there should be a sense of continuity. This doesn't mean you can't switch from sixteenth-century Florentine damask to Nineties plastic sheeting in a single house – but you need to give visual warning of what is about to happen. Once again, complementary colours will do the trick, as will a consistent theme – roses through the centuries, say, or checks and tartans.

Most professional decorators work with a colour board, and it makes good sense to do so.

Above: **In a restrained room, the single pattern on the fake fur draws the eye.**

Left: **Real ingenuity has gone into these textured cushions, made from woven elastic bands. The upholstery is a bland honey-brown felt.**

Right: **This disciplined bedroom is utterly plain to show off the handblocked throw.**

Not only does a colour board look swanky, it actually works. Paint or cover the card with what's going on the walls, then attach to it swatches of the fabrics for curtains, covers and cushions. If the scale of a fabric's pattern is enormous, try to get a colour photocopy of it reduced in scale to give an idea of its entire pattern. Move all the bits around, pin them by your breakfast table and keep considering whether they work and why. If you are doubtful, make a change or two. If you are still doubtful, scrap the whole lot and think again. The effort will give enormous satisfaction – and a much better result at a tenth of the cost.

Top right: **Lots of antique finds cover this bed, from lace-edged linen to the embroidered and bemirrored spread, but they are all kept in one colour palette.**

Centre right: **Indigo and white always works, even with complex patterns, as here. Order is kept by the pure white bedhead and soft blue walls.**

Above: **Loose covers are very useful in changing a room's emphasis. Here an old chair has a plain, light loose cover, over which is a neat woollen throw, a shade darker. Darker yet are the cushions on the window seat. This is a summer scheme which could change utterly for colder weather.**

Above right:
Plain off-white loose covers reduce the bulk of this large sofa – but keep a spare set to make laundering easier. The pale fabric also increases the light levels in the room.

Right: **Ugly brown wood furniture can become beautiful when painted white, revealing its lines. This small table and large seat have been given a Swedish feel by adding cushions in a gingham of Gustavian green shadowed with tan.**

Loose covers

A loose cover is meant to be practical, but it can still look good. The secret is to pick a fabric which can cope with the curves and angles that make up a chair or sofa. Plains are obviously excellent, as are all-over florals of a restrained nature. Geometrics can cause problems – though stripes and checks are generally easy. Another good choice is a faded, tea-stained chintz which looks as though it's had a thousand washes. The secret is to avoid anything too new looking or over-powering – most armchairs and sofas are not beautiful in themselves and are best dressed discreetly rather than in garish florals.

Once the fabric has been chosen (not all chairs in a room need to match – better if they don't, in fact), decide the style of cover. Ruched petticoats are unfashionable (and ugly) so go for a plain valance and the minimum of fuss. Edges can be piped to give shape and emphasis, and this works well with chintzes and many geometrics. Plain fabrics rarely look good with contrast piping.

Cushion covers are a form of loose cover and are extremely adaptable. They are also very easy and cheap to make. In certain rooms – kitchens, dining rooms and studies – where there are fewer soft furnishings, a variation in the cushion covers can alter the entire decor. The obvious time to change is between winter and summer. Winter cushions need an element of snuggle and come in heavy fabrics such as tweed, corduroy, velvet and, if you are very lucky, cashmere, the cosiest of all. Colours should suit the season: warm autumnal browns and rusts, scarlets and crimsons. Summer brings out sari fabrics, ginghams, tickings and antique French linens. Florals come into their own, as do checks, tickings and maritime colours.

When you've got it all planned, it's tempting to buy two of everything just to ensure longer wear, easier washing and no more hassle for a decade. It depends on how fickle your tastes are and how often you are likely to change whole schemes – but for some there's nothing more comforting in a room than a squashy old sofa dressed in a floppy cover which welcomes muddy fingers and paws.

Top left: **The complex patterns of ticking make fine cushions and curtains. Back cushions are tied onto casual seats in front of a table in a different version.**

Centre left: **When you buy furniture, go for line rather than upholstery. If pieces are good, ugly covers can be disguised by bandaging up the backs and seats in soft linen. But keep the fabric simple.**

Above: **Details – how curtains are hung and cushions fixed to chairs – are key. Here, plain dining chairs have cushions with long ties which are cross-gartered down the legs.**

Left: **Big, squashy chairs or sofas seem even more inviting covered in traditional – but worn – chintz. 'Faded' or tea-stained floral cottons can now be bought new – and strong.**

Cushions & accessories

The most changeable parts of any room scheme are the accessories which you add at the end. Today's styles mean that lots of these will be made of fabric, as well as plants, flowers, paintings and tablescapes. Indeed, you can use fabric for realistic silk plants such as orchids or bowls of flowers such as deep magenta lilies, while modern tapestries in bright abstracts are much in vogue, as is the idea of hanging a special antique dress or Chinese costume on the wall. If you have large and important areas of wall, do watch out for these finely embroidered robes – they are beautifully sewn in brilliant colours, exotic and, what's more, really good value.

More prosaically, modern living has gone overboard on the throw. From cashmere to synthetic fleece, knitted Aran to silk tartan, no fabric designer has ignored the possibilities. They have come up with deeply luxurious alpacas to snuggle up to in winter, glossily handsome fake furs, brilliantly coloured Welsh blankets with contrast stitching, and bright tartan weaves that are as good around your shoulders as on the sofa.

But don't feel the need to buy designer chic if the cost is too high; market finds such as old blankets, plaids and travel rugs can be improved with the addition of a wide, complementary or contrast border, with contrast stitching, or by adding appliqué patterns cut from other vintage fabrics. Find faded old curtains and sew them onto plain, matching backgrounds for added strength. Buy fake furs from the fabric merchants and back them with matching felt.

These throws fulfil multiple purposes: they change the feeling of a room in an instant; they disguise ugly furniture or unfortunate upholstery; they soften the harsh lines of beds and sofas; and they give a casual feeling to a formal room. Use them over sofas and easy chairs, drop them on side tables and dining tables. Layer them over each other as you would shirts and sweaters, or fold them neatly and drape them over chair arms.

Then you can add cushions on top. They must be filled with down or feathers – slightly under-

Above left: **Tweed is the most helpful fabric for furniture because so many patterns, textures and colours match each other. Here throws have been given presence and formality by heavy, contrasting borders.**

Below left: **Don't overlook texture – see how this cube covered in bobbly ostrich skin immediately takes centre stage in an all-neutral living room. Place it so it catches the light for full effect.**

Above and centre right: **The pretty greens of a fragile sari fabric – with a thin strip of pink – contrast with soft leathers, velvet and cotton. Notice how the vibrant green plant emphasizes the colour in the room.**

Below: **When choosing fabrics for accessories, think what the room already offers. Here it is a thin stripe of blue in the window. Avoiding the obvious (quantities of gingham or blue ticking), a single piped cushion is a bright note.**

Above left: **Slipcovers protect stored furniture. But why not dress your chairs in transparent slips, to show their lines – but not their ages?**

Above right: **Texture is key in an off-white living room containing two suede cubes. The chair and sofa are in a slightly sharper cotton.**

Left: **Many materials can make accessories. This tablecloth is made of heavily textured artist's canvas, appliquéd with perky petals and border.**

stuffed if you want the current floppy look – but can be in any size from bolster to handkerchief as long as they are round, square or rectangular. No triangles, hexagons or stars, please. The choice of fabrics for cushions should be as carefully chosen as the rest of the scheme but, keeping up the fashion analogy, cushions are like ties in a man's outfit – a chance to show a sense of colour and humour, to break away from the formality of the rest. When you have your scheme, pile them high.

Like large sofas, beds benefit from cushion power – especially spare beds, which can look awfully sad. Your bed looks good dressed up, too – if you are prepared to dress it as well as yourself every morning and reverse the process every night. If you are, then your bedroom will always be a haven during the day, a comfort zone when things go wrong.

Because fabric around the place helps soften the acoustics, use plenty in rooms which are intended to be comforting. As well as bedrooms, these include living rooms, bathrooms and children's rooms. Bathrooms should be packed with fleecy white towels and such items as sponge bags, make-up boxes and nests of flannels, preferably in white with soft touches of colour. Grey, beige, stone and dark brown are very soothing.

Children's rooms, by contrast, thrive on bright primary shades, but keep the scheme under control by sticking to one bright colour – scarlet, denim blue, lemon yellow – and contrasting this with black, white or neutral stone. Try having toys, bags and boxes, chair cushions and laundry bags in nothing but shades of scarlet combined with

stone. Both adults and children will appreciate the stunning effect.

Living rooms can be accessorized rather more subtly. Again, pick a colour and play games with it. Lacquer red, chocolate brown or leaf green can be mixed in dozens of tones, textures and fabrics and teamed with real Chinese lacquer, ebony pieces or leafy plants. Use fabric for lampshades, as mats under houseplants, as backing to wall-hung mirrors or to cover piles of notebooks.

Left: **There is absolutely no adornment in this pale green tropical-style bedroom but the ceiling fan and the lines of the mosquito net. Both valance and floor match the walls. Throws and a trail of cushions in a variety of pinks provide the only colour interest.**

Above right: **Subtle mixes of natural colours – seashell, granite, cream, string and straw – are highly fashionable in our environmentally conscious age. And they all work together, as they do in nature.**

Below right: **If you are unenthusiastic about paintings, interesting fabrics make good wall hangings and, as in this bedroom, make sense of an overall colour scheme. The hanging should have some pretensions to be more than just a fabric strip. Here, it's the ornate edging.**

Far right: **Fabric can not only be used for wall hangings, it can act as a frame for a painting, print or photograph. This two-tone cotton hanging with its monochrome centre picture matches the satin bedspread, feathers, lampshade and even the organized files.**

Accessories will pin down the theme of a room. Take tartan: you may want to have a Scottish effect in your dining room without going overboard with tartan curtains and carpets. So use tartans to cover the table and for the napkins, emphasized, perhaps, with horn-handled knives and prints of Scottish castles. If you want a seaside effect, the living room can have cushions of bleached, natural canvas and old pennants, ropes and flags draped over sofas or hung on the wall. Country rooms can take up those brilliantly coloured horse blankets. Great sources of unusual accessories are specialist shops such as ship's chandlers, riding stores and tropical outfitters.

Even offices benefit from being cleverly accessorized. Computers come in vibrant colours and their raspberry or aqua shades can be echoed by fabric-covered boxes for papers and files. Ugly reference books can be covered in similar fabrics and marshalled together on a shelf, and even tubs for pencils can be matched in. Don't go over the top, however: aim at a smart, organized office.

DIRECTORY OF SUPPLIERS

INSPIRATIONAL INTERIORS

Search department stores and home shops for basics. Define your style with finds from boutiques and specialist outlets (see the Living Rooms section for ideas).

BoConcept
158 Tottenham Court Road
London W1T 7NH
020 7388 2447
www.boconcept.com
Fresh contemporary furniture from Denmark.

Cargo Home Shop
231 Banbury Road
Summertown
Oxford OX2 7HN
01865 515559
And branches.
www.cargohomeshop.com
Pale wood furniture and a range of big, comfy sofas.

The Conran Shop
Michelin House
81 Fulham Road
London SW3 6RD
020 7589 7401
www.conran.co.uk
Cutting-edge design from furniture to forks.

Debenhams
334–348 Oxford Street
London W1C 1JG
020 7580 3000
And branches nationwide.
www.debenhams.com
Furniture and accessories for every room. Mail-order and online shopping available.

General Trading Company
2 Symons Street, off Sloane Square
London SW3 2TJ
020 7730 0411
Antique and modern style.

Habitat
196 Tottenham Court Road
London W1T 9LD
020 7631 3880
Phone 0845 6010740 for details of other branches.
www.habitat.net
Exciting modern design for all areas of the home.

Harrods
87–135 Brompton Road
London SW1X 7XL
020 7730 1234
www.harrods.com
Classic British furniture in traditional style.

Heal's
196 Tottenham Court Road
London W1T 7LQ
020 7636 1666
www.heals.co.uk
Cool and elegant classic style for the home.

House of Fraser
Metro Centre
Gateshead
Tyne & Wear NE11 9YE
0191 4932424
And stores nationwide.
www.houseoffraser.co.uk
Home collection of lighting, furniture and soft furnishings.

IKEA
255 North Circular Road
London NW13 0JQ
020 8208 5600
And branches nationwide.
www.ikea.co.uk
Huge range of furniture and accessories from kitchens to kids' rooms.

InHouse
28 Howe Street
Edinburgh EH3 6TG
0131 225 2888

24–26 Wilson Street
Glasgow G1 1SS
0141 552 5902
Wide-ranging contemporary design.

John Lewis
Oxford Street
London W1A 1EX
020 7629 7711
And branches nationwide.
www.johnlewis.com
Affordable modern style.

Marks and Spencer
48 Donegal Place
Belfast BT1 5BY
01232 235235
And branches nationwide.
www.marksandspencer.co.uk
Affordable furnishings and accessories.

McCord
Phone 0870 9070870 for a catalogue.
www.emccord.com
Furniture and accessories, by mail order and online.

Next
Stores nationwide. Phone 0116 2866411 for your nearest Next Home stockist.
www.next.co.uk
Furniture and accessories for every room. Mail order available.

The Pier
Pavilions Shopping Centre
Birmingham B4 7SL
0121 6438441
And branches nationwide.
For mail order, call 020 7814 5004.
www.pier.co.uk
Stained pine, wicker and rattan furniture a speciality.

Purves & Purves
220–224 Tottenham Court Road
London W1T 7QE
020 7580 8223
Call 020 8453 1827 for a mail-order catalogue.
www.purves.co.uk
Design-led furniture, lighting and accessories.

Selfridges
400 Oxford Street
London W1A 1AB
020 7629 1234

1 The Dome
The Trafford Centre
Manchester M17 8DA
0161 6291234
www.selfridges.co.uk
Designer furniture and accessories from around the world.

ROOM BY ROOM

KITCHENS & EATING AREAS

Aga Rayburn
Phone 08457 125207 for stockists.
www.agarayburn.co.uk
Cast-iron heat storage cookers.

Alno
Call 020 8898 4781 for your nearest stockist.
www.alno.co.uk
Modern kitchen units.

Atag
Phone 01275 877301 for stockists.
www.atag.co.uk
Ovens, fridges and other kitchen fittings.

Bulthaup
37 Wigmore Street
London W1U 1PN
Phone 020 7495 3663 for stockists.
www.bulthaup.com
Hi-tech and cutting-edge kitchen designs.

Chalon
The Plaza
535 Kings Road
London SW10 0SZ
020 7351 0008
Call 01458 254600 for other stockists.
www.chalon.com
Formal country kitchen furniture.

Crabtree Kitchens
The Sorting Office
17 Station Road
London SW13 0LF
020 8392 6955
www.crabtreekitchens.co.uk
Interpretations of classic styles such as Arts & Crafts, Mackintosh and Provençal.

Divertimenti
139–141 Fulham Road
London SW3 6SD
020 7581 8065
www.divertimenti.co.uk
Complete range of cookware and kitchen accessories. Online shopping available.

Forneaux de France
Phone 01202 733011 for stockists.
www.lacanche.co.uk
French makers of Lacanche and Fornair range cookers and extraction systems.

Gaggenau
Phone 01780 722144 for stockists.
www.gaggenau.com
Built-in appliances including many stainless-steel models.

John Lewis of Hungerford
Park Street
Hungerford
Berkshire RG17 0EF
01488 688100
And branches.
www.john-lewis.co.uk
Bespoke kitchens with an emphasis on country style.

MFI
Phone 0800 192192 for your nearest store.
www.mfi.co.uk
Fitted kitchens including Hygena and Schreiber.

Miele
Fairacres
Marcham Road
Abingdon
Oxfordshire OX14 1TW
01235 554455
And stocked nationwide.
www.miele.co.uk
Kitchens and appliances in a range of styles.

Newcastle Furniture Company
4 Green Lane Buildings
Pelaw
Tyne and Wear NE10 0UW
Phone 0191 4381342 for stockists.
www.newcastlefurniture.com
Country-style and Shaker designs, plus free-standing kitchen furniture.

Poggenpohl
Phone 0800 243781 for stockists.
www.Poggenpohl.de
Modern German designs.

Rhode Design Furniture
137–139 Essex Road
London N1 2NR
020 7354 9933
Individually crafted kitchens influenced by Arts & Crafts and early American designs.

Smallbone of Devizes
The Hopton Workshop
London Road
Devizes
Wiltshire SN10 2EU
01380 729090
Phone for details of other showrooms; London showroom 020 7581 9989.
www.smallbone.co.uk
Well-established company with a diverse range of designs.

Smeg
Phone 08708 437373 for stockists and information.
www.smeguk.com
Italian cookers and white goods.

UK Marble
21 Burcott Road
Hereford HR4 9LW
01432 352178
www.ukmarble.co.uk
Granite and marble surfaces.

Watts & Wright
The Woodworks
Bentley Road North
Walsall WS2 0DF
01922 622247
www.wattsandwright.com
Handmade kitchens in traditional styles.

Whitehall Fabrications
Phone 0113 2223000
for stockists.
www.whitehall-uk.com
*Luxury worksurfaces
including granite and Corian.*

LIVING ROOMS

Aero
96 Westbourne Grove
London W2 5RT
020 7221 1950
Modern classics.

The Antiques Emporium
The Old Chapel
Long Street
Tetbury
Gloucestershire GL8 8AA
01666 505281
Antique furniture.

Aram
110 Drury Lane
London WC2B 5SG
020 7557 7557
www.aram.co.uk
*Five storeys of
contemporary furniture.*

Century Design
68 Marylebone High Street
London W1U 5JH
020 7487 5100
www.centuryd.com
*Retro pieces, original
and reissued.*

The Chair Company
60 Eden Street
Kingston upon Thames
Surrey KT11 1EE
020 8547 2211
www.thechair.co.uk
Chair specialists.

Coexistence
288 Upper Street
London N1 2TZ
020 7354 8817
www.coexistence.co.uk
*Vast range of modern
home design.*

Geoffrey Drayton Interiors
85 Hampstead Road
London NW1 2PL
020 7387 5840
www.geoffrey-drayton.co.uk
Modern furniture.

Graham & Green
4 Elgin Crescent
London W11 2HX
020 7727 4594
www.grahamandgreen.co.uk
*Luxurious finishing touches
from leather cushions to
tableware. Some furniture.
Online shopping available.*

Inhouse
28 Howe Street
Edinburgh EH3 6TG
0131 2252888
*Wide selection of
modern design.*

Interiors bis
60 Sloane Avenue
London SW3 3DD
020 7838 1104
*Contemporary interior
design.*

Kingdom of Leather
Unit 1A
Edge Lane Retail Park
Montrose Way
Liverpool L13 1EN
0151 2542468
And showrooms nationwide.
www.kingdomofleather.co.uk
Leather seating.

Monsoon
60 Queen Street
Cardiff CF10 2GQ
029 20398442
And shops nationwide:
phone 020 7313 3000 for
stockists of the Home
collection. Phone 020 7313
4018 for mail order.
www.monsoon.co.uk
*Textiles and soft furnishings
with global influences.*

Ocean
0870 8484840
www.oceancatalogue.com
*Mail-order and online
retailer of furniture
and accessories.*

SCP
135–139 Curtain Road
London EC2A 3BX
020 7739 1869
And stocked nationwide.
www.scp.co.uk
*Contemporary furniture,
lighting and accessories
for home and office.*

Shaker
72–73 Marylebone High
　Street
London W1U 5JW
020 7935 9461
*Shaker-style accessories
and furniture, traditionally
made. Mail order available.*

Sixty 6
66 Marylebone High Street
London W1U 5JF
020 7224 6066
*Vintage furniture, clothes
and accessories.*

Skandium
72 Wigmore Street
London W1H 9DL
020 7935 2077
www.skandium.com
Modern Scandinavian design.

Sofa Workshop
Stores nationwide and mail
order. Phone 01798 343400
for branches.
www.sofaworkshop.com
*Sofas in all styles from
classic to modern.*

twentytwentyone
274 Upper Street
London N1 2VA
020 7288 1996
www.twentytwentyone.co.uk
*Twentieth-century classic
furniture and reproductions.
Online shopping available.*

BEDROOMS

After Noah
121 Upper Street
London N1 1QP
020 7359 4281
*Antique and new beds,
in eclectic style.*

Amazing Emporium
249 Cricklewood Broadway
London NW2 6NX
020 8208 1616
www.amazingemporium.com
*Beds including bateaux
lits, daybeds and Art
Deco styles, plus other
bedroom furniture.*

And So To Bed
Showrooms nationwide.
Phone 0808 1444343 for
details of your nearest
stockist.
www.andsotobed.co.uk
*Full range of bedsteads,
mattresses and bed linen.*

Couverture
310 Kings Road
London SW3 5UH
Phone 020 7795 1200
for mail order.
www.couverture.co.uk
Pretty bed linen.

The Cross
141 Portland Road
London W11 4LR
020 7727 6760
*Luxurious bed linen,
pyjamas and towels.
Also mail order.*

Dreams
Mail order and showrooms
in England. Phone 01628
530800 for details.
www.dreamsplc.com
*Divans, sofa beds and
bedsteads.*

The Iron Bed Company
470 Great Western Road
Glasgow G12 8EW
0141 337 6600
Branches nationwide: call
01243 578888 for details of
your nearest store.
www.ironbed.com
*Iron bedsteads, also
available in children's
designs. Mail order
available.*

J & M Davidson
42 Ledbury Road
London W11 2AB
020 7313 9532
*Bed linen in gingham,
chambray and linen.*

Harriet Ann Sleigh Beds
Cherry Garden Farm
Hastings Road
Rolvenden
Cranbrook
Kent TN17 4PL
Phone 01580 243005 for
stockists.
*A wide range of wooden
beds, including antique and
reclaimed pine models.*

Hypnos
Station Road
Princes Risborough
Bucks HP27 9DN
01844 348200
www.hypnosbeds.com
*Handcrafted beds including
models with pull-out beds
underneath and bedsteads.*

Sealy
Station Road
Aspatria
Wigton
Cumbria CA7 2AS
01697 320342
www.sealyuk.com
*Wide range of beds,
including many with
built-in storage drawers.*

BATHROOMS

Armitage Shanks
Phone 0800 866966 for
stockists.
*Comprehensive selection of
bathroom furniture.*

Aston Matthews
141/147A Essex Road
London N1 2SN
020 7226 7220
www.astonmatthews.co.uk
*Large selection of baths and
taps, from period to modern.*

Kenneth Clark Ceramics
Southover Grange
Southover High Street
Lewes
East Sussex BN7 1TP
01273 476761
*Manufacturer of unusual
ceramic tiles.*

C. P. Hart
Newnham Terrace
Hercules Road
London SE1 7DR
020 7902 1000
And branches.
www.cphart.co.uk
*Wide range of sanitary ware
and accessories, including
Philippe Starck designs,
Duravit, Hansgrohe and
Hoesch. (Also do kitchens.)*

Heating World
Excelsior Works
Eyre Street
Hockley
Birmingham B18 7AA
0121 4542244
*Hot-water and electric
towel rails.*

Matki
Churchward Road
Yate
Bristol BS37 5PL
01454 322888
*Shower enclosures
with lightweight and
watertight frames.*

Old Fashioned Bathrooms
The Foresters Hall
52 High Street
Debenham
Suffolk IP14 6QW
01728 860926
www.oldfashioned
　bathrooms.co.uk
*Large range of Victorian,
Edwardian and reproduction
baths, basins and toilets.
They restore cast-iron baths.*

Showeristic Ltd
Unit 10
Manor Industrial Estate
Flint
Clwyd CH6 5UY
01352 735381
Made-to-measure showers.

Teuco
Phone 020 7704 2190
for stockists.
www.teuco.com
*Hydro and multifunction
showers, corner and
round bathtubs.*

Triton
Stocked nationwide. Call
024 76372222 for details.
www.tritonshowers.co.uk
*Full range of electric and
power showers.*

WORK SPACES

Besk
Lawn Farm Business Centre
Grendon Underwood
Aylesbury
Buckinghamshire HP18 0QX
0870 7524842
www.besk.co.uk
*Desks that convert into
spare beds.*

Hülsta Furniture
22 Bruton Street
London W1X 7DA
Phone 020 7629 4881
for stockists.
www.huelsta.co.uk
Stocked nationwide.
Modular home-office units.

Ryman
Phone 0800 801901 for
details of your nearest store.
www.ryman.co.uk
*Stationery, storage, office
furniture, computers and
accessories.*

System 180
387 King Street
London W6 9JN
020 8748 6200
www.system180.co.uk
*Configure your own modular
metal storage system.*

CHILDREN'S ROOMS

Casaidea Kids
01621 810201
www.casaidea.co.uk
*Modern furniture and
storage solutions for
children's bedrooms.*

Mothercare
461 Oxford Street
London W1R 1DB
020 7629 6621
And branches nationwide.
Call 01923 210210 for details
of your nearest store.
www.mothercare.com
*Baby bedding and nursery
furniture.*

Parma Lilac
020 8960 9239
*Furnishings and accessories
for the nursery.*

Stokke
Phone 01895 442990 for
details of your nearest
stockist.
www.stokke.com
*Manufacturers of the Tripp
Trapp chair, a Scandinavian
design classic which adapts
to the growing child.*

Urchin
Phone 01672 872873 for
mail order.
www.urchin.co.uk
*Practical and stylish
furniture and accessories
for babies and children.*

Wigwamkids
PO Box 15105
Glasgow G3 8BR
0870 9027500
www.wigwamkids.co.uk
*Mail-order furniture and
accessories for babies and
children, with fun themes.*

HALLS & AWKWARD SPACES

Goddard & Gibbs
Marlborough House
Cooks Road
London E15 2PW
020 8536 0300
www.goddard.co.uk
*Glass art; stained, leaded
and sandblasted panels.*

Roger Oates Design
The Long Barn
Eastnor, Ledbury
Herefordshire HR8 1EL
01531 631611
www.rogeroates.com
*Rugs and runners in a wide
variety of materials, plus
stair rods. Mail order
available.*

ESSENTIAL ELEMENTS

COLOUR

Auro Organic Paints
Unit 2, Pamphillions Farm
Purton End
Debden
Saffron Walden
Essex CB11 3JT
01799 543077
www.auroorganic.co.uk
Natural and organic paints.

B & Q
Phone 0845 3093099 for
your nearest branch.
www.diy.com
*Paints and varnishes from
Benetton, Crown and Dulux.*

Brats
281 Kings Road
London SW3 5EW
020 7351 7674 for mail order
*Specialist paints, including
the Mediterranean Palette
and the Chalk Collection.*

Farrow & Ball
Uddens Estate
Wimborne
Dorset BH21 7NL
Phone 01202 876141 for
stockists.
www.farrow-ball.com
*Traditionally manufactured
papers, paints, varnishes
and stains, including the
National Trust paint range.*

Fired Earth
Twyford Mill
Oxford Road
Adderbury
near Banbury
Oxfordshire OX17 3HP
01295 814399
www.firedearth.com
*Quality paints including
designer ranges from Kelly
Hoppen, Kevin McCloud and
the V&A Museum. (Also do
flooring.)*

Homebase
Branches nationwide; phone
0870 9008098 for details of
your nearest store.
www.homebase.co.uk
*Wide range of interior and
exterior paints.*

The Paint Library
5 Elystan Street
London SW3 3NT
020 7823 7755
www.paintlibrary.co.uk
*Wide selection of paint and
wallpaper, including Nina
Campbell paints and a range
of 32 shades of off-white.*

Sanderson
Stocked nationwide; phone
01895 830044 for details.
www.sanderson-uk.com
*Wallpaper, fabric and paint
in classic English style.*

LIGHTING

Bella Figura
Unit G5
Chelsea Harbour
London SW10 0XL
020 7376 4564
*Manufacturers of decorative
lighting including wall and
table lamps.*

British Home Stores
252–258 Oxford Street
London W1N 9DC
020 7629 2011
And branches nationwide.
www.bhs.co.uk
*Interesting and unusual
light fittings at affordable
prices.*

John Cullen Lighting
585 Kings Road
London SW6 2EH
020 7371 5400
www.johncullenlighting.co.uk
*A wide range of
contemporary light fittings
as well as innovative made-
to-measure lighting design.*

Lloyd Davies
14 John Dalton Street
Manchester M2 6JR
0161 8323700
www.lloyddavies.co.uk
*Classic lighting and
furniture.*

**The London Lighting
Company**
135 Fulham Road
London Sw3 6RT
020 7589 3612
*A wide range of modern
and work lights.*

Mathmos
20 Old Street
London EC1V 9AP
020 7549 2700
www.mathmos.co.uk
*Cutting-edge modern
lighting, including lava
lamps in many colours.*

McCloud Lighting
269 Wandsworth Bridge Road
London SW6 2TX
020 7371 7151
www.mccloud.co.uk
*Contemporary and
decorative lights, many
designed by Kevin McCloud.*

Ryness Electrical
45A Old Compton Street
London W1D 6HH
020 7437 8833
And branches nationwide.
www.ryness.co.uk
*Lighting from lava lamps to
chandeliers, plus switch
plates, dimmers and a large
range of bulbs.*

SKK
34 Lexington Street
London W1F 0LH
020 7434 4095
*The latest from young
lighting designers, plus
lighting consultancy.*

Stiffkey Lamp Shop
Wells Road
Stiffkey
Wells-next-the-Sea
Norfolk NR23 1AJ
01328 830460
*Original Victorian and
Edwardian lights, plus wall
brackets and oil lamps.*

Tsé Tsé
at Maryse Boxer Design
26 Sloane Street
London SW1X 7QL
020 7245 9493

and at

Galerie Sentou
26 boulevard Raspail
75007 Paris
+33 1 45 49 00 05
*Elegant, quirky lighting
designs by a stylish young
French company.*

Christopher Wray Lighting
8–10 Headingley Lane
Leeds LS6 2AS
0113 2782653
And branches nationwide.
Phone 020 7751 8701 for
details.
www.christopherwray.co.uk
*Over 4,000 lights and
lighting accessories.*

FLOORING

Allied Carpets
Call 0800 192192 for your
nearest store.
www.alliedcarpets.com
All types of flooring.

Amtico
Phone 02476 861400 for
details of your nearest
stockist.
www.amtico.com
*Flooring for every room,
including sheet and soft
tiling.*

Crucial Trading Ltd
79 Westbourne Park Road
London W2 5QH
020 7221 9000
*Carpets and rugs including
natural fibres: sisal, coir,
rush, jute and others.*

Dalsouple
Phone 01984 667233
for stockists.
www.dalsouple.com
*Rubber flooring in many
colours.*

The Delabole Slate Company
Pengelly
Delabole
Cornwall PL33 9AZ
01840 212242
www.delaboleslate.com
Riven slate tiles or slate slabs from England's oldest slate quarry. For flooring, paving, sills and fireplaces.

English Timbers
1a Main Street
Kirkburn
Driffield
North Humberside YO25 9DU
01377 229301
Finishes include English oak, ash and elm; Canadian maple; and yellow birch.

First Floor Ltd
174 Wandsworth Bridge Road
London SW6 2UQ
020 7736 1123
Hard-wearing floor coverings, plus linoleum.

Hanson Bath and Portland Stone
Monks Park Mine
Monks Lane
Corsham
Wiltshire SN13 9PH
01255 811154
Bath and Portland stone, available in various sizes and thicknesses.

Harvey Maria
Phone 020 8516 7788
for stockists.
www.harveymaria.co.uk
Cork tiles laminated with fun photographic images, from pebbles to green grass.

Junckers
Phone 01376 517512
for stockists.
www.junckers.co.uk
Solid hardwood flooring and worktops in beech, oak and ash, from managed forests.

Original Tile Company
23a Howe Street
Edinburgh EH3 6TF
0131 5562013
Terracotta, limestone, slate and marble, Victorian and Moroccan encaustic tiles.

Paris Ceramics
583 Kings Road
London SW6 2EH
020 7371 7778
Limestone and terracotta flooring, mosaics and decorative tiles.

The Rug Company
124 Holland Park Avenue
London W11 4UE
020 7229 5148
www.rugcompany.co.uk
Contemporary and traditional rugs. Also mail order.

STORAGE & DISPLAY

Cubbins & Co
Unit 1, Rampisham Manor
Dorchester DT2 0PT
01935 83060
View the Cubbins & Co page at www.idda.co.uk
Essential finishing touches: wastepaper baskets, linen baskets and storage boxes. Mail order available.

The Holding Company
241–245 Kings Road
London SW3 5EL
020 7352 1600
Phone 020 8445 2888 for mail order and details of other branches.
www.theholding company.co.uk
A complete range of innovative storage solutions for every area of the home.

IKEA
255 North Circular Road
London NW13 0JQ
020 8208 5600
And branches nationwide.
www.ikea.co.uk
Self-assembly adjustable shelves in a wide range of finishes, plus all manner of small and large storage and display items.

Lakeland Limited
Alexandra Buildings
Windermere
Cumbria LA23 1BQ
And branches nationwide.
Phone 01539 488100 for details and mail-order catalogue.
www.lakelandlimited.com
Small-scale storage ideas.

Muji
Call 020 7323 2208 for details of your nearest store.
Steel and cardboard modular shelving, plus cardboard, acrylic, fabric and polypropylene storage boxes.

Paperchase
213 Tottenham Court Road
London W1T 7PS
020 7467 6200
Phone 0161 8391500 for mail-order information and stockists nationwide.
www.paperchase.co.uk
Bright, fun small storage and office items.

WINDOW TREATMENTS

Adams & Co
The Courtyard
24 Silver Street
Bradford-on-Avon
Wiltshire BA15 1JZ
01225 865744
Make up curtains, blinds, pelmets, bed linen and bed hangings.

Bancroft Soft Furnishings
Brook Mill
Parker Street
Macclesfield
Cheshire SK11 7BQ
Phone 01625 423828 for stockists.
Curtain-making supplies.

The Curtain Exchange
11 Widcombe Parade
Bath BA2 4JT
01225 422078
And branches.
www.thecurtainexchange.net
Ready-made and bespoke curtains.

Eclectics
25 Leigh Road
Ramsgate
Kent CT12 5EU
01843 852888
www.eclectics.co.uk
Made-to-measure contemporary blinds, by mail order.

Faber Blinds
Kilvey Road
Brackmills
Northampton NN4 7BQ
Phone 01604 766251
for stockists.
www.faberblinds.co.uk
Blinds, sunscreens and blind components.

McKinney & Co
71 Warriner Gardens
London SW11 4XW
020 7627 5077
Finials and poles, pelmets and coronas, tie-backs.

Tidmarsh & Sons
32 Hyde Way
Welwyn Garden City
Herts AL7 3AW
01707 886226
Blindmakers since 1828.

SOFT FURNISHINGS

Bennison Fabrics
10 Holbein Place
London SW1W 8NL
020 7730 8076
Tea-stained and muted floral period-style fabrics.

Colefax and Fowler
39 Brook Street
London W1K 4JE
020 7493 2231
Traditional English-style fabrics.

Designers Guild
Phone 020 7351 5775 for stockists or 0845 6021189 for mail order.
www.designersguild.com
Colourful fabrics, cushions, rugs and throws.

The Easy Chair Company
30 Lyndhurst Road
Worthing
West Sussex BN11 2DF
01903 201081
Mail-order upholstery and soft furnishing equipment.

Cath Kidston
8 Clarendon Cross
London W11 4AP
020 7221 4000
Phone 020 7229 8000
for mail order.
www.cathkidston.co.uk
Floral fabrics (including oilcloths) and wallpapers with a retro influence.

Laura Ashley
Branches nationwide. Call 0870 5622116 for details of your nearest store.
www.lauraashley.com
The traditional English country look updated. Mail order available.

Liberty
210–220 Regent Street
London W1R 6AH
020 7734 1234
www.liberty.co.uk
Home accessories with global influences, including the classic Liberty prints.

Melin Tregwynt
28–30 Royal Arcade
Cardiff CF10 1AE
029 20224997
Phone 01348 891644
for mail order.
www.melintregwynt.co.uk
Contemporary-style woollen rugs and cushions from a Pembrokeshire mill.

Morris & Co
233 Kings Road
London SW3 5EJ
Phone 01895 830044 for details of stockists.
www.william-morris.co.uk
Fabrics and wallpapers inspired by the Arts & Crafts movement.

Mulberry
62 King Street
Manchester M2 4ND
0161 8393333
Phone 01202 575457 for other stockists of the Mulberry Home collection.
www.mulberry.com
Textiles and accessories with an emphasis on luxurious fabrics and rich, classic colours.

Natural Fabric Co.
Wessex Place
127 High Street
Hungerford
Berkshire RG17 0DL
01488 684002
Fabrics from toile to tartan via gingham, denim and plain cotttons.

Nina Campbell Shop
7 Walton Street
London SW3 2JD
020 7225 1011
www.ninacampbell.com
Bold florals in adaptable colours.

Osborne & Little
304–308 Kings Road
London SW3 5UH
020 7352 1456
And stocked nationwide.
www.osborneandlittle.com
Wide range of fabrics and trimmings, including hand-printed materials.

The White Company
0870 1601610
www.thewhiteco.com
Mail-order company supplying bed and table linen, cushions, throws and accessories – all in classic white.

PICTURE CREDITS

KEY: **a**=above, **b**=below, **c**=centre, **l**=left, **r**=right, *ph*=photographer.

1 *ph* Andrew Wood/the Shell Beach, California home of Chuck & Evelyn Plemons; **2–3** *ph* Chris Everard/an apartment in London designed by Littman Goddard Hoggarth, light courtesy of Skandium; **4** *ph* Polly Wreford/Courtney Brennan's apartment in New York designed by Ken Foreman; **6–7** *ph* Polly Wreford/Mary Foley's house in Connecticut; **8–9** *ph* Chris Everard/Reuben Barrett's apartment in London, light courtesy of Coexistence; **10l** *ph* James Merrell; **10–11** *ph* James Merrell/Gabriele Sanders's apartment in New York; **11a** *ph* Tom Leighton/blanket and candle, Interiors Bis; **11b** *ph* Andrew Wood/a house near Antwerp designed by Claire Bataille & Paul ibens; **12l** *ph* Tom Leighton/Roger & Fay Oates' house in Herefordshire, The Long Barn, Eastnor, Ledbury, Herefordshire HR8 1EL (01531 632718); **12–13** *ph* Andrew Wood/Bernie de Le Cuona's home in Windsor; **13a** *ph* James Merrell/a house in Sydney designed by Larcombe & Soloman; **13b** *ph* Andrew Wood/a house near Antwerp designed by Claire Bataille & Paul ibens; **14al** *ph* Catherine Gratwicke/Kimball Mayer & Meghan Hughes's apartment in New York designed by L. A. Morgan, painting by Erin Parrish; **14ar** *ph* James Merrell; **14b** *ph* David Montgomery/Sheila Scholes's house near Cambridge; **15al** *ph* Chris Everard/the Sugarman–Behun house on Long Island; **15ar** *ph* Andrew Wood/Roger & Suzy Black's apartment in London designed by Johnson Naylor; **15cl & bl** *ph* Andrew Wood/Bernie de Le Cuona's home in Windsor; **15cr** *ph* Chris Everard/a house in Hampstead, London designed by Orefelt Associates; **15br** *ph* Chris Everard/a house in London by Seth Stein; **16al** *ph* Alan Williams/the architect Voon Wong's own apartment in London; **16ar** *ph* Andrew Wood/Alastair Hendy and John Clinch's apartment in London designed by Alastair Hendy; **16bl** *ph* Chris Everard/Jonathan Wilson's apartment in London, light courtesy of SCP; **16br** *ph* Alan Williams/Jennifer & Geoffrey Symonds's apartment in New York designed by Jennifer Post Design; **17** *ph* David Montgomery/Carlton Gardens apartment in London designed by Claire Nelson at Nelson Design; **18al** *ph* James Merrell/Dominique Lubar for IPL Interiors; **18ar** *ph* Alan Williams/private apartment in West London, designed by Hugh Broughton Architects; **18bl** *ph* James Merrell/Rose Gray's flat in London designed by Hester Gray; **19al** *ph* Alan Williams/apartment for Richard Oyarzarbal by Urban Research Laboratory, London; **19ar** *ph* Alan Williams/the architect Voon Wong's own apartment in London; **19bl** *ph* Alan Williams/Alannah Weston's house in London designed by Stickland Coombe Architecture; **19br** *ph* Ray Main/an apartment in London designed by Circus Architects; **20al** *ph* Tom Leighton/a house in London designed by Charles Rutherfoord; **20ac** *ph* Chris Everard/Paul Brazier & Diane Lever's house in London designed by Carden & Cunietti; **20ar** *ph* Chris Everard/Calvin Tsao & Zack McKown's apartment in New York designed by Tsao and McKown; **20b** *ph* Alan Williams/Alannah Weston's house in London designed by Stickland Coombe Architecture; **21al** *ph* Chris Everard/Mark Weinstein's apartment in New York designed by Lloyd Schwan; **21ar** *ph* Alan Williams/Selworthy apartment in London designed by Gordana Mandic and Peter Tyler at Buildburo (www.buildburo.co.uk); **21b** *ph* Andrew Wood/Alastair Hendy and John Clinch's apartment in London designed by Alastair Hendy; **22al** *ph* Christopher Drake/Nelly Guyot's house in Ramatuelle, France, styled by Nelly Guyot; **22ar** *ph* Christopher Drake/designer Barbara Davis's own home in upstate New York; **22cl** *ph* Fritz von der Schulenburg/Robert Kinnaman & Brian Ramaekers' house in Wainscott; **22cr** *ph* Simon Upton; **22bl** *ph* Christopher Drake/Ali Sharland's home in Gloucestershire; **22br** *ph* Tom Leighton; **24a** *ph* Christopher Drake/designer Barbara Davis's own home in upstate New York; **24b** *ph* Alan Williams/the Arbuthnott family's house near Cirencester designed by Nicholas Arbuthnott, fabrics designed by Vanessa Arbuthnott; **25al** *ph* Simon Upton; **25ar** *ph* Tom Leighton; **25bl** *ph* Christopher Drake/Enrica Stabile's house in Brunello; **25br** *ph* Jan Baldwin/Elena Colombo's cottage on the east end side of Long Island; **26a** *ph* Simon Upton; **26c** *ph* David Montgomery/a house in Connecticut designed by Lynn Morgan Design; **26bl** *ph* Christopher Drake/designer Barbara Davis's own home in upstate New York; **26br** *ph* Christopher Drake/refurbishment & interior design by Chicchi Meroni Fassio, Parnassus; **27a** *ph* Simon Upton; **27ar** *ph* Christopher Drake/Enrica Stabile's house in Milan; **27cr** *ph* Christopher Drake/designed by Lorraine Kirke; **27br** *ph* Tom Leighton; **28a** *ph* Chris Everard/Bob & Maureen Macris's apartment on Fifth Avenue in New York designed by Sage Wimer Coombe Architects; **28bl** *ph* Andrew Wood/Norma Holland's house in London; **28br** *ph* Chris Everard/the London apartment of The Sheppard Day Design Partnership; **29al** *ph* Chris Everard/an apartment in Milan designed by Daniela Micol Wajskol, interior decorator, prints from Cristina Ballini Antiquario, Milan; **29ar** *ph* Alan Williams/Stanley and Nancy Grossman's apartment in New York designed by Jennifer Post

Design; **29br** *ph* Tom Leighton/Keith Varty & Alan Cleaver's apartment in London designed by Jonathan Reed/Reed Boyd (020 7565 0066); **30al** *ph* Ray Main/an apartment in New York designed by Laura Bohn Design Associates Inc., light from Lightforms; **30ar** *ph* Ray Main/Jonathan Reed's apartment in London, lighting designed by Sally Storey, Design Director of John Cullen Lighting; **30bl** *ph* Andrew Wood/Chelsea loft apartment in New York, designed by The Moderns; **30br** *ph* Andrew Wood/an apartment in London designed by James Gorst; **31al** *ph* Ray Main/a house in Pennsylvania designed by Jeffrey Bilhuber; **31ar** *ph* Ray Main/Gai Harris's apartment in London designed by François Gilles and Dominique Lubar, IPL Interiors; **31cl** *ph* Ray Main; **31cr** *ph* Chris Everard/Florence Buchanan, Steve Harrison & Octavia Spelman's house in Tribeca, New York, designed by Sage Wimer Coombe Architects; **31b** *ph* Andrew Wood/media executive's house in Los Angeles, architect: Stephen Slan, builder: Russell Simpson, original architect: Carl Maston c.1945; **32a** *ph* Polly Wreford/Mary Foley's house in Connecticut; **32c** *ph* Ray Main/Jonathan Reed's apartment in London, lighting designed by Sally Storey, Design Director of John Cullen Lighting; **32b** *ph* Alan Williams/Stanley and Nancy Grossman's apartment in New York designed by Jennifer Post Design; **33al** *ph* Tom Leighton/Keith Varty & Alan Cleaver's apartment in London designed by Jonathan Reed/Reed Boyd (020 7565 0066); **33ac** *ph* David Montgomery/Annabel Astor's house in London is full of furniture and accessories designed exclusively for her OKA Direct Mail Order Catalogue; **33ar** *ph* David Montgomery/house in South London designed by Todhunter Earle Interiors; **33cr** *ph* David Montgomery/Carlton Gardens apartment in London designed by Claire Nelson at Nelson Design; **33b** *ph* Chris Everard/interior designer Ann Boyd's own apartment in London; **34a** *ph* Verity Welstead/Lulu Guinness's house in London; **34b** *ph* Andrew Wood/the apartment of Michel Hurst & Robert Swope, owners of Full House NYC; **35a** *ph* David Montgomery/Sabina Fay Braxton's apartment in Paris; **35b** *ph* Fritz von der Schulenburg/Michael & Ruth Burke's house in Mississippi designed by Vicente Wolf of Vicente Wolf Associates; **36al** *ph* Chris Everard/Gentucca Bini's apartment in Milan; **36ar** *ph* Polly Wreford/Ros Fairman's house in London; **36b** *ph* Ray Main/Jonathan Leitersdorf's apartment in New York designed by Jonathan Leitersdorf/Just Design Ltd; **37a** *ph* Polly Wreford/The Sawmills Studio; **37bl** *ph* Polly Wreford/Ros Fairman's house in London; **37br** *ph* Chris Everard/Gentucca Bini's apartment in Milan; **38–39** *ph* Andrew Wood/John Cheim's apartment in New York; **39al** *ph* Chris Everard/Gentucca Bini's apartment in Milan; **39ar** *ph* Polly Wreford/Ros Fairman's house in London; **39b** *ph* Polly Wreford/Carol Reid's apartment in Paris; **40–41** *ph* Chris Everard/an apartment in London designed by Littman Goddard Hoggarth, light courtesy of Skandium; **42–43** *ph* Andrew Wood; **44al & br** *ph* Andrew Wood/Phillip Low, New York; **44r** *ph* Andrew Wood/Kurt Brendenbeck's apartment at the Barbican, London; **45** *ph* James Merrell/Sophie Sarin's flat in London; **46** *ph* James Merrell; **47al, cl & ar** *ph* James Merrell/Felix Bonnier's apartment in Paris; **47bl & br** *ph* James Merrell/Christine Walsh & Ian Bartlett's house in London designed by Jack Ingham of Bookworks; **48b** *ph* James Merrell/a house in London designed by François Gilles and Dominique Lubar, IPL Interiors; **48al & 48–49** *ph* Andrew Wood/Norma Holland's house in London; **49** *ph* Andrew Wood/Gabriele Sanders's apartment in New York; **50** *ph* James Merrell/Grant Ford & Jane Bailey's house in London/kitchen by Rhode Design; **51l & ar** *ph* James Merrell/Nigel Rowe's house in Middlesex/kitchen by Crabtree Kitchens; **51b** *ph* Henry Bourne/a mews house in London designed by McDowell & Benedetti; **52al & bl** *ph* James Merrell/Charles Morris Mount & Harold Gordon's house on Long Island designed by Charles Morris Mount; **52r** *ph* Andrew Wood/the loft of Peggy & Steven Learner designed by Steven Learner Studio; **52br** *ph* Andrew Wood/a house in London designed by Guy Stansfeld (020 7727 0133); **52–53** *ph* Ray Main/Alastair Gordon & Barbara de Vries' house near Princeton designed by Smith-Miller + Hawkinson Architects; **53bl & br** *ph* James Merrell/John Alexander & Fiona Waterstreet's loft in New York designed by Lorraine Kirke; **54a** *ph* James Merrell/designed by Interni Interior Design Consultancy; **54b** *ph* James Merrell/Douglas & Dorothy Hamilton's apartment in New York; **55al & ar** *ph* Fritz von der Schulenburg/a house in Pennsylvania designed by Laura Bohn Design Associates; **55b** *ph* James Merrell; **56bl & ac** *ph* Christopher Drake/refurbishment & interior design by Chicchi Meroni Fassio, Parnassus; **56bc** *ph* Christopher Drake/Enrica Stabile's house in Milan; **56r** *ph* Henry Bourne; **57al** *ph* Henry Bourne; **57ar** *ph* James Merrell/Mr & Mrs Barrow's house in Surrey designed by architects Marshall Haines + Barrow/kitchen by Chalon; **57bl & br** *ph* James Merrell/Sally Butler's house in London; **58al & ar** *ph* James Merrell/the Ash house in London designed by Ash Sakula Architects; **58bl** *ph* James Merrell/Etienne and Mary Millner's house in London; **58br** *ph* Polly Wreford/Ann Shore's house in London; **59bl** *ph* James Merrell; **59ar** *ph* Christopher Drake/Melanie Thornton's house in Gloucestershire; **59cr** *ph* Fritz von der Schulenburg/Bunny Williams's house in Connecticut; **59br** *ph* James Merrell/a house in London designed by

François Gilles and Dominique Lubar, IPL Interiors; **60–61** *ph* Andrew Wood/ Robert Kimsey's apartment in London designed by Gavin Jackson (07050 097561); **62** *ph* Andrew Wood/Bernie de Le Cuona's home in Windsor; **63a** *ph* Andrew Wood/Aude Cardinale's house near Paris; **63bl** *ph* Chris Everard/an apartment in New York designed by Gabellini Associates; **63br** *ph* Tom Leighton; **64–65** *ph* Andrew Wood/Rosa Dean & Ed Baden-Powell's apartment in London designed by Urban Salon (020 7357 8800); **66a** *ph* James Merrell; **66b** *ph* Chris Everard/ Mark Weinstein's apartment in New York designed by Lloyd Schwan; **67a** *ph* Simon Upton/Barefoot Elegance; **67b** *ph* Andrew Wood/Andrew Noble's apartment in London designed by Nico Rensch Architeam; **68l** *ph* Andrew Wood/Brian Johnson's apartment in London designed by Johnson Naylor; **68–69** *ph* Andrew Wood/Roger & Suzy Black's apartment in London designed by Johnson Naylor; **69al & r** *ph* Chris Everard/Eric de Queker's apartment in Antwerp; **70a & 70–71** *ph* Andrew Wood/an apartment in Bath designed by Briffa Phillips Architects; **70cl, bl & br** *ph* Andrew Wood/Jamie Falla & Lynn Graham's house in London; **71a & b** *ph* Andrew Wood/Han Feng's apartment in New York designed by Han Feng; **72** *ph* Andrew Wood/Brian Johnson's apartment in London designed by Johnson Naylor; **73a** *ph* Alan Williams/Gail & Barry Stephens's house in London; **73c** *ph* James Merrell; **73b** *ph* Chris Everard/François Muracciole's apartment in Paris; **74a** *ph* Henry Bourne/Frédéric Mérchiche's apartment in Paris; **74b** *ph* Alan Williams/Margot Feldman's house in New York designed by Patricia Seidman of Mullman Seidman Architects; **74–75** *ph* Ray Main/Vicente Wolf's house on Long Island, lights designed by Vicente Wolf; **76bl** *ph* Alan Williams/designer Barbara Davis's own house in upstate New York; **76ar** *ph* Chris Everard/an apartment in New York designed by Steven Learner; **76br** *ph* James Merrell; **76–77** *ph* Ray Main/Julie Prisca's house in Normandy; **77a** *ph* Alan Williams/ Miv Watts's house in Norfolk; **77b** *ph* Chris Everard/an apartment in Milan designed by Nicoletta Marazza; **78–79** *ph* Tom Leighton; **80** *ph* Andrew Wood/ Nicki de Metz's flat in London designed by de Metz Architects; **81a** *ph* Andrew Wood/Michael Benevento–Orange Group; **81b** *ph* Henry Bourne; **82al & bl** *ph* Andrew Wood/an apartment in London designed by Littman Goddard Hogarth Architects; **82ar** *ph* Andrew Wood/Johanne Riss's house in Brussels; **82–83 & 83al** *ph* Andrew Wood/Brian Johnson's apartment in London designed by Johnson Naylor; **83ar** *ph* Alan Williams/the Arbuthnott family's house near Cirencester designed by Nicholas Arbuthnott, fabrics designed by Vanessa Arbuthnott; **83b** *ph* Chris Everard/the London apartment of the Sheppard Day Design Partnership; **84al** *ph* Jan Baldwin/Fern Mallis's house in Southampton, Long Island; **84bl** *ph* Alan Williams/Stanley and Nancy Grossman's apartment in New York designed by Jennifer Post Design; **84ar** *ph* Andrew Wood/Johanne Riss's house in Brussels; **84–85** *ph* Jan Baldwin/Robert & Gabrielle Reeves's house in Clareville designed by Stutchbury & Pape Architecture + Landscape Architecture; **85al & ac** *ph* Catherine Gratwicke/the brownstone in New York of Bonnie Young, director of global sourcing and inspiration at Donna Karan International, styled by Gaby Karan; **85ar** *ph* Henry Bourne; **86** *ph* Catherine Gratwicke/Bryan Purcell, an artist living in New York; **87al** *ph* Chris Everard/an apartment in New York designed by Gabellini Associates; **87ar** *ph* Fritz von der Schulenburg/Irene & Giorgio Silvagni's house in Provence; **87bl** *ph* Fritz von der Schulenburg/Frank Faulkner's loft in New York; **87br** *ph* Chris Everard/an apartment in New York designed by Steven Learner; **88al** *ph* Polly Wreford/Glenn Carwithen & Sue Miller's house in London; **88al** *ph* Jan Baldwin/Camp Kent designed by Alexandra Champalimaud; **88bl** *ph* Chris Everard/Eric de Queker's apartment in Antwerp; **88br** *ph* Andrew Wood/ Century (020 7487 5100); **89al** *ph* Ray Main/Central London apartment designed by Ben Kelly Design; **89bl** *ph* Andrew Wood/Philip & Barbara Silver's house in Idaho designed by Mark Pynn A.I.A. of McMillen Pynn Architecture L.L.P.; **89r** *ph* Andrew Wood/Jo Shane, John Cooper & family apartment, in New York; **90l** *ph* Polly Wreford/Glenn Carwithen & Sue Miller's house in London; **90ac & ar** *ph* Andrew Wood/Andrew Noble's apartment in London designed by Nico Rensch Architeam; **90c** *ph* Polly Wreford/home of 27.12 Design Ltd, Chelsea, NYC; **90b** *ph* Tom Leighton/a loft in London designed by Robert Dye Associates; **91ar** *ph* Christopher Drake/Josephine Ryan's house in London; **91bl & br** *ph* James Merrell; **92–93** *ph* Andrew Wood; **94** *ph* Polly Wreford/Kimberly Watson's house in London; **94–95a** *ph* Chris Everard/the London apartment of the Sheppard Day Design Partnership; **94–95b** *ph* Andrew Wood/'Melwani House' designed by Bedmar & Shi Designers in Singapore; **95** *ph* Chris Everard/Hilton McConnico's house near Paris; **96al** *ph* Christopher Drake/Ali Sharland's home in Gloucestershire; **96br** *ph* Chris Everard/a house in Highbury, London designed by Dale Loth Architects; **96–97** *ph* Andrew Wood/a house near Antwerp designed by Bataille & ibens; **97al** *ph* Chris Everard/the Sugarman–Behun house on Long Island; **97ar** *ph* Fritz von der Schulenburg/Frédéric Méchiche's apartment in Paris; **97bl** *ph* Chris Everard/Emma & Neil's house in London, walls painted by Garth Carter;

97br *ph* Andrew Wood/Roger & Fay Oates's house in Herefordshire, The Long Barn, Eastnor, Ledbury, Herefordshire HR8 1EL (01531 632718); **98** *ph* Chris Everard/ Richard Oyarzarbal's apartment in London designed by Jeff Kirby of Urban Research Laboratory; **99al & ar** *ph* Chris Everard/Fred Wadsworth's flat in London designed by Littman Goddard Hogarth; **99c** *ph* Andrew Wood/an apartment in London designed by Littman Goddard Hogarth Architects; **99b** *ph* Chris Everard/ designer Alan Tanksley's own apartment in Manhattan; **100** *ph* James Morris/ a loft apartment in London designed by Simon Conder Associates; **101al** *ph* Chris Everard/One New Inn Square, a private dining room and home of chef David Vanderhook (all enquiries to 020 7729 3645); **101ac & al** *ph* Chris Everard/an apartment in Paris designed by Bruno Tanquerel; **101bl** *ph* Simon Upton; **101br** *ph* Chris Everard/Freddie Daniells's apartment in London designed by Brookes Stacey Randall; **102al** *ph* Andrew Wood/a house in London designed by Bowles & Linares; **102ar** *ph* Chris Everard/One New Inn Square, a private dining room and home of chef David Vanderhook (all enquiries to 020 7729 3645); **102bl** *ph* Chris Everard/ Richard Hopkin's apartment in London designed by HM2; **102br** *ph* Andrew Wood/ a house near Antwerp designed by Bataille & ibens; **103al** *ph* Chris Everard/ architect Nigel Smith's apartment in London; **103ar & br** *ph* Simon Upton; **103bl** *ph* Chris Everard/Stephen Schulte's loft apartment in London; **104al** *ph* Andrew Wood/Alastair Hendy and John Clinch's apartment in London designed by Alastair Hendy; **104cl** *ph* Chris Everard/a house in Hampstead, London designed by Orefelt Associates; **104bl** *ph* Chris Everard/a house in Highbury, London designed by Dale Loth Architects; **104ar** *ph* Chris Everard/Tiffany Ogden's house in London designed by Andy Martin of Fin Architects & Designers; **104br** *ph* Tom Leighton/a house in London designed by Charles Rutherfoord, 51 The Chase, London SW4 0NP (020 7627 0182); **105al** *ph* Chris Everard/Richard Oyarzarbal's apartment in London designed by Jeff Kirby of Urban Research Laboratory; **105bl** *ph* Chris Everard/Paul Brazier & Diane Lever's house in London designed by Carden & Cunietti; **105ar** *ph* Chris Everard/Gomez/Murphy loft, London designed by Urban Salon Ltd; **105br** *ph* Chris Everard/Suzanne Slesin & Michael Steinberg's apartment in New York designed by Jean-Louis Ménard; **106l** *ph* Alan Williams/ Gail & Barry Stephens's house in London; **106ar** *ph* Andrew Wood/a house near Antwerp designed by Bataille & ibens; **106br & 107cl** *ph* Andrew Wood/a house in London designed by Guy Stansfeld (020 7727 0133); **107al** *ph* Chris Everard/ an apartment in New York designed by Steven Learner; **107bl & c** *ph* Chris Everard/ Calvin Tsao & Zack McKown's apartment in New York designed by Tsao & McKown; **107r** *ph* Andrew Wood/Dawna & Jerry Walter's house in London; **108–109** *ph* Andrew Wood; **110al** *ph* Andrew Wood/Chelsea studio in New York City, designed by Marino + Giolito; **110ar** *ph* Andrew Wood/Heidi Kingstone's apartment in London; **110bl & br** *ph* Andrew Wood/Kurt Bredenbeck's apartment at the Barbican, London; **111al** *ph* Andrew Wood/Gabriele Sanders's apartment in New York; **111ar** *ph* Catherine Gratwicke; **111bl** *ph* Catherine Gratwicke/Frances Robinson & Eamonn McMahon's house in London; **111bc** *ph* Polly Wreford/Clare Nash's house in London; **111br** *ph* Ray Main/Kenneth Hirst's apartment in New York; **112al** *ph* Ray Main/Thierry Watorek's house near Paris; **112ar** *ph* Ray Main/Century (020 7487 5100); **112b** *ph* James Morris/Joan Barnett's house in West Hollywood, designed by William R Hefner A.I.A., interior design by Sandy Davidson Design; **113bl** *ph* Chris Everard/Bob & Maureen Macris's apartment on Fifth Avenue in New York designed by Sage Wimer Coombe Architects; **113ar & br** *ph* Andrew Wood/Jo Shane, John Cooper & family apartment, in New York; **114al & br** *ph* Andrew Wood/Ian Bartlett & Christine Walsh's house in London; **114bl & ar** *ph* Andrew Wood; **115b** *ph* Andrew Wood/Century (020 7487 5100); **115a** *ph* Andrew Wood/Phillip Low, New York; **116–117** *ph* Debi Treloar/Eben & Nica Cooper's bedroom, the Cooper family playroom; **118al & b** *ph* Debi Treloar/Belén Moneo & Jeff Brock's apartment in New York designed by Moneo Brock Studio; **118ar** *ph* Debi Treloar/Vincent & Frieda Plasschaert's house in Brugge, Belgium; **118c** *ph* Debi Treloar/Ab Rogers & Sophie Braimbridge's house, London, designed by Richard Rogers for his mother. Furniture design by KRD – Kitchen Rogers Design; **118–119** *ph* Debi Treloar/Michele Johnson's house in London designed by Nico Rensch Architeam; **120al** *ph* Debi Treloar/Ab Rogers & Sophie Braimbridge's house, London, designed by Richard Rogers for his mother. Furniture design by KRD – Kitchen Rogers Design; **120a** *ph* Debi Treloar/designed by Sage Wimer Coombe Architects New York; **120br** *ph* Debi Treloar/Sophie Eadie's house in London; **121 al** *ph* Debi Treloar/Rudi, Melissa & Archie Thackry's house in London; **121** *ph* Debi Treloar/Vincent & Frieda Plasschaert's house in Brugge, Belgium; **121bl** *ph* Debi Treloar/Victoria Andreae's house in London; **121br** *ph* Debi Treloar/ an apartment in London, by Malin Iovino Design; **122 & 123al** *ph* Debi Treloar/ the Boyes home in London designed by Circus Architects; **123cl & c** *ph* Debi Treloar/the Zwirner's loft in New York; **123cr** *ph* Debi Treloar/Ben Johns & Deb Waterman Johns's house in Georgetown; **123b** *ph* Christopher Drake/Enrica

Stabile's house in Brunello; **124al & bl** *ph* Debi Treloar/Sudi Pigott's house in London; **124bc** *ph* Debi Treloar/Julia & David O'Driscoll's house in London; **124ar** *ph* Debi Treloar/the Zwirner's loft in New York; **124br** *ph* Debi Treloar/Victoria Andreae's house in London; **125al** *ph* Debi Treloar/Elizabeth Alford & Michael Young's loft in New York; **125bl** *ph* Debi Treloar/Suzanne & Christopher Sharp's house in London; **125ar & br** *ph* Debi Treloar/Sera Hersham-Loftus's house in London; **126al** *ph* Christopher Drake/Melanie Thornton's house in Gloucestershire; **126cl** *ph* Debi Treloar/Suzanne & Christopher Sharp's house in London; **126bl** *ph* Debi Treloar/Sue & Lars-Christian Brask's house in London designed by Susie Atkinson; **126ca & cb** *ph* Debi Treloar/Ben Johns & Deb Waterman Johns's house in Georgetown; **126br, 126–127 & 127bl** *ph* Debi Treloar/Eben & Nica Cooper's bedroom, the Cooper family playroom; **127br** *ph* Debi Treloar/Victoria Andreae's house in London; **128–129** *ph* Tom Leighton; **130al** *ph* Christopher Drake/designer Barbara Davis's own home in upstate New York; **130cl** *ph* Polly Wreford/Sheila Scholes & Gunter Schmidt's house in Cambridgeshire; **130bl** *ph* Simon Upton; **130br** *ph* Christopher Drake/designed by Lorraine Kirke; **131al** *ph* Chris Everard/Bob & Maureen Macris's apartment on Fifth Avenue in New York designed by Sage Wimer Coombe Architects; **131ar** *ph* Chris Everard/an apartment in Milan designed by Nicoletta Marazza; **131bl** *ph* Andrew Wood/Heidi Kingstone's apartment in London; **131br** *ph* Christopher Drake/designer Barbara Davis's own home in upstate New York; **132l** *ph* James Merrell; **132ar** *ph* Ray Main/Marina & Peter Hill's barn in West Sussex designed by Marina Hill, Peter James Construction Management, Chichester, The West Sussex Antique Timber Company, Wisborough Green, and Joanna Jefferson Architects; **132br** *ph* Simon Upton/Barefoot Elegance; **133al** *ph* Simon Upton; **133bl** *ph* Andrew Wood/Vanessa & Robert Fairer's studio in London designed by Woolf Architects (020 7428 9500); **133ar & br** *ph* Andrew Wood/Patricia Ijaz's house in London designed by Jonathan Woolf of Woolf Architects; **134–135** *ph* Chris Everard/Jonathan Wilson's apartment in London, light courtesy of SCP; **136–137** *ph* Alan Williams; **138a** *ph* James Merrell/Milly de Cabrol's apartment in Paris; **138bl** *ph* Simon Upton; **138br** *ph* James Merrell; **138–139** *ph* Alan Williams/Warner Johnson's apartment in New York designed by Edward Cabot of Cabot Design Ltd; **139a** *ph* Tom Leighton; **140a** *ph* Alan Williams/Donata Sartorio's apartment in Milan; **140b** *ph* Alan Willams/Géraldine Prieur's apartment in Paris, an interior designer fascinated with colour; **140–141 & 141a** *ph* James Merrell; **141b** *ph* Andrew Wood/Aude Cardinale's house near Paris; **142** *ph* Polly Wreford/Clare Nash's house in London; **142–143** *ph* Chris Everard/an apartment in Antwerp designed by Claire Bataille & Paul ibens; **143bl & ar** *ph* Alan Williams/Stanley and Nancy Grossman's apartment in New York designed by Jennifer Post Design; **143cr & br** *ph* Tom Leighton; **144l** *ph* James Merrell; **144r** *ph* Alan Williams/Gail & Barry Stephens's house in London; **145a** *ph* Andrew Wood/a house in London designed by Bowles & Linares; **145b** *ph* Tom Leighton/bed, bed linens & table Interiors Bis; wooden cylinder David Champion; **146** *ph* Tom Leighton/paint Farrow & Ball: floor Mouse's Back floor paint no.40, cupboards Green Smoke no.47 and interiors Red Fox no. 48, walls and woodwork String no.8, ceiling Off White no.3; **147al** *ph* Alan Williams/the Arbuthnott family's house near Cirencester designed by Nicholas Arbuthnott, fabrics designed by Vanessa Arbuthnott; **147bl & ar** *ph* Simon Upton; **147br** *ph* Alan Williams/Alannah Weston's house in London designed by Stickland Coombe Architecture; **148al** *ph* Christopher Drake/Marisa Cavalli's home in Milan; **148ar** *ph* James Merrell/Sally Butler's house in London; **148b** *ph* Alan Williams/New York apartment designed by Bruce Bierman; **149l** *ph* Christopher Drake/Juan Corbella's apartment in London designed by HM2, Richard Webb with Andrew Hanson; **149r** *ph* James Merrell/an apartment in Paris designed by Hervé Vermesch; **150a** *ph* Alan Williams/the Arbuthnott family's house near Cirencester designed by Nicholas Arbuthnott, fabrics designed by Vanessa Arbuthnott; **150b** *ph* Simon Upton; **151a** *ph* Christopher Drake/Juan Corbella's apartment in London designed by HM2, Richard Webb with Andrew Hanson; **151b** *ph* Alan Williams/Lindsay Taylor's apartment in Glasgow; **152al** *ph* Simon Upton; **152bl** *ph* Alan Williams/interior designer and managing director of the Société Yves Halard, Michelle Halard's own apartment in Paris; **152br** *ph* Andrew Wood/Neil Bingham's house in Blackheath, London; **152–153** *ph* Alan Williams/apartment for Richard Oyarzabal by Urban Research Laboratory, London; **153bl** *ph* Chris Everard/architect's house in London designed by Dale Loth Architects; **153br** *ph* Alan Williams/Selworthy apartment in London designed by Gordana Mandic and Peter Tyler at Buildburo (www.buildburo.co.uk); **154–155** *ph* Ray Main; **156** *ph* Ray Main/Mark Jennings's apartment in New York designed by Asfour Guzy; **157a** *ph* Andrew Wood/an apartment in The San Remo on the Upper West Side of Manhattan, designed by John L. Stewart and Michael D'Arcy of SIT; **157c** *ph* Ray Main/Gai Harris's apartment in London designed by François Gilles and Dominique Lubar, IPL Interiors; **157b** *ph* Ray Main/John Howell's loft in London

designed by Circus Architects; **158b** *ph* Ray Main/Vicente Wolf's house on Long Island, lights designed by Vicente Wolf; **158cr** *ph* Ray Main/Greg Yale's house in Southampton, New York; **158br** *ph* Ray Main/Nello Renault's loft in Paris; **158–159** *ph* Ray Main/an apartment in New York designed by Laura Bohn Design Associates, Inc.; **159bl** *ph* Andrew Wood/Jane Collins of Sixty 6 in Marylebone High Street, home in central London; **159ar** *ph* Ray Main/Lee F. Mindel's apartment in New York, lighting designed by Johnson Schwinghammer; **159br** *ph* Ray Main/Greg Yale's house in Southampton, New York; **160a** *ph* Chris Everard/Simon Crookall's apartment in London designed by Urban Salon, light courtesy of London Lighting; **160b** *ph* Andrew Wood/Heidi Kingstone's apartment in London; **161l** *ph* Ray Main/a loft in London designed by Nico Rensch; **161ar** *ph* Ray Main/Malin Iovino's apartment in London; **161br** *ph* Ray Main/Andrea Luria & Zachary Feuer's house in Los Angeles designed by Studio Works, Robert Mangurian & Mary-Ann Ray; **162al** *ph* Ray Main/an apartment in New York designed by Laura Bohn Design Associates, Inc.; **162cl** *ph* Ray Main/a house in Pennsylvania designed by Jeffrey Bilhuber, light from The Light Center; **162bl** *ph* Ray Main/an apartment in New York designed by Lucretia Moroni; **162br** *ph* Ray Main/a house in London designed by François Gilles and Dominique Lubar, IPL Interiors; **163a** *ph* Ray Main/an apartment in New York designed by Laura Bohn Design Associates, Inc.; **163b** *ph* Ray Main/Nello Renault's loft in Paris; **164l** *ph* Chris Everard/Gentucca Bini's apartment in Milan; **164ar** *ph* Chris Everard; **164cr** *ph* Ray Main; **164br** *ph* Chris Everard/an apartment in Milan designed by Daniela Micol Wajskol, interior designer; **165ar & l** *ph* Ray Main/Malin Iovino's apartment in London; **165b** *ph* Andrew Wood/Nanna Ditzel's home in Copenhagen; **166al, ac & ar** *ph* Ray Main; **166bl** *ph* Ray Main/a house in East Hampton, interior by Vicente Wolf; **165cr & bc** *ph* Ray Main; **166br** *ph* Andrew Wood; **167l** *ph* Andrew Wood/an apartment in The San Remo on the Upper West Side of Manhattan, designed by John L. Stewart and Michael D'Arcy of SIT; **167r** *ph* Andrew Wood; **168al** *ph* Ray Main/light from Babylon Design; **167ac** *ph* Chris Everard/Christina Wilson's house in London, light courtesy of SCP; **168bl** *ph* Chris Everard/Jonathan Wilson's apartment in London, light courtesy of SCP; **168bc** *ph* Chris Everard/Glenn Carwithen & Sue Miller's house in London, light courtesy of Coexistence; **168br** *ph* Andrew Wood/Guido Palau's house in North London, designed by Azman Owens Architects; **168–169a** *ph* Andrew Wood/Freddie Daniells's loft apartment in London designed by Brookes Stacey Randall; **169bl** *ph* Chris Everard/Reuben Barrett's apartment in London, light courtesy of Purves & Purves; **169c** *ph* Chris Everard/Simon Crookall's apartment in London designed by Urban Salon, light courtesy of Geofrey Drayton; **169ar & br** *ph* Andrew Wood/Guido Palau's house in North London, designed by Azman Owens Architects; **170al** *ph* Ray Main/light from Ingo Maurer for London Lighting; **170bl** *ph* Ray Main/light from Tsé Tsé associées, Catherine Levy & Singoléne Prébois; **170ar** *ph* Ray Main/Greg Yale's house in Southampton, New York; **170cr** *ph* Catherine Gratwicke/an apartment in Paris designed by Bruno Tanquerel; **170br** *ph* Andrew Wood/the Pasadena, California home of Susan D'Avignon; **170–171a** *ph* Chris Everard/an apartment in London designed by Littman, Goddard & Hogarth; **171al** *ph* Chris Everard/Reuben Barrett's apartment in London, light courtesy of Purves & Purves; **171ar** *ph* Ray Main/light from Mathmos; *ph* Andrew Wood/The Caroline De Forest House in Pasadena, California, home to Michael Murray & Kelly Jones; **171bcl** *ph* Andrew Wood/Jane Collins of Sixty 6 in Marylebone High Street, home in central London; **171bcr** *ph* Ray Main/Lee F. Mindel's apartment in New York, lighting designed by Johnson Schwinghammer; **171br** *ph* Ray Main/light by Tom Kirk from Space; **172–173** *ph* Ray Main; **174al** *ph* Andrew Wood/Roger & Fay Oates's house in Herefordshire, The Long Barn, Eastnor, Ledbury, Herefordshire HR8 1EL (01531 632718); **174cl** *ph* Chris Everard; **174bl** *ph* Chris Everard/Gentucca Bini's apartment in Milan; **174br** *ph* Chris Everard/David Mullman's apartment in New York designed by Mullman Seidman Architects; **174–175** *ph* Chris Everard/an apartment in New York designed by Steven Learner; **175bl** *ph* Chris Everard/Eric De Queker's apartment in Antwerp; **175ar** *ph* Henry Bourne; **175cr** *ph* Chris Everard/the London apartment of the Sheppard Day Design Partnership; **175br** *ph* Chris Everard/an apartment in London designed by Jo Hagan of USE Architects; **176 below, top row l** *ph* Henry Bourne; **top row r** *ph* Ray Main; **middle row l** *ph* Simon Upton; **middle row r** *ph* Tom Leighton; **bottom row both** *ph* Catherine Gratwicke; **176–177a** *ph* Chris Everard/an apartment in Antwerp designed by Claire Bataille & Paul ibens; **177al** *ph* Chris Everard/François Muracciole's apartment in Paris; **177ar** *ph* James Merrell/a house in Sydney designed by Luigi Rosselli; **177bl** *ph* Chris Everard/a house in Paris designed by Bruno Tanquerel; **177br** *ph* Chris Everard/Stephan Schulte's loft apartment in London; **178a** *ph* Simon Upton; **178b** *ph* James Merrell/Frédéric Méchiche's house near Toulon; **179bl** *ph* James Merrell/Khai Liew & Sue Kellett; **179ac** *ph* Andrew Wood/Bernie de Le Cuona's house in Windsor; **179c** *ph* Chris Everard; **179br** *ph* Andrew Wood; **179ar** *ph* Chris Everard/

an apartment in New York designed by Gabellini Associates; **179cr** *ph* Chris Everard; **180al & bl** *ph* Chris Everard; **180cl** *ph* Andrew Wood; **180ar** *ph* Chris Everard/Eric De Queker's apartment in Antwerp; **180br** *ph* Chris Everard/François Muracciole's apartment in Paris; **181** *ph* Chris Everard/Mrs Venturini's apartment in Milan; **182a** *ph* Chris Everard/Simon Crookall's apartment in London designed by Urban Salon, light courtesy of London Lighting; **182bl** *ph* Chris Everard/an apartment in Antwerp designed by Claire Bataille & Paul ibens; **182br** *ph* Ray Main/Jonathan Leitersdorf's apartment in New York designed by Jonathan Leitersdorf/Just Design; **183a** *ph* Ray Main/the contemplative space of Greville Worthington; **183c** *ph* Ray Main; **183bl** *ph* James Merrell; **183r** *ph* James Merrell/a house in Sydney designed by Interni Interior Design Consultancy; **184** *ph* Henry Bourne/Circus Architects/floor by First Floor; **185a** *ph* Henry Bourne; **185bl** *ph* Henry Bourne/John Raab's apartment in London/floor by Sinclair Till; **185br** *ph* James Merrell/Sue & Andy's apartment in Blackheath; **186al** *ph* James Merrell/an apartment in New York designed by Marino & Giolito; **186al** *ph* Chris Everard; **186–187** *ph* Henry Bourne/Richard Mabb & Kate Green's apartment in London; **187a** *ph* Henry Bourne/a house in London designed by Charles Rutherfoord; **187b** *ph* Henry Bourne/an apartment in London designed by Emily Todhunter; **188al** *ph* Henry Bourne/a mews house in London designed by McDowell & Benedetti; **188bl** *ph* Henry Bourne/rug by Christopher Farr; **188ar** *ph* Henry Bourne/an apartment in London designed by Ash Sakula Architects; **188br** *ph* Chris Everard/an apartment in London designed by Jo Hagan of USE Architects; **189al** *ph* Andrew Wood/Jane Collins of Sixty 6 in Marylebone High Street, home in central London; **189bl** *ph* Andrew Wood/Roger & Suzy Black's apartment in London designed by Johnson Naylor; **189ar** *ph* Henry Bourne/designed by François Gilles & Dominique Lubar, IPL Interiors/floor by Helen Yardley; **189br** *ph* Polly Wreford/Louise Jackson's house in London; **190al** *ph* Henry Bourne/Roger & Fay Oates's house in Herefordshire; **190ac** *ph* James Merrell/a house in London designed by François Gilles & Dominique Lubar, IPL Interiors; **190ar** *ph* Ray Main/client's residence, East Hampton, New York, designed by ZG DESIGN; **190b** *ph* Andrew Wood/Heidi Kingstone's apartment in London; **191al & b** *ph* Andrew Wood/Roger Oates and Fay Morgan's house in Eastnor; **191ar** *ph* Andrew Wood/a house near Antwerp designed by Claire Bataille & Paul ibens; **192–193** *ph* Polly Wreford; **194al** *ph* Andrew Wood/Vanessa & Robert Fairer's studio in London designed by Woolf Architects (020 7428 9500); **194cl** *ph* Andrew Wood/Roger Oates and Fay Morgan's house in Eastnor; **194bl** *ph* Jan Baldwin/a house in Cape Elizabeth designed by Stephen Blatt Architects; **194r** *ph* Andrew Wood/a house in London designed by François Gilles and Dominique Lubar, IPL Interiors; **195a** *ph* James Merrell; **195b** *ph* Chris Everard/an apartment in Milan designed by Nicoletta Marazza; **196al** *ph* Tom Leighton; **196ar** *ph* Polly Wreford/an apartment in New York designed by Belmont Freeman Architects; **196–197** *ph* Henry Bourne/Frédéric Méchiche's apartment in Paris; **197al** *ph* Chris Everard/interior designer Ann Boyd's own apartment in London; **197ac** *ph* Andrew Wood/Ian Bartlett & Christine Walsh's house in London; **197r** *ph* Verity Welstead/Lulu Guinness's house in London; **198al, ac & cl** *ph* Andrew Wood/a house in London designed by Guy Stansfeld (020 7727 0133); **198bl & br** *ph* Tom Leighton; **198–199** *ph* Alan Williams/Katie Bassford King's house in London designed by Touch Interior Design; **199bl** *ph* Chris Everard/Mark Weinstein's apartment in New York designed by Lloyd Schwan; **199ar** *ph* Tam Nhu Tran/Ian Chee's apartment in London; **200al** *ph* Fritz von der Schulenburg/Frédéric Méchiche's apartment in Paris; **200ar** *ph* Andrew Wood/Paula Pryke's house in London; **200bl** *ph* Chris Everard/an apartment in Antwerp designed by Claire Bataille & Paul ibens; **201l** *ph* James Morris/a house in Wiltshire designed by Ken Shuttleworth; **201ar** *ph* Chris Everard/interior designer Ann Boyd's own apartment in London; **202a** *ph* Andrew Wood; **202bl & br** *ph* Chris Everard/Mark Weinstein's apartment in New York designed by Lloyd Schwan; **203** *ph* Andrew Wood; **204al** *ph* James Merrell/a house in London designed by stylist Baba Bolli/kitchen by Smallbone; **204bl** *ph* Andrew Wood/Dawna & Jerry Walter's house in London; **204cb** *ph* Ray Main/Thierry Watorek's house near Paris; **204br & 204–205a** *ph* Andrew Wood/a house in London designed by François Gilles and Dominique Lubar, IPL Interiors; **205b** *ph* Simon Upton; **205c** *ph* Tom Leighton/Siobhan Squire and Gavin Lyndsey's loft in London designed by Will White, 326 Portobello Road, London W10 5RU (020 8964 8052); **205r** *ph* Andrew Wood/Ian Bartlett & Christine Walsh's house in London; **206a** *ph* Andrew Wood/Vanessa & Robert Fairer's studio in London designed by Woolf Architects (020 7428 9500); **206b** *ph* Andrew Wood; **206–207** *ph* Chris Everard/Gentucca Bini's apartment in Milan; **207a** *ph* Andrew Wood; **207bl** *ph* Polly Wreford/Jen Harte's apartment in New York, home of 27.12 Design Ltd, Chelsea NYC; **207br** *ph* Andrew Wood/Dawna & Jerry Walter's house in London; **208–209** *ph* James Merrell; **210a** *ph* James Merrell/Interni Interior Design Consultancy; **210b** *ph* James Merrell/a house in London designed by François Gilles & Dominique Lubar, IPL Interiors; **211al** *ph* James Merrell/designed by Charlotte Barnes; **211ar** *ph* James Merrell/an apartment in New York designed by Jacqueline Coumans, Le Décor Français with the help of Olivier Glebsmann; **211bl** *ph* James Merrell/Amy & Richard Sachs's apartment in New York designed by Vicente Wolf; **211cr** *ph* Polly Wreford/Glenn Carwithen & Sue Miller's house in London; **211br** *ph* James Merrell/Vicente Wolf's apartment in New York; **212al** *ph* Simon Upton; **212cl** *ph* James Morris/The Lew House, originally designed by Richard Neutra in 1958, architect and contractor Marmol Radziner + Associates, Architecture and Construction; **212bl** *ph* James Merrell/Nigel Greenwood's apartment in London; **212cr** *ph* James Merrell/Interni Interior Design Consultancy; **212bc & br** *ph* James Merrell; **212–213a** *ph* James Morris/a loft in London designed by Simon Conder Associates; **213cl & bl** *ph* James Merrell; **213ar** *ph* James Merrell/a house in London designed by François Gilles & Dominique Lubar, IPL Interiors; **214l & r** *ph* Polly Wreford/the Sawmills Studio; **214c** *ph* James Merrell; **215l** *ph* Ray Main/Nello Renault's loft in Paris; **215ar** *ph* James Merrell/Larcombe & Soloman; **215br** *ph* Christopher Drake/Nelly Guyot's house in Ramatuelle, France, styled by Nelly Guyot; **216al** *ph* James Merrell; **216bl** *ph* James Merrell/an apartment in New York, architect Campion A. Platt; **216ar** *ph* James Merrell/a house in London designed by François Gilles & Dominique Lubar, IPL Interiors; **217al** *ph* James Merrell/designed by Charlotte Barnes; **217bl** *ph* Polly Wreford/Daniel Jasiak's apartment in Paris; **217r** *ph* James Merrell/Frédéric Méchiche's house near Toulon; **218al & bl** *ph* James Merrell; **218–219a** *ph* James Merrell/Nigel Greenwood's apartment in London; **218–219b** *ph* James Merrell/an apartment in London designed by François Gilles & Dominique Lubar, IPL Interiors; **219cr** *ph* James Merrell/an apartment in London designed by Charles Rutherfoord; **219ar, br & bc** *ph* James Merrell; **220al** *ph* James Merrell/a house in Sydney designed by Interni Interior Design Consultancy; **220bl** *ph* James Merrell/Richard Ronald's house in London; **220ar** *ph* James Merrell/Nigel Greenwood's apartment in London; **220br** *ph* David Montgomery/Annabel Astor's house in London is full of furniture and accessories designed exclusively for her OKA Direct Mail Order Catalogue; **221a** *ph* Ray Main/a house in East Hampton, interior by Vicente Wolf; **221b** *ph* James Merrell/Amy & Richard Sachs's apartment in New York designed by Vicente Wolf; **222a** *ph* James Merrell/Andrew Parr's house in Melbourne; **222bl** *ph* James Merrell/Kelly Hoppen's apartment in London; **222br** *ph* James Merrell/William Hayes & Annie Har's house near Brisbane; **223al** *ph* James Merrell; **223bl** *ph* James Merrell/Robyn & Simon Carnachan's house in Auckland; **223ar** *ph* Ray Main/a house in London designed by Seth Stein and Sarah Delaney; **223br** *ph* Ray Main/a house in London designed by Mark Guard Architects; **224** *ph* James Merrell/Kelly Hoppen's apartment in London; **225 main** *ph* Christopher Drake/Marisa Cavalli's home in Milan; **225 all details** *ph* James Merrell **except 225bl & ac** *ph* David Montgomery; **226–227** *ph* Polly Wreford; **228bl** *ph* James Merrell; **228ar & 228–229** *ph* Polly Wreford/Ros Fairman's house in London; **229ar** *ph* Alan Williams/owner of Gloss, Pascale Bredillet's own apartment in London; **229br** *ph* Polly Wreford/Clare Nash's house in London; **230al** *ph* Andrew Wood; **230acl** *ph* Andrew Wood/Bernie de Le Cuona's home in Windsor; **230bcl** *ph* Polly Wreford; **230bl** *ph* David Montgomery/Annabel Astor's house in London is full of furniture and accessories designed exclusively for her OKA Direct Mail Order Catalogue; **230c** *ph* David Montgomery; **230ar** *ph* Polly Wreford/The Sawmills Studio; **230br** *ph* Henry Bourne; **231ar** *ph* Chris Everard; **231br** *ph* Simon Upton; **232al** *ph* Polly Wreford/Glenn Carwithen & Sue Miller's house in London; **230bl & c** *ph* Polly Wreford; **232ar** *ph* Polly Wreford/Ros Fairman's house in London; **232br** *ph* Andrew Wood/a house in London designed by Bowles & Linares; **233l** *ph* Alan Williams/Janice Kirkpatrick's apartment in Glasgow, director of design consultants Graven Images; **233ar** *ph* Catherine Gratwicke/antique mirrored bedthrow from the Gallery of Antique Costume & Textiles, striped throw from Selfridges; **233cr** *ph* Catherine Gratwicke/Agnès Emery's house in Brussels, tiles and bedding from Emery & Cie; **233br** *ph* Polly Wreford/an apartment in New York designed by Belmont Freeman Architects; **234al** *ph* Polly Wreford/Mary Foley's house in Connecticut; **234ar** *ph* Henry Bourne; **234b & 235al & ar** *ph* David Montgomery/Sasha Waddell's house in London; **235bcl** *ph* Polly Wreford/Daniel Jasiak's apartment in Paris; **235b** *ph* Polly Wreford/Adria Ellis's apartment in New York; **236al** *ph* Andrew Wood/Mary Shaw's Sequana apartment in Paris; **236bl** *ph* Andrew Wood/Bernie de Le Cuona's home in Windsor; **236ar & cr** *ph* Polly Wreford/Kimberly Watson's house in London; **236br, 237al & bl** *ph* James Merrell; **237r** *ph* Chris Everard/interior designer Ann Boyd's own apartment in London; **238l** *ph* James Merrell/Gabriele Sanders's apartment in New York; **238–239a** *ph* Tom Leighton/Roger & Fay Oates's house in Herefordshire, The Long Barn, Eastnor, Ledbury, Herefordshire HR8 1EL (01531 632718); **238–239b** *ph* Alan Williams/owner of Gloss, Pascale Bredillet's own apartment in London; **239** *ph* Polly Wreford/Liz Stirling's apartment in Paris; **endpapers** *ph* Andrew Wood/Charlotte Crosland's home in London, designed by Charlotte Crosland, Wingrave Crosland Interiors.

ARCHITECTS & DESIGNERS WHOSE WORK IS FEATURED IN THIS BOOK:

Elizabeth Alford Design
60 Thomas Street
New York
NY 10013 USA
t. +1 212 385 2185
f. +1 212 385 2186
e. esa799@banet.net
Page 125al

Anthropologie
375 West Broadway
New York
NY 10012 USA
Pages 27br, 63br

Nicholas Arbuthnott
Arbuthnott Ladenbury
Architects
15 Gosditch Street
Cirencester GL7 2AG
*Architects & urban
designers.*
Pages 24b, 83ar, 147al, 150a

Vanessa Arbuthnott Fabrics
The Tallet, Calmsden
Cirencester GL7 5ET
www.vanessaarbuthnott.co.uk
Pages 24b, 83ar, 147al, 150a

Asfour Guzy
594 Broadway, Suite 1204
New York
NY 10012 USA
t. +1 212 334 9350
f. +1 212 334 9009
Page 156

Ash Sakula Architects
24 Rosebery Avenue
London EC1R 4SX
t. 020 7837 9735
f. 020 7837 9708
e. info@ashsak.com
www.ashsak.com
Pages 58al & ar, 188ar

Susie Atkinson Design
t. 0468 814 134
Page 126bl

Azman Owens Architects
18 Charlotte Road
London EC2A 3PB
t. 020 7739 8191
f. 020 7739 6191
www.azmanowens.com
Pages 168br, 169ar&br

Babylon Design Ltd
301 Fulham Road
London SW10 9QH
t. 020 7376 7233
e. info@babylon
    design.demon.co.uk
*Lighting designers. Lights
by up-and-coming
designers such as Peter
Wylly, Ross Menuez and
Roland Simmons.*
Page 168al

Barefoot Elegance
3537 Old Conejo Road
Suite 105
Newbury Park
CA 91320 USA
t. +1 805 499 5959
*Dot Spikings & Jennifer
Castle, Interior Designers.*
Pages 67a, 132br

Charlotte Barnes Interiors
26 Stanhope Gardens
London SW7 5QX
*An interior decorator,
Charlotte Barnes provides
elegant, beautiful and
practical solutions, tailored
to each client and property.*
Pages 211al, 217al

Claire Bataille & Paul ibens
Design NV, Architects
Vekestratt 13 Bus 14
2000 Antwerpen, Belgium
t. +32 3 231 3593
f. +32 3 213 8639
*Pages 11b, 13b, 102br, 106ar,
142–143, 176–177a, 182bl,
191ar, 200bl*

Bedmar & Shi Designers
Pte Ltd
12a Keong Saik Road
Singapore 089119
t. +65 22 77117
f. +65 22 77695
*A Singapore-based firm
established in 1980
specializing in residential
projects and interior
design, mainly for
restaurants and offices.*
Pages 94–95b

behun / ziff design
153 East 53rd Street,
43rd Floor
New York
NY 10022 USA
t. +1 212 292 6233
f. +1 212 292 6790
Pages 15al, 97al

Michael Benevento
Orange Group
515 Broadway
New York
NY 10012 USA
t. +1 212 965 8617
Page 81a

Bruce Bierman Design, Inc.
29 West 15th Street
New York
NY 10011 USA
t. +1 212 243 1935
f. +1 212 243 6615
www.Biermandesign.com
*Residential interior
design firm.*
Page 148b

Bilhuber Inc.
330 East 59th Street
6th Floor
New York
NY 10022 USA
t. +1 212 308 4888
Pages 31al, 162cl

Laura Bohn Design
Associates, Inc.
30 West 26th Street
New York
NY 10010 USA
t. +1 212 645 3636
f. +1 212 645 3639
*Pages 30al, 55al&ar,
158–159, 162al, 163a*

Felix Bonnier
7 rue St Claude
75003 Paris, France
t. +33 142 26 09 83
Pages 47al, cl & ar

Bowles & Linares
32 Hereford Road
London W2 5AJ
t. 020 7229 9886
Pages 102al, 145a, 232br

Ann Boyd Design Ltd
33 Elystan Street
London SW3 3NT
t. 020 7591 0202
Pages 33b, 197al, 201ar, 237r

Nancy Braithwaite Interiors
2300 Peachtree Road
Suite C101
Atlanta
Georgia 30309 USA
Page 103ar & br

Sabrina Fay Braxton
Cloth of Gold
Grennan Watermill
Thomastown
Co Kilknenny, Ireland
t. +353 565 4383
by appointment in New York:
t. +1 212 535 2587
by appointment in Paris:
t. +33 1 46 57 11 62
Page 35a

Caroline Breet
Caroline's Antiek &
Brocante
Nieuweweg 35A
1251 LH Laren, Holland
Page 22br

Briffa Philips
19–21 Holywell Hill
St Albans
Hertfordshire AL1 1EZ
t. 01727 840 567
Pages 70a, 70–71

Brookes Stacey Randall
16 Winchester Walk
London SE1 9AQ
t. 020 7403 0707
f. 020 7403 0880
e. info@bsr-architects.com
www.bsr-architects.com
Pages 101br, 168–169a

Hugh Broughton Architects
4 Addison Bridge Place
London W14 8XP
t. 020 7602 8840
f. 020 7602 5254
e. hugh@hbarchitects.
    demon.co.uk
Award-winning architects.
Page 18ar

Buildburo Design & Build
7 Tetcott Road
London SW10 0SA
t. 020 7352 1092
f. 020 7351 3986
e. gordanamandic@
    buildburo.co.uk
e. petertyler@buildburo.co.uk
www.buildburo.co.uk
Pages 21ar, 153br

Cabot Design Ltd
1925 Seventh Avenue
Suite 71
New York
NY 10026 USA
t. +1 212 222 9488
e. eocabot@aol.com
Interior design.
Pages 138–139

Milly de Cabrol Ltd
150 East 72nd Street
Suite 2–C
New York
NY 10021 USA
Interior decorator.
Page 138a

Aude Cardinale, Designer
12 Avenue de Madrid
92000 Neuilly, France
Pages 63a, 141b

Garth Carter
t. 0958 412953
Specialist interiors painter.
Page 97bl

Marisa Tadiotto Cavalli
via Solferino, 11
20121 Milano, Italy
t. +39 03 48 41 01 738
    +39 02 86 46 24 26
f. +39 02 29 00 18 60
e. marisscavalli@hotmail.com
Pages 148al, 225 main

Alexandra Champalimaud &
Associates Inc.
One Union Square West, #3
New York
NY 10003 USA
t. +1 212 807 8869
f. +1 212 807 1742
www.acainteriordesign.com
*Interior architecture and
design.*
Page 88al

Ian Chee
VX Design & Architecture
t. 020 7370 5496
e. ianchee@vxdesign.com
www.vxdesign.com
Page 199ar

Circus Architects
Unit 1, Summer Street
London EC1r 5BD
t. 020 7833 1999
*Pages 19br, 122, 123al, 157b,
184*

Simon Conder Associates
Nile Street Studios
8 Nile Street
London N1 7RF
t. 020 7251 2144
f. 020 7251 2145
e. simon@simonconder.co.uk
Architects & designers.
Pages 100, 212–213a

Conner Prairie Museum
134000 Alisonville Road
Fishers
Indiana 46038 USA
Pages 25al, 150bl

Jaqueline Coumans
Le Décor Français
1006 Lexington Avenue
New York
NY 10021 USA
t. +1 212 734 0032
f. +1 212 988 0816
Page 211ar

Charlotte Crosland Interiors
62 St Mark's Road
London W10 6NN
t. 020 8960 9442
f. 020 8960 9714
e. mail@charlotte
   crosland.com
www.charlottecrosland.com
Endpapers

Carden Cunietti
83 Westbourne Park Road
London W2 5QH
t. 020 7229 8559
f. 020 7229 8799
www.carden-cunietti.com
Pages 20ac, 105bl

Barbara Davis
t. +1 607 264 36736
Interior design; antique hand-dyed linen, wool, and silk textiles by the yard; soft furnishings & clothes to order.
Pages 22ar, 24a, 26bl, 76bl, 130al, 131br

De Le Cuona Textile Home Collection
Head Office:
9–10 Osborne Mews
Windsor SL4 3DE
e. bernie@softech.co.uk
Please call De Le Cuona for stockists: 01753 830301
Pages 12–13, 15cl, 15bl, 62, 179ac, 230bcl, 236bl

Eric De Queker
DQ Design In Motion
Koninklijkelaan 44
2600 Bercham, Belgium
Pages 69al&r, 88bl, 175bl, 180ar

De Metz Architects
Unit 4, 250 Finchley Road
London NW3 6DN
t. 020 7435 1144
Page 80

Ischa van Delft
September
Vughterstraat 72
5211 GK's Hertogenbosch
Holland
Interior decorator.
Page 66a

Nanna Ditzel MDD FCSD
Nanna Ditzel Design
Klareboderne 4
DK-1115 Copenhagen K
Denmark
www.nanna.ditzel.design.dk
Industrial designer specializing in furniture, textiles, jewellery & exhibitions.
Page 165b

Agnès Emery
Emery & Cie and Noir D'Ivorie
Rue de l'Hôpital 25–29
Brussels, Belgium
t. +32 2 513 5892
f. +32 5 513 3970
Page 233cr

Jamie Falla
MooArc
198 Blackstock Road
London N5 1EN
t. 020 7345 1729
Page 70bl, cl & br

Han Feng, Fashion Designer
333 West 39th Street
12th Floor
New York
NY 10018 USA
t. +1 212 695 9509
Page 71a & b

Ken Foreman, Architect
105 Duane Street
New York
NY 10007 USA
t./f. +1 212 924 4503
Page 4

Belmont Freeman Architects
Sangho Park
110 West 40th Street
New York
NY 10018 USA
t. +1 212 382 3311
f. +1 212 730 1229
Project Team: Belmont Freeman (Principal Designer), Alane Truitt.
Pages 196ar, 233br

Full House
38 Renwick Street
New York
NY 10013 USA
t. +1 646 486 4151
Page 34b

Gabellini Associates
665 Broadway, Suite 706
New York
NY 10012 USA
t. +1 212 388 1700
f. +1 212 388 1808
Pages 63bl, 87al, 179ar

Zina Glazebrook
ZG Design
10 Wireless Road
East Hampton
NY 11937 USA
t. +1 631 329 7486
f. +1 631 329 2087
e. dzina@ATT.net
www.zgdesign.com
Page 190ar

Gloss Ltd
274 Portobello Road
London W10 5TE
t. 020 8960 4146
f. 020 89604842
e. pascale@
   glossltd.u-net.com
Home-accessory designers.
Pages 229ar, 238–239b

James Gorst Architects
35 Lamb's Conduit Street
London WC1N 3NG
t. 020 7831 8300
Page 30br

Hester Gray
25 Pembridge Villas
London W11 3EP
t. 020 7229 3162
Page 18bl

Mark Guard Architects
161 Whitfield Street
London W1P 5RY
t. 020 7380 1199
Page 223br

Nelly Guyot
12 rue Marthe Edouard
92190 Meudon, France
Interior designer & photographic stylist.
Pages 22al, 215br

Yves Halard Interior Decoration
27 Quai de la Tournelle
75005 Paris, France
t. +33 1 4407 14 00
f. +33 1 44 07 1030
Page 152bl

Annie Har
Sunnit Architects
10 Attunga Lane
Mount Glorious
Queensland 4520, Australia
Page 222br

William R. Hefner A.I.A.
William Hefner Architect L.L.C.
5820 Wilshire Boulevard
Suite 601
Los Angeles CA 90036 USA
t. +1 323 931 1365
f. +1 323 931 1368
e. wh@williamhefner.com
www.williamhefner.com
Page 112b

Alastair Hendy
f. 020 7739 6040
Food writer, art director and designer.
Pages 16ar, 21b, 104al

Hirst Pacific Ltd
250 Lafayette Street
New York
NY 10012 USA
t. +1 212 625 3670
f. +1 212 625 3673
e. hirstpacific@earthlink.net
Page 111br

HM2 Architects
33–37 Charterhouse Square
London EC1M 6EA
t. 020 7600 5151
f. 020 7600 1092
e. andrew.hanson@
   harper-mackay.co.uk
Architects & designers. Richard Webb, Project Director. Andrew Hanson, Director.
Pages 102bl, 149l, 151a

The Holding Company
241–245 Kings Road
London SW3 5EL
t. 020 7352 1600
Innovative storage solutions for every room in the home.
Pages 107r, 204bl, 207br

Kelly Hoppen Interiors
2 Alma Studios
32 Stratford Road
London W8 6QF
Pages 222bl, 224

Hotel de la Mirande
Avignon, France
Page 218

Hotel Villa Gallici
Aix-en-Provence, France
Page 218

Jack Ingham
Bookworks
34 Ansleigh Place
London W11 4BW
t. 020 7792 8310
Page 47bl & br

Interni Pty Ltd
15–19 Boundary Street
Rushcutters Bay
Sydney 2010, Australia
Interior design consultancy.
Pages 54a, 183r 210a, 212cr, 220al

Malin Iovino Design
t. 020 7252 3542
f. 020 7252 3542
e. iovino@btinternet.com
Pages 121br, 161ar, 165ar & l

IPL Interiors
François Gilles & Dominique Lubar
25 Bullen Street
London SW11 3ER
t. 020 7978 4224
f. 020 7978 4334
Pages 18al, 31ar, 48b, 59br, 157c, 162br, 190ac, 194r, 204br, 204–205a, 210b, 213ar, 216ar, 218–219b

Jacomini Interior Design
1701 Brun, Suite 101
Houston
Texas 77019 USA
Pages 27al, 152al, 212al

Daniel Jasiak, Designer
12 rue Jean Ferrandi
Paris 75006, France
t. +33 1 45 49 13 56
f. +33 1 45 49 23 66
Pages 217bl, 235bcl

Joanna Jefferson Architects
222 Oving Road
Chichester
West Sussex PO19 4EJ
t. 01243 532398
f. 01243 531 550
e. jjeffearch@aol.com
Page 132ar

Brian Johnson
Johnson Naylor
13 Britton Street
London EC1M 5SX
t. 020 7490 8885
f. 020 7490 0038
e. brian.johnson@
   johnsonnaylor.co.uk
Pages 15ar, 68l, 72, 82–83, 83al, 189bl

Just Design Ltd
80 Fifth Avenue, 18th Floor
New York
NY 10011 USA
t. +1 212 243 6544
f. +1 212 229 1112
e. wbp@angel.net
Pages 36b, 182br

Ben Kelly Design
10 Stoney Street
London SE1 9AD
t. 020 7378 8116
f. 020 7378 8366
e. bkduk@dircon.co.uk
Page 89al

Khai Liew Design
166 Magill Road
Norwood
South Australia 5067
Australia
Page 179bl

Robert E. Kinnaman & Brian A. Ramaekers Inc.
2466 Montauk Highway
Bridgehampton
NY 11932 USA
Postal address:
P.O. Box 1140
Wainscott
NY 11975 USA
t. +1 516 537 0779
American folk art & early painted furniture.
Page 22cl

KRD Kitchen Rogers Design
t. 020 8944 7088
e. ab@krd.demon.co.uk
Pages 118c, 120al

Bruno & Hélène Lafforgue Mas de l'Ange
Maison d'Hôte
Petite route de St. Remy-de Provence
13946 Mollégès, France
Page 178al & ar

Larcombe & Soloman Architects
Level 3, 397 Riley Street
Surry Hills 2010
New South Wales, Australia
Pages 13a, 215ar

Steven Learner Studio
307 Seventh Avenue
New York
NY 10001 USA
t. +1 212 741 8583
f. +1 212 741 2180
www.stevenlearner studio.com
Pages 52r, 76ar, 87br, 107al, 174–175

Littman Goddard Hogarth Architects
12 Chelsea Wharf
15 Lots Road
London SW10 0QJ
t. 020 7351 7871
f. 020 7351 4110
www.lgh-architects.co.uk
Pages 82al & bl, 99al & ar, 99c, 170–171a

Dale Loth Architects
1 Cliff Road
London NW1 9AJ
t. 020 7485 4003
f. 020 7284 44920
e. mail@daleloth architects.ltd.uk
Pages 96br, 104bl, 153bl

Hilton McConnico
8 rue Antoine Panier
93170 Bagnolet, France
t. +33 1 43 62 53 16
f. +33 1 43 62 73 44
e. hmc@club-internet.fr
Interior home designer.
Page 95

McDowell + Benedetti
62 Rosebury Avenue
London EC1R 4RR
t. 020 7278 8810
Pages 51b, 188al

Nicoletta Marazza
via G Morone, 8
20121 Milan, Italy
t./f. +39 2 7601 4482
Pages 77b, 131ar, 185b

Marino + Giolito
161 West 16th Street
New York
NY 10011 USA
t./f. +1 212 675 5737
Pages 110al, 186al

Andy Martin Fin Architects and Designers
73 Wells Street
London W1P 3RD
e. finbox@globalnet.co.uk
Page 104ar

Marshall Haines & Barrow
35 Alfred Place
London WC1E 7DP
Page 57ar

Frédéric Méchiche
4 rue de Thorigny
75003 Paris, France
Pages 97ar, 178b, 196–197, 200al, 217r

Jean-Louis Ménard
32 Boulevard de l'Hôpital
75005 Paris, France
t. +33 146 34 44 92
Page 105br

Philippe Model
33 Place du Marché St. Honoré
75001 Paris, France
t. +33 1 4296 8902
Decoration, home furnishing & coverings.
Pages 174cl, 179cl, 180al

The Moderns
900 Broadway, Suite 903
New York
NY 10003 USA
t. +1 212 387 8852
f. +1 212 387 8824
e. moderns@aol.com
Page 30bl

Belén Moneo & Jeff Brock Moneo Brock Studio
Francisco de Asis Mendez
Casariego, 7 – bajo
28002 Madrid Spain
t. +34 661 340 280
e. contact@moneobrock.com
www.moneobrock.com
Architecture & interior design.
Page 118al & b

L. A. Morgan, Interior Designer
P.O. Box 39
Hadlyme
CT 06439 USA
t. +1 860 434 0304
f. +1 860 434 3013
Page 14al

Lynn Morgan Design
19 Hilltop Road
Norwalk
CT 06854 USA
t. +1 203 854 5037
Page 26c

Charles Morris Mount
300 West 108th Street/2c
New York
NY 10025 USA
t. +1 212 864 2937
Page 52al & bl

Mullman Seidman Architects
443 Greenwich Street
New York
NY 10013 USA
t. +1 212 431 0770
f. +1 212 431 8428
e. mullseid@monmouth.com
Architecture & interior design.
Pages 74b, 174br

François Muracciole, Architect
54 rue de Montreuil
75011 Paris, France
t. +33 1 43 71 33 03
e. francois.muracciole@ libertysurf.fr
Pages 73b, 177al, 180br

Claire Nelson Nelson Design
169 St John's Hill
London SW11 1TQ
t. 020 7924 4542
Pages 17, 33cr

Roger Oates Design
The Long Barn
Eastnor
Ledbury
Herefordshire HR8 1EL
t. 01531 631611
Pages 12l, 97br, 174al, 190al, 191al&b, 194cl, 238–239a

OKA Direct
www.okadirect.com
For a catalogue, please call
0870 160 6002.
A unique collection of mail-order furniture & home accessories including rattan, painted furniture, leather and horn.
Pages 33ac, 220br, 230bl

Orefelt Associates
4 Portobello Studios
5 Haydens Place
London W11 1LY
t. 020 7243 3181
f. 020 7792 1126
e. orefelt@msn.com
Design Team: Gunner Orefelt, John Massey, Gianni Botsford, Jason Griffiths.
Pages 15cr, 104cl

Parnassus
Corso Porta Vittoria, 5
Milan, Italy
t. +39 02 78 11 07
Pages 26br, 56bl&ac

Andrew Parr SJB Interior Design Pty, Ltd
Studio Southbank
5 Haig Street
South Melbourne 3205
Australia
Page 222a

Plain English Kitchen Design
The Tannery
Tannery Road
Coombs, Stowmarket
Suffolk IP14 2EN
Pages 133al, 138bl

Campion A. Platt
64l Fifth Avenue
New York
NY 10022 USA
Page 216bl

Jennifer Post Design
25 East 67th Street, 8D
New York
NY 10021 USA
t. +1 212 734 7994
f. +1 212 396 2450
e. jpostdesign@aol.com
Spatial & interior designer.
Pages 16bl, 29ar, 32b, 84bl, 143bl&ar

Géraldine Prieur, Interior Designer
7 rue Faraday
75017 Paris, France
t. +33 1 44 40 29 12
f. +33 1 44 40 29 17
Page 140b

Lena Proudlock Denim in Style
Drews House
Leighterton
Gloucestershire GL8 8UN
t./f. 01666 890230
Pages 26a, 147bl & ar

Brian Purcell, Artist
436 Fort Washington Avenue
New York
NY 10033 USA
Page 86

Mark Pynn A.I.A. McMillen Pynn Architecture LLP
P.O. Box 1068
Sun Valley
Idaho 83353 USA
t. +1 208 622 4656
f. +1 208 726 7108
e. mpynn@sunvally.net
www.sunvallyarchitect.com
Page 89bl

Reed Creative Services Ltd
151a Sydney Street
London SW3 6NT
t. 020 7565 0066
Pages 29br, 30ar, 32c, 33al

Nico Rensch Architeam
t. 0411 412 898
Pages 67b, 90ac&ar, 118–119, 161l

Johanne Riss
35 Place du Nouveau Marché aux Graens
1000 Brussels, Belguim
t. +32 2 513 0900
f. +32 2 514 3284
Stylist, designer & fashion designer.
Pages 82ar, 84ar

Frances Robinson Detail
t. 020 7582 9564
f. 020 7587 3783
Jewellery designers & consultants.
Page 111bl

Richard Ronald
c/o Manuel Canovas
2 North Terrace
London SW3 2BA
Page 220bl

Luigi Rosselli
Surry Hills
2010 Sydney
New South Wales, Australia
t. +61 2 9281 1498
Page 177ar

Charles Rutherfoord
51 The Chase
London SW4 ONP
*Pages 20al, 104br, 187a,
219cr*

**Sage Wimer Coombe
Architects**
480 Canal Street Room 1002
New York
NY 10013 USA
t. +1 212 226 9600
*Project Team: Jennifer Sage,
Peter Coombe, Suzan
Selcuk, Peggy Tan.*
*Pages 28a, 31cr, 113bl,
120a, 131al*

Sophie Sarin
c/o The Ground Floor
201 Mitcham Lane
London SE16 6PW
t. 020 8769 4204
Page 45

Sheila Scholes, Designer
t. 01480 498 241
Pages 14b, 130cl

Lloyd Schwan/Design
195 Chrystie Street, # 908
New York
NY 10002 USA
t. +1 212 375 0858
f. +1 212 375 0887
*Pages 21al, 66b, 199bl,
202bl & br*

Johnson Schwinghammer
339 West 38th Street # 9
New York
NY 10018 USA
t. +1 212 643 1552
Pages 159ar, 171bcr

Sequana
64 Avenue de la Motte
Picquet
75015 Paris, France
t. +33 1 45 66 58 40
f. +33 1 45 67 99 81
e. sequana@wandoo.fr
Page 236al

Sharland & Lewis
45 Long Street
Tetbury
Gloucestershire
t. 01666 502440
Page 22bl, 96al

**Shelton, Mindel &
Associates**
216 West 18th Street
New York
NY 10011 USA
t. +1 212 243 3939
Pages 159ar, 171bcr

Sheppard Day Design
t. 020 7821 2002
*Pages 28br, 83b, 94–95a,
175cr*

Ann Shore
t./f. 020 7377 6377
*London-based designer &
stylist, owner of Story.
Personal selection of old and
new furniture and accessories.
Appointment only.*
Pages 10, 58br

**Stephen Slan A.I.A.
Variations In Architecture Inc.**
2156 Hollyridge Drive
Los Angeles
CA 90068 USA
t. +1 323 467 4455
f. +1 323 467 6655
Page 31b

Nigel Smith, Architect
t. 020 7278 8802
e. n-smith@dircon.co.uk
Page 103al

**Henry Smith-Miller and
Laurie Hawkinson, Architects**
305 Canal Street
New York
NY 10013 USA
t. +1 212 966 3875
f. +1 212 966 3877
www.smharch.com
Pages 52–53

Enrica Stabile
via della Spiga, 46
Milan, Italy
t. +39 02 76 00 84 20
e. e.stabile@enrica
 stabile.com
www.enricastabile.com
*Antiques dealer, interior
decorator & photographic
stylist.*
Pages 25bl, 27ar, 56bc, 123b

Seth Stein
15 Grand Union Centre
West Row
London W10
t. 020 8968 8581
Pages 15br, 223ar

John L. Stewart CIT, L.L.C.
113–115 Bank Street
New York
NY 10014–2176 USA
t. +1 212 620 777
f. +1 212 620 0770
e. JLSCollection@aol.com
Pages 157a, 167l

**Stickland Coombe
Architecture**
258 Lavender Hill
London SW11 1LJ
t. 020 7924 1699
f. 020 7652 1788
e. nick@scadesign.
 freeserve.co.uk
Pages 19bl, 20b, 147br

Studio Works
6775 Centinela Avenue,
 Building #3
Culver City
CA 90230 USA
t. +1 301 390 5051
f. +1 301 390 2763
Page 161br

**Stutchbury & Pape
Architecture + Landscape
Architecture**
4/364 Barrenjoey Road
Newport
New South Wales 2106
Australia
t. +61 2 9979 5030
f. +61 2 9979 5367
e. snpala@ozemail.com.au
*Have a reputation for
innovative thinking and
environmental sensitivity.
The land, site and place are
seen as directives toward
the solution of formulating
a building.*
Pages 84–85

Tia Swan Bed & Breakfast
Crooked House
P.O. Box 13
Knighton D 0
Powys LD8 2WE
Page 22cr

Alan Tanksley, Inc.
114 East 32nd Street
Suite 1406
New York
NY 10016 USA
t. +1 212 481 8458
f. +1 212 481 8456
Interior design.
Page 99b

Bruno Tanquerel, Artist
2 Passage St. Sébastien
75011 Paris, France
t. +33 1 43 57 03 93
*Pages 101ac & al, 170cr,
171bl*

Todhunter Earle Interiors
Chelsea Reach
1st Floor, 79–89 Lots Road
London SW10 0RN
t. 020 7349 9999
Pages 33ar, 187b

Touch Interior Design
t. 020 7498 6409
Pages 198–199

Tsao & McKown, Architects
20 Vandam Street
10th Floor
New York
NY 10013 USA
t. +1 212 337 3800
f. +1 212 337 0013
Pages 20ar, 107bl & c

27.12 Design Ltd
451 Greenwich Street
Suite 504
New York
NY 10013 USA
t. +1 212 334 5245
Pages 90c, 207bl

Urban Research Laboratory
3 Plantain Place
Crosby Row
London SE1 1YN
t. 020 7403 2929
e. jeff@urbanresearch
 lab.com
*Pages 19al, 98, 105al,
152–153*

Urban Salon Architects
Unit D, Flat Iron Yard
Ayres Street
London SE1 1ES
t. 020 7357 8000
*Pages 64–65, 105ar, 160a,
169c, 182a*

USE Architects
Unit 12
47–49 Tudor Road
London E9 7SN
e. use.arch@virgin.net
Pages 175br, 188br

Sasha Waddell
269 Wandsworth Bridge
 Road
London SW6 2TX
t. 020 7736 0766
Pages 234b, 235al, 235ar

**Miv Watts
House Bait Interior
Decoration**
Market Place
Burnham Market
Norfolk PE31 8HV
t. 01358 730557
f. 01485 52 8970
e. miv.watts@virgin.net
Page 77a

Bunny Williams Inc.
306 61st Street, Fifth Floor
New York
NY 10021–8752 USA
Page 59cr

**Vicente Wolf Associates,
Inc.**
333 West 39th Street
New York
NY 10018 USA
t. +1 212 465 0590
*Pages 35b, 74–75, 158b,
166bl, 211bl, 211br, 221a,
221b*

Woolf Architects
39–51 Highgate Road
London NW5 1RT
t. 020 7428 9500
*Pages 133ar, br & bl, 194al,
206a*

Voon Wong Architects
Unit 27, 1 Stannary Street
London SW11 4AD
t. 020 7587 0116
f. 020 7840 0178
e. Voon@dircon.co.uk
Pages 16al, 19ar

**Greg Yale Landscape
Illumination**
27 Henry Road
Southampton
NY 11968 USA
t. +1 516 287 2312
f. +1 516 287 2182
Pages 158cr, 159br, 170ar

Bonnie Young
t./f. +1 212 228 0832
*Director of global sourcing
and inspiration, Donna
Karan International.*
Page 85al & ac

INDEX

Page numbers in *italic* refer to the illustrations

ACKNOWLEDGMENTS

In addition to the homeowners mentioned the publishers would like
to thank the following people:

Rodney Archer, Katsuji Asada, Ann Boyd, Caroline & Michael Breet,
Conner Prairie Museum, Ischa van Delft, Sherri Donghia & Robert Eulau, Tricia Foley,
Katie Fontana & Tony Niblock, Daniel Gabay, Janie Jackson, Beverly Jacomini,
Glen Senk & Keith Johnson of Anthroplogie, Monsieur Jouve, Marie Kalt,
Bruno & Hélène Lafforgue, James Lynch & Sian Tucker, Alf & Wendy Martensson,
Ellen O'Neill, Kristin Perers, Lena Proudlock, Lars Røtterud, Gabriele Sanders, Ann Shore,
Dot Spikings, Monsieur & Madame Stein, Mark & Tia Swan.